# FERNS / TO KNOW AND GROW

**Ferns Around the World**

Ferns have world-wide distribution and may be found growing almost anywhere between the equator and the near-polar regions. Most ferns have feather-like leaves; others have such unconventional leaves as to have little or no resemblance to the plants seen in our garden.

Upper left: *Drynaria rigidula,* **Oak-leaf Fern,** an epiphytic species growing high on a coconut palm on the island of Fiji. Upper right: A group of miscellaneous tree ferns growing in the bush of New Zealand. Lower left: *Psilotum nudum,* **Whisk Fern,** attached to a palm tree on the island of Tahiti. Lower right: *Botrychium lunaria,* **Moonwort,** growing in an exposed area near Mt. McKinley, Alaska.

# FERNS
# TO KNOW AND GROW

*Third revised and enlarged edition of*
*THE GARDENER'S FERN BOOK*

*by F. Gordon Foster*

TIMBER PRESS
*1984, Portland, Oregon*

ISBN 0-917304-98-5

TIMBER PRESS
P.O. Box 1631
Beaverton, Oregon 97075

TO MY WIFE
ETHEL B. FOSTER
who through the years has
assisted me in the study of
the ferns.

# Contents

## List of Illustrations

*(The illustrations are by the author unless otherwise credited.)*

# Foreword

Ferns are becoming increasingly popular, whether used as background plantings or as major focal points in the garden. Many of them will grow vigorously and can be used in places where other desirable plants will not thrive. They are perennial plants demanding relatively little attention and offering a variety of attractive and distinctive leaves. This book is based upon Gordon Foster's own experience with ferns, developing out of enthusiasm and curiosity, his interest in growing and observing, and finally his study and lectures about them. The pleasure derived from these experiences is apparent throughout the book. The chapters on the use of ferns in the garden and those on growing them as houseplants will be of interest to beginning gardeners as well as experienced ones. The methods of growing ferns from spores and the many observations on the seasonal development of the plants will open new fields of interest to many readers. This will be a stimulating source of information for those who wish to use ferns effectively in house or garden.

ROLLA TRYON
*Gray Herbarium,*
*Harvard University*

# Acknowledgments

Preparing the manuscript and drawings for this book has led me to a greater knowledge of these fascinating plants. My association with many fern-loving people has been a stimulating experience.

To acknowledge all by name would be a difficult task and the danger of omission is ever present. I wish, however, to thank all of these people in general—friends, members of the American Fern Society, horticulturists, librarians, and authors of other fern books.

Dr. Rolla M. Tryon, Curator and Curator of Ferns, Gray Herbarium, Harvard University, has guided me in the verification of correct identity and correct names of the ferns, and in checking the botanical terms and their usage.

Dr. Alice F. Tryon, Associate Curator, Gray Herbarium, has made many helpful suggestions during the preparation of the manuscript.

To all of these people I am sincerely grateful.

F. G. F.

# FERNS TO KNOW AND GROW

# 1. Getting Acquainted with Ferns

Sharing a hobby is one of its most enjoyable aspects. Certainly this has been my experience for many years. When I first became interested in ferns, I had the help of others with far greater knowledge; but soon I found myself introducing beginners to the pleasure of studying these primitive, flowerless plants. This book and its predecessor, *The Gardener's Fern Book,* are the result of these many associations and experiences.

My early interest in ferns was casual. Then a friend introduced me to the beautiful and symmetrical structure of the plants seen through the microscope. I still recall my first sight of the little mounds on the underside of the leaves, uniform in size and shape, definite in pattern. I discovered that ferns had a great variety of leaves and that the little mounds underneath were not the same. After this awakening experience, and with only a small fern manual as a guide, I started on a venture that now seems to have no end.

Vacations in New England—a fern-lover's paradise—followed. For twelve years, ferns, large and small, were found throughout the area. At home a fern garden was planted—first with only a few hardy northeastern ferns, then the less common species were introduced. Rare plants and those difficult to grow out of their habitat were left for others to enjoy. My fern garden grew; plants neatly arranged and labeled with their botanical names became a living reference library for students, gardeners, and nature lovers. Like myself years before, they were amazed to see the tiny structures under the microscope.

Later I combined my thrilling hobby of fern study with photography. Black-and-white photographs, then color transparencies recorded the unique life cycle of the fern. Particular attention was given to accurately depicting each species in its natural environment with its associated plant life, whether it grew in a swamp or on a mountainside. Pictures showing the architecture of the leaf followed, illustrating the character of the blade, whether simple or multi-pinnate. In the laboratory, diagnostic areas were selected to show details of the crosiers, sori, scales, and trichomes, all at higher magnification so that the reader might readily know the individual species.

Talks to garden and nature clubs followed, all illustrated with colorful slides to bring life to these little known plants. These discussions brought many questions regarding identification and growth habits, horticultural applications, and photography. The most common question was, "Why don't you write a book on ferns?" The books that have followed on growing and identifying ferns for both the home and garden enthusiast, and the nature lover, have been my answer.

## The Book and the Illustrations

In writing this book, my purpose has been to bring specialized horticultural knowledge to the gardener or houseplant enthusiast, and to provide an understandable and reliable reference guide for the serious-minded nature lover. Originally written with only the people of northeastern United States in mind, the present volume has been expanded to include ferns of the southern and western areas of our country. No book could be considered complete in this vast family of foliar plants, but it is believed that the reference material given here will more than supply the needs of most readers.

My presentation of this material is based on personal experience in observing, collecting, growing, and collaborating with people recognized as authorities in given areas. Propagating new plants from spores, and further culture for observation, have complemented my reading of journals and monographs. Of no little value has been the building of a library of worldwide 19th and 20th century reference books and maintaining a photographic file of thousands of pictures.

As trees have different types of leaves, ferns also have leaf patterns that are distinctive. Each page of drawings includes a silhouette, made with photographic accuracy, to bring the architecture of the leaf quickly to mind. Wherever possible, details of the leaf have been projection-traced through the camera and microscope. The accompanying individual text includes a description of the plant, its range and culture. *Sori,* little mounds of sporangia with encapsulated spores on the underside of the leaves have been shown in enlarged views to assist in the identification of the plant.

## Names and Knowledge

As one becomes acquainted with ferns, he will recognize their differences and will want to learn their names, many of which are descriptive and provide a clue to identification. This may seem difficult at first, particularly when it is discovered that there is disagreement among botanists as to the scientific names, and that common names differ with locality. It helps to decide on one authority and follow his taxonomy. In this book the botanical names of the northeastern ferns are essentially the same as those used by Dr. E. T. Wherry in his book *The Fern Guide.** Notable exceptions used here are:

*Thelypteris hexagonoptera* instead of *Phegopteris hexagonoptera*
*Thelypteris phegopteris* instead of *Phegopteris connectilis*
*Woodwardia areolata* instead of *Lorinseria areolata*
*Athyrium filix-femina* instead of *Athyrium angustum*

For common names of the North American ferns, I have been guided by a list prepared by the late Mrs. Una Foster Weatherby and published in the *American Fern Journal,* Volume 42, No. 4, October-December, 1952. This list gives several common names for each species and indicates the name generally used. To be consistent with current taxonomy, I have made two important changes:

*Glade Fern* instead of *Narrow-leaved Spleenwort*
*Silvery Glade-fern* instead of *Silvery Spleenwort*

Differences also exist in the botanical and common names of some exotic ferns. Here I have used recognized botanical names suggested by Dr. Rolla M. Tryon. Some species appear to be either without common names or have many names varying with the locality.

Originally, the ranges of the North American ferns were taken from the *Index to the North American Ferns,* by Dr. Maurice Braun. The present edition of this book, with its

---

*E. T. Wherry, *The Fern Guide,* revised edition. Available through Morris Arboretum, 9414 Meadowbrook Avenue, Philadelphia, Penna. 19118.

added material, has extended some ranges, using sources believed to be reliable.

Books can guide and stimulate interest; much can be gained from field trips under competent leadership, particularly if the groups are small; but learning from ferns growing in one's own garden is best of all. To watch a fern develop day by day, especially as the plant emerges from the ground, is truly revealing.

Keeping records of observations and experiences will also add pleasure and understanding. A loose-leaf notebook, file cards, and photographs all help. Notes for each plant should include the source and natural growing conditions, the dates the first crosier appears in the spring and the last leaf turns brown in the fall.

A notebook page or file card might look like this:

| FERN RECORD | | | | |
|---|---|---|---|---|
| NAME | DATE | PHOTO | LEAF | REMARKS |
| Marginal Shield | 7-16-83 | #63-127 f 5 @ 1/50 K II | Blue green 21" long 10" wide sori mature | Gaskill property Leicester, Vt. Edge of Birch-pine grove. Crown well formed. Leaves uniformly spread |
| Rattlesnake | 7-22-83 | #63-128 + 129 f 8 @ 1/25 flash | 26" high Lush green— Sporangia open | Near Plymouth, Vt. Pine-Maple-Birch Gr. 200' from Highway 100. Damp slope—Deep Humus—stony |

Most of my fern study has been recorded by means of color slides. Data considered pertinent has been entered on 5" × 8" filing cards ruled for tabulating this information. A similar set of cards is maintained for my spore growing schedule, giving name of species, where and when collected, date of sowing and first sign of germination.

Use a magnifying glass whenever possible, for seemingly insignificant features may indicate the species or variant. An inexpensive magnifying glass will be found helpful in seeing many of the smaller details of the ferns. For those wanting a better magnifier, a Hastings triplet, preferably 10-power, is recommended. Glasses lower than 10-power will not provide sufficient magnification for some observations, whereas a glass of higher power with limited field area, close working distance, and shallow depth of field may be annoying.

For those who wish to study the ferns in a more serious manner, a herbarium or collection of dried fern leaves all neatly mounted and labeled is helpful. Immediately after collecting, carefully press fresh specimens between blotters or several sheets of newspaper until thoroughly dry. Heavy white or buff paper or light card stock 11½" × 16½" can be cut or obtained from biological suppliers. Fasten leaves with small straps of gummed paper tape, and label each sheet with name, date, source, and growing conditions.

### American Fern Society

Founded in 1893, this society has been a constantly growing organization of fern-loving people from all parts of the world. Dues are nominal, and since 1910 a well-edited journal has been issued four times each year. Field trips under excellent leadership are planned to all parts of the country, and a library of books and herbarium sheets is available to members. For years the society has operated a spore bank for those interested in propagation.

### Los Angeles International Fern Society

This organization has a membership of several hundred amateur and professional fern people who live in all parts of the world. The group meets each month for the study of practical fern growing, and every year has a large exhibit of plants. Members receive monthly lesson sheets and can obtain spores from the society's spore bank.

### British Pteridological Society

Founded in 1891, the society disseminates fern knowledge through its "Fern Gazette" and the "Bulletin," meetings and field trips. The society has a wide membership composed of gardeners, nurserymen and botanists, both amateur and professional, in Britain and overseas.

### Addresses of Societies

Names and addresses of society officers change each year, making a list here of little value. For latest information, it is suggested that inquiry be made at a local library.

# 2. Ferns, Then and Now

Ferns are among the oldest known plants. Before dinosaurs roamed the earth, these plants were well established, growing, reproducing, and decomposing throughout the ages. Fossil remains in rocks and coal record their past and indicate their vastness and grandeur. Today in their native woodland haunts, they gain the awe and admiration of the nature lover. Relocated in the house or garden, ferns adapt themselves to new surroundings, adding a delicate beauty to either situation. Foliage of varying shades of green, soft and plume-like or coarse and rugged, makes ferns delightful additions to any collection of plants. The home gardener, selecting hardy plants for the summer months, can bring these woodland gems to his outdoor garden. This garden pleasure can be continued indoors through the winter months with exotic species from warmer climates.

In medieval times, mysticism, fear, and superstition surrounded the ferns. People "knew" that without flowers ferns could have no seeds; they questioned how such plants could reproduce. As knowledge increased, man discovered that the *seedless* ferns were the most prolific "seed" producers of all plants. Unlike flowering plants with a few seed pods, the ferns shed their dust-like reproductive organs or *spores* by the millions. The spores still seemed supernatural with magic powers to cast spells of good and evil.

## Life Cycle of the Fern

Although spores come from the leaves of ferns, fern leaves or plants do not come directly from spores. Flowering plants grow from seeds which at one time are single cells, but ferns have a different way of life. Twice in the life of a fern it exists as a single-celled organism.

Spores from the parent plant fall to the ground or are air-borne a few feet or perhaps over many miles. With moisture and light, these tiny single-celled organisms start to grow, the first cells dividing, and later new cells dividing and redividing. Soon orderly arrangements of cells form little green heart-shaped plants or *prothallia* (singular, *prothallium*). So small are the prothallia that not only was medieval man unaware of them but most people today have never seen these marvelous plants.

As the prothallia grow, *rhizoids* which function as rootlets reach down for nourishment and moisture. *Antheridia* (singular, *antheridium*) or male organs, and *archegonia* (singular, *archegonium*) or female organs develop on the underside of the prothallia. At

5

maturity, with a drop of moisture as a path between the two organs, motile sperm cells or *spermatozoids* find their way to the archegonia to fertilize the egg cell. The egg cell then divides and redivides to form a young *sporophyte,* the start of a new generation. Different in every respect from their progenitors, the prothallia have all they require to support life in the new-born ferns. At first, miniature leaves entirely unlike the parent appear. Later leaves become fern-like, as seen in their habitat or in the garden. Thus, the spore comes from the fern, the prothallium from the spore, and the sporophyte from the prothallium, a succession known as the life cycle, Figure 1.

Here is a plant that has been evolving over a long period—a plant of beauty and a plant with an unusual way of life. Thoughts now turn to how ferns can beautify both house and garden. Whether a home has limited or extensive garden area, each planting will challenge the gardener's talent and ingenuity. If his knowledge already includes gardening, planning, and arrangement, he has an excellent start.

## Ferns Today

Besides valuing ferns for their beauty, consider their advantages. Avoid a haphazard start. Only by reading, studying, and observing, can one get a sound foundation. The following chapters suggest ways to begin, and later they will serve as a reference. When ready, consider indoor and outdoor ferns separately; this will be less confusing.

Start with the indoor garden. It will be helpful to visit a well-stocked florist's shop or greenhouse specializing in ferns. Here one will see many species and learn something of their appearance and cultural requirements. Plants differ widely; some are short and bushy, others tall and stately; some are lacy, others leathery; some climb, others gracefully flow over their containers. Think of how they may be used—in window gardens and on shelves, in combination with flowering plants, or as foliage alone for planters and room dividers.

Spring is the time to think of the outdoor garden. After resting all winter, *crosiers* or *fiddleheads* of the hardy ferns awaken and unwind as a reminder that spring has returned for another year. Again, imagination is challenged. What can these plants do for today's garden? Fortunately there are many native ferns suitable for different locations in the garden. Their subtle, blending shades of green harmonize with the more colorful neighboring flowers. While small ferns are always pleasing in a neatly arranged rock garden, large stately ones can serve many useful purposes. Numerous ferns grow best in tree-shaded spots where flowers would fail. Some are useful as a transitional planting where the garden adjoins a woodland. Tall species can hide house foundations and lower architectural lines. In the absence of flowers, ferns can be a garden highlight, always interesting to visiting gardeners. Long after the leaves have fallen and the first snow covers the ground, evergreen varieties are a reminder that the ferns will perpetuate themselves in the ages to come.

Bulldozers of civilization are rapidly making inroads on meadowlands and chain saws topple giant forest trees. Fauna has been pushed back and flora has been annihilated as native land gives way to modern development. If plants can be removed and placed in home gardens or transferred to similar growing areas, conservation will be served well. In many cases it is already too late; in others, only by fast and careful action can this beautiful heritage be saved for future generations to enjoy.

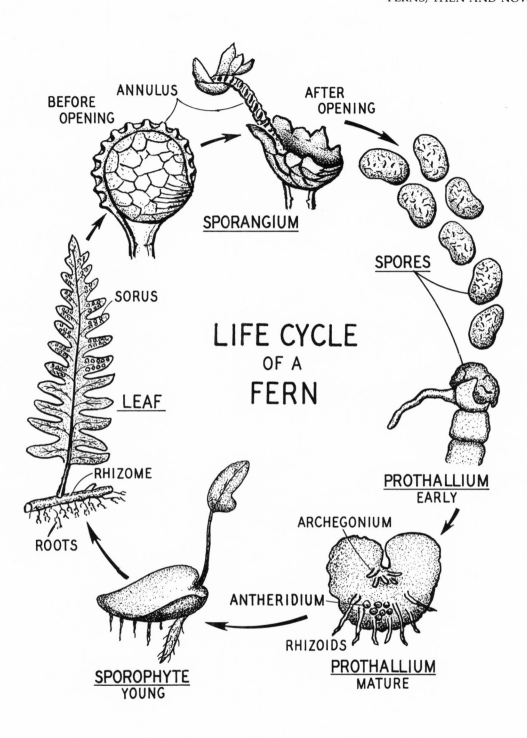

BEFORE OPENING
ANNULUS
AFTER OPENING
SPORANGIUM
SPORES
SORUS
LEAF
LIFE CYCLE OF A FERN
RHIZOME
ROOTS
PROTHALLIUM EARLY
ARCHEGONIUM
SPOROPHYTE YOUNG
ANTHERIDIUM
RHIZOIDS
PROTHALLIUM MATURE

1. These parts of the fern are not drawn proportionally, but in a size to show their function.

# 3. The Plant and Its Components

The most conspicuous feature of a fern is its leaf. Other structures, such as the spores, are so small that they defy the keenest vision. To have a better appreciation of the ferns, a knowledge of their structure and nomenclature is helpful. As the names and functions of the different parts are learned, the identification of each species will be easier.

## The Plant

The entire plant, thumb-size or tree-high, is known as a *sporophyte* or spore-bearing plant. Regardless of its size, it has three general parts—the *leaf*, the *rhizome* or stem, and the *roots*. Through the ages, ferns have developed distinct habitat preferences, probably in response to different environmental conditions. Some have become *terrestrial*, at home in woods and fields, swamps and marshlands, mountains and cliffs. Others have become *epiphytic*, making their homes on trees. A third group have become *aquatic*, living in lakes and ponds. Their degree of hardiness differs widely so that ferns are found growing from the tropics almost to the Arctic Circle.

## The Roots

Roots gather sustenance for the plant; they are dark and divided and grow down from the rhizome. In some genera, like *Thelypteris, Dennstaedtia,* and *Adiantum,* roots are uniformly spread along the rhizome; in others like *Humata* and *Davallia,* the roots grow as occasional clusters.

## The Rhizomes

The rhizome is really a modified stem, growing either above or below the surface of the ground. Many are covered with black or colored scales. Species like the New York Fern or Virginia Chain-fern have dark scale-covered subterranean rhizomes that are not commonly seen. Many epiphytic ferns, like the Golden Polypody, have erect or crawling rhizomes clinging to the bark of trees or extending over rocks. Often these intertwining and odd-shaped rhizomes have white or orange-brown scales which add

9

much to the beauty of the plant, Figure 2. Scars on some rhizomes indicate areas of attachment of previous leaves. The Golden Polypody is an excellent example of both colorful rhizome scales and leaf scars.

## The Leaves

### CROSIERS

The leaf buds that expand in the spring are the *crosiers*. These differ greatly among genera; a few typical ones are shown in Figure 3. The crosiers of some species first appear as large, hairy or scale-covered coils, as in the genus *Osmunda* with its Cinnamon and Interrupted Ferns. Others, like the Fragile Bladder-fern, have little unprotected brilliant green balls.

After a few warm days the crosiers rise and uncoil, looking like violin scrolls or, in fern language, *fiddleheads.* Prominent examples are the Lady Ferns and various Shield Ferns. Most ferns follow this method of simultaneous unwinding and growing, a process known as *circinate vernation.* As vertical unwinding advances, the *pinnae* or leaflets also unwind, in this case in a lateral direction.

Some ferns lift themselves from the winter ground cover by pushing their folded structure upward and outward at the same time, a method known as *straight* or *erect vernation.* The Rattlesnake Fern shows this unusual method best.

The advancing crosiers are seldom the color of the mature leaves. Some are light yellow-green like the Lady Ferns. Others, like the Common Maidenhair, are reddish-brown and are hardly noticeable. Christmas Ferns while young are silvery-white with just a tinge of light green striking through.

Late winter and early spring are critical times in the life of a fern. Any damage done to the dormant or unfolding crosier will be reflected in malformation of the leaf.

### MATURE LEAVES

The beauty of a fern is in its leaves, whether of *simple* or *compound* structure. The expanded part of the leaf is called the *blade.* Between the blade and the rhizome is the *petiole* or stalk. Regardless of its size or shape, a leaf is said to be *fertile* when it bears *spores* capable of producing a new generation. Leaves of many species are entirely or partly fertile. Other species have leaves that are *dimorphic,* the fertile and the sterile leaves differing in appearance.

The degree of dimorphism may be slight or obvious. In the Glade Fern there is a great similarity between the fertile and sterile leaves, while in the Sensitive Fern the sterile leaf is broad and deeply segmented, the fertile leaf forming the characteristic "bead stick." Although both fertile and sterile leaves are important to the plant and its perpetuation, it is generally the sterile leaves that are more beautiful and lasting. Depending on the species, the leaves of a plant may be *deciduous* or *evergreen.* Notice that no mention has been made of a sex designation of the leaf, for at this stage the plant is asexual.

Some leaves are not *cut* or divided in any way; these are known as simple leaves, Figure 4. For example, *Schizaea pusilla,* the Curly-grass Fern, a very rare species, looks like a blade of Merion bluegrass from a well-kept lawn. *Phyllitis scolopendrium,* the Hart's-tongue Fern, another uncommon fern, seems more like a rhododendron leaf. *Camptosorus rhizophyllus,* the Walking Fern, has a long, tapering blade and no divisions.

Blades divided into leaflets are called *compound.* The leaflets or divisions of the leaf extending from the rachis are known as *pinnae* (pinna, singular). Where further division of the pinnae occurs, the divisions are called *pinnules.* Ferns complex in their leaf structure are classified according to their cutting or subdivisions as 1-, 2-, or 3-*pinnate.* In fern literature this designation is sometimes indicated as once-pinnate, twice-pinnate, and thrice-pinnate, or pinnate, bipinnate, and tripinnate. An example of a 1-pinnate leaf

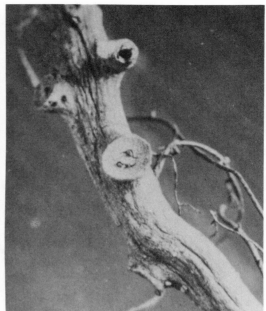

**2. Ferns with Unusual Rhizomes**

Upper left: *Polypodium aureum,* **Golden Polypody,** with heavy scale-covered rhizome extending itself beyond redwood hanging basket. Upper right: *Polypodium virginianum,* **Common Polypody.** Dead rhizome showing leaf scars of previous articulate leaves and venation pattern on remaining surfaces. Old roots can be seen in lower right area. Lower left: *Humata tyermannii,* **Bear's-foot Fern,** with rhizome covering of colorful white and light green scales. Lower right: *Aglaomorpha meyenianum,* **Bear's-paw Fern,** featuring heavily scale-clad rhizome with brilliant green, sessile leaf in background.

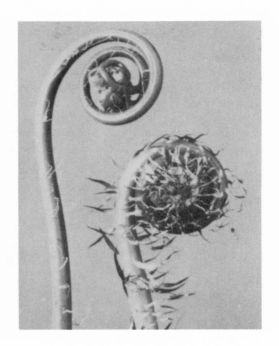

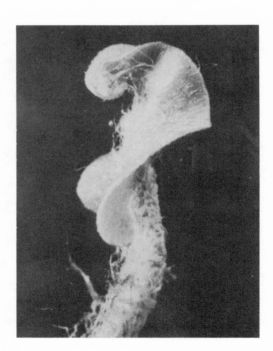

3. **Examples of Typical Crosiers**

Upper left: *Polystichum acrostichoides*, **Christmas Fern,** showing tightly wound, silver-scaled leaf bud. Upper right: *Adiantum pedatum*, **Common Maidenhair Fern,** having simultaneous vertical and lateral uncoiling of pinnae and pinnules. Lower left: *Botrychium virginianum*, **Rattlesnake Fern,** illustrating straight vernation. Lower right: *Phyllitis scolopendrium*, **Hart's-tongue Fern,** showing uncoiling of simple, tongue-like leaf.

would be *Polystichum acrostichoides*, the Christmas Fern; a 2-pinnate leaf, *Dryopteris marginalis*, the Marginal Shield-fern; and *Dryopteris spinulosa*, the Spinulose Shield-fern would be classified as 3-pinnate, at least in part.

When a blade or pinna is deeply cut, that is, more than halfway, but the cutting does not fully reach the rachis or midrib, the blade or pinna is said to be *pinnatifid*. The silhouettes of the Christmas Fern and Common Polypody illustrate the difference between blades pinnate and pinnatifid. In some ferns, like the Interrupted Fern, the primary division is pinnate and the secondary division is pinnatifid, giving the blade a "pinnate-pinnatifid" designation.

### PETIOLE, RACHIS, AND COSTA

The complete central stalk of a compound leaf is composed of the *petiole* and *rachis;* in a simple leaf this is known as the petiole and *costa.* The petiole is the portion between the rhizome and the blade, and the rachis or costa the portion that continues through the blade to the *apex* or tip. Generally this combination is of a fibrous structure, although in some species, like the Rattlesnake Fern, it is quite *succulent.* The petiole contains a *vascular* system which provides support and a means of transporting water, food, and nutrients between the blade and the rhizome. The round or horseshoe shape of the petiole and the central vascular system can be observed by slicing the petiole directly across with a razor blade.

### PINNAE AND PINNULES

The *pinnae* and *pinnules* are the primary and secondary divisions of the blade. Some pinnules, like those of the Hairy Lip-fern, are *pubescent* or hairy, giving them a soft, whitish appearance. Tiny *glands* grow along the veins and the underside of the pinnules of some ferns. A common example is the Hay-scented Fern.

### VEINS

Veins are the thread-like vascular elements in the leaf tissue. They form definite patterns that may be either *free* or *anastomosing.* Free veins are of two types, *simple* or *dichotomous.* Simple veins are unbranched and extend between the midrib and *sori* or edge of pinnule. Dichotomous veins fork and refork but never cross each other. Anastomosing veins are those that form a complex network. In most leaves the veins are visible; a flashlight held behind the leaf will reveal the pattern.

### SORI

Since ferns are propagated by dust-like spores rather than seeds, nature has provided miniature sacks or capsules known as *sporangia* (*sporangium,* singular), each containing many spores. Several sporangia are grouped in a cluster called a *sorus* (*sori,* plural), Figure 5. As a rule these sori are geometrically arranged on the underside of the leaf, as in Goldie's Fern, but there are many exceptions. Some ferns do not have sori, but rather the sporangia grow in confluent masses as in the Cinnamon Fern. These masses are so dense that the identity of the pinnae may seem to be lost.

### SPORANGIA

The *morphology* or structure of the sporangia differs with each *family* or group of genera. As a guide in the study of the sporangia, typical ones from five families are shown in Figure 6.

Since the family *Polypodiaceae* is the largest group of ferns, its sporangium is used in the life-cycle diagram, Figure 1. The sporangia of this family are spheroidal, membranous little capsules having an *annulus* or stiffened ring placed in a nearly vertical position around the sphere. The ring is not continuous, but is interrupted on one side by *lip cells.* From the base of the sphere a small stalk connects each sporangium to the surface of the pinna.

At maturity, a strong force breaks the annulus at the lip cells and discharges the spores. This important action, so necessary to scatter the spores, is known as *dehiscence*. The convulsive snapping and recoiling of the annulus and outward thrust of the spores can be seen easily through a magnifier.

### INDUSIA

The sori of many species have an *indusium* (*indusia,* plural) or thin protective covering over their clustered sporangia. These vary in shape with the species, some being round as in the Christmas Fern, or kidney-shaped as in the Marginal Shield-fern. Others, like the Spleenworts and the Silvery Glade-fern, have linear indusia. In some species, the edge of the pinna is rolled over, or *reflexed,* to form a more or less continuous protective covering.

Glands are present on the indusia of some ferns, an example being the Intermediate Shield-fern. They are so small that a magnifier will be needed to see them. If no indusia are present, the sori are said to be *exindusiate* or naked. These sori, their indusia and arrangement, as well as the sporangia and spores, aid in the identification and classification of ferns.

### SPORES

Spores, like seeds, carry the germ of life for succeeding generations. Under the microscope, some appear oval, some round, and some triangular, with colors of yellow, green, black, brown and cream.

The spore, developing within the sporangium, comes from a *spore-mother-cell.* This expanding cell divides to form a unit of four spores which is known as the *tetrad.* The manner in which the divisions occur can be one of two ways (Figure 7), depending on the particular fern. Spores that follow *bilateral* arrangement are known as monolete; those that follow *tetrahedral* arrangement are known as trilete. At first, these nearly transparent microscopic spores have remarkable geometrical symmetry and adhere to each other along their cleavage planes. As the spores mature, they become more strongly sculptured and separate from the tetrad. The original planes of contact and scars, however, are usually retained in the mature spore and may be seen when examined under the microscope.

Examples of Character and Size of Spores of Some Common Species.

| | | |
|---|---|---|
| *Cystopteris bulbifera,* Bulblet Bladder-fern, | monolete | 22 × 33μm |
| *Dryopteris marginalis,* Marginal Shield-fern, | monolete | 24 × 33μm |
| *Pellaea atropurpurea,* Purple Cliff-brake, | trilete | 53 × 61μm |
| *Osmunda regalis,* Royal Fern, | trilete | 53 × 67μm |
| *Athyrium filix-femina,* Lady Fern, | monolete | 25 × 38μm |
| *Schizaea pusilla,* Curly-grass Fern, | monolete | 65 × 90μm |

Dimensions shown in this list range between 22 and 90 microns. For comparison, an average human hair is 75 microns in diameter. (A micron, μm, equals one thousandth of a millimeter or 0.000039 inches.)

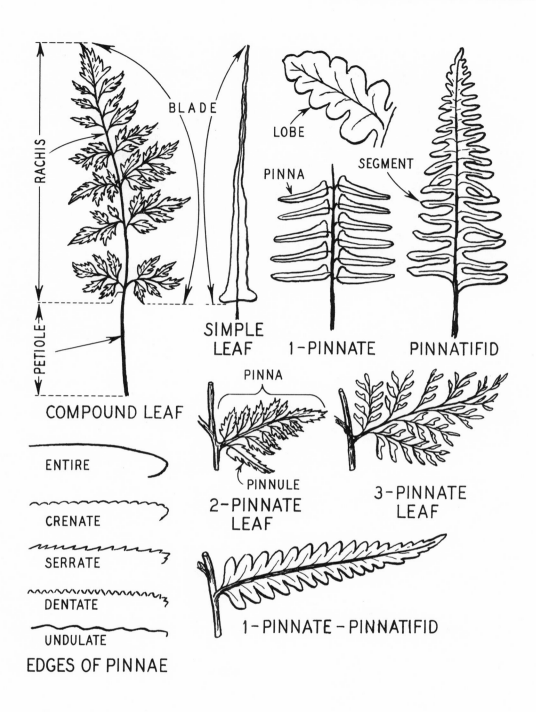

BLADE

RACHIS

PETIOLE

COMPOUND LEAF

SIMPLE LEAF

LOBE

PINNA

SEGMENT

1-PINNATE

PINNATIFID

PINNA

PINNULE

2-PINNATE LEAF

3-PINNATE LEAF

ENTIRE

CRENATE

SERRATE

DENTATE

UNDULATE

EDGES OF PINNAE

1-PINNATE-PINNATIFID

4. Types of leaves and details of pinnae.

15

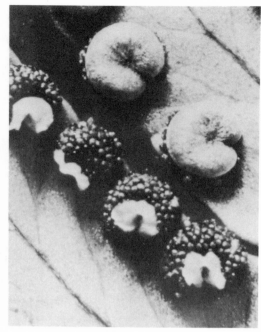
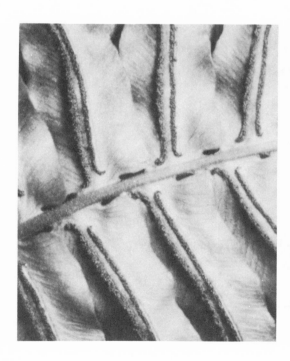

5. **Examples of Typical Fertile Areas**

Upper left: *Onoclea sensibilis,* **Sensitive Fern,** with bead-like covering of sori. Upper right: *Dryopteris marginalis,* **Marginal Shield-fern,** showing orbicular soral pattern. Lower left: *Blechnum occidentale,* **Hammock Fern,** with linear soral pattern following each side of midrib. Lower right: *Pteris cretica,* **Cretan Brake,** illustrating marginal soral pattern.

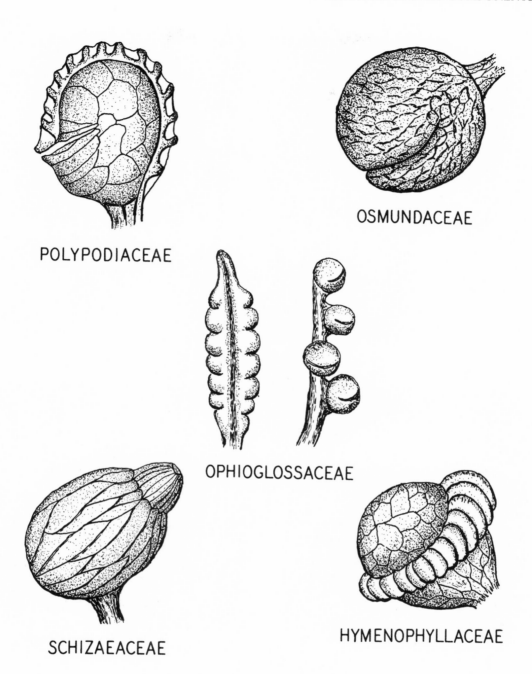

POLYPODIACEAE

OSMUNDACEAE

OPHIOGLOSSACEAE

SCHIZAEACEAE

HYMENOPHYLLACEAE

6. **Typical sporangia of five fern families.**

## 7. FORMATION OF SPORES

**Two types of tetrads showing geometrical arrangement of spores.**
The spores result from the division
of the spore-mother-cell.

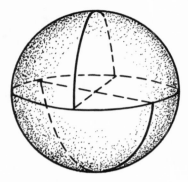 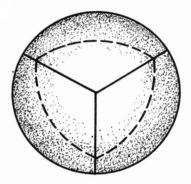

Bilateral division          Tetrahedral division

Photographs of Mature Spores

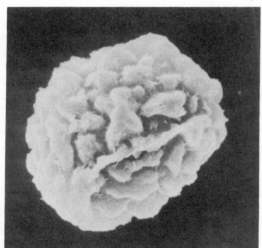

*Scanning Electron Microscope Pictures*
*Courtesy of Dr. Alice F. Tryon, Gray Herbarium*

Monolete spore                Trilete spore
x 1000                        x 2000
*Dryopteris fragrans,*         *Pteridium aquilinum,*
**Fragrant Fern**             **Bracken**

Scanning electron microscope pictures illustrating individual mature spores after separation from the tetrad.

Pictures at these magnifications reveal structure far greater than ever seen with a conventional microscope.

# 4. Easy Steps to Identification

For centuries, botanists have attempted to group members of the plant kingdom in an orderly arrangement, providing a method for identification, classification, and study. Different classification systems have been proposed; one frequently used places the ferns and their allies in a large category known as the DIVISION *Pteridophyta*.

Divisions are separated into smaller groups known as CLASSES. True ferns are represented by the class known as *Filicopsida*. Further division known as ORDERS follows in which the ferns we know are designated *Filicales*. Next in line of descent is the FAMILY level which is composed of GENERA (GENUS, singular), finally dividing to form SPECIES of ferns having common features. Occasionally, species are divided into VARIETIES. As an example:

|  |  |
|---|---|
| DIVISION: | *Pteridophyta* |
| CLASS: | *Filicopsida* |
| ORDER: | *Filicales* |
| FAMILY: | *Osmundaceae* |
| GENUS: | *Osmunda* |
| SPECIES: | *regalis* |
| VARIETY: | *spectabilis* |

In studying different fern books, it will be noticed that the number of families and their subsequent divisions are quite variable, a condition to be expected when various methods of classification are used.

While it is helpful to know that orderly grouping exists, identification throughout this book will be confined mainly to the genus-species level.

## Binomial System

With the binomial or genus-species naming system, the names of ferns are akin to those of people—each has a surname, the *genus*, and a given name, the *species*. Thus, in looking up the telephone number of John Brown, the family name of Brown is found. With a list of many Browns from which to select, search is continued until Brown, John, is found. Likewise, using a fern index or key, the botanical name is found listed as genus, then species, an example being *Osmunda regalis*, the Royal Fern. The genus Osmunda has many species, the other two more commonly known are *O. cinnamomea*, the Cinnamon Fern, and *O. claytoniana*, the Interrupted Fern.

Notice that the generic name is capitalized, and when the genus is first mentioned it is spelled out completely. Where reference to the same genus immediately fellows, it is often abbreviated, using only the capital letter and a period. Lower case letters, omitting the initial capital, are used for species, as *cinnamomea*.

In previous editions of this book, initial capital letters were used in the names of species when the name honored a botanist, as *Claytoniana*, or when it had been derived from a genus, *Asplenium Trichomanes*, a practice in accordance with Gray's Manual of Botany, 8th edition. In the present edition of this book, however, this capitalization has been discontinued, and all species are given in lower case letters.

A further classification follows in some ferns—*Pteridium aquilinum* var. *latiusculum* and *Davallia fejeensis* cv. 'Plumosa'. The *variety* (var.) name indicates a naturally occurring plant that is similar to a species but does not warrant species status. The *cultivar* (cv.) name is given to a minor variation that arises under cultivation, and is usually maintained only in horticulture. The word *form* (Latin: *forma*) appears occasionally in fern literature, indicating a minor variant of species. As an example, see *Botrychium dissectum* f. *obliquum,* page 92.

Generic names honoring botanists are of historical significance but provide no direct clue to identification. Regardless of these names, each genus has definite characteristics that are helpful in identifying the plant. As an example, in the genus *Woodwardia* a significant feature is the chain-like sori borne on the underside of the fertile leaf.

Some of the species carry latinized names of geographical locations which are generally of no help in identification. Fortunately there are many names of species that are descriptive. Here are some examples of the sources of names:

Generic names honoring botanists
    *Davallia* . . . Edmund Davall, 19th century, Switzerland
    *Dennstaedtia* . . . August Wilhelm Dennstaedt early 19th century, Germany
    *Matteuccia* . . . Carlo Matteucci, 1800-1868, Italy
    *Woodsia* . . . Joseph Woods, 1776-1864, England
    *Woodwardia* . . . Thomas Jenkinson Woodward, 1745-1820, England

Species names honoring botanists
    *braunii* . . . Alexander Braun, 1805-1877, Germany
    *claytoniana* . . . John Clayton, ?-1773, America
    *clintoniana* . . . George William Clinton, 1807-1885, America
    *goldiana* . . . John Goldie, 1793-1886, America

Generic names of Greek origin
    *Asplenium* . . . referring to the curative powers of the genus for disorders of the spleen
    *Botrychium* . . . meaning "cluster of grapes" in reference to the exposed spheroidal sporangia
    *Cryptogramma* . . . meaning "hidden line" in reference to the line of sori beneath the reflexed margin
    *Cystopteris* . . . meaning "bladder fern" in reference to the bladder-like pockets formed by the indusia
    *Dryopteris* . . . meaning "oak fern"

Species names of geographical origin
    *ilvensis* . . . Island of Elba
    *occidentale* . . . Western hemisphere
    *pensylvanica* . . . Pennsylvania
    *tsus-simense* . . . Japanese Island of Tsus-sima
    *virginianum* . . . Virginia

Species names that are strongly definitive
  *aureum* . . . golden
  *bulbiferum* . . . bulb-bearing
  *cristata* . . . crested
  *falcatum* . . . sickle-shaped
  *fragilis* . . . fragile
  *macrophylla* . . . large-leaved
  *marginalis* . . . marginal
  *obtusa* . . . blunt
  *palmatum* . . . palmate
  *palustris* . . . swamp
  *pentaphylla* . . . five-leaved
  *rotundifolia* . . . round-leaved
  *spinulosa* . . . spine-like
  *tremula* . . . trembling

The leaf in its entirety is the significant part of a fern, and the starting point for identification; size alone is insufficient. In some gardens, Interrupted Ferns when fully developed and mature do not exceed 24 inches, yet in their constantly damp, native areas they will often exceed 60 inches.

The age of a plant can also be misleading in identification. Young Spinulose Shield-ferns and Intermediate Shield-ferns are virtually impossible to distinguish. Only tentative identification can be made until the plant reaches maturity.

Color is another misleading variable. Healthy Christmas Ferns may range in color from light yellow-green to dark green. *Ecology* or environmental conditions of light, soil, and moisture influence the size, color, fertility, and health of a plant.

Do not overlook growth habits. Some ferns have normal growing seasons or periods when most of the leaves appear, after which the plant is somewhat dormant for the remainder of the year. Fertile leaves of the Osmundas—the Cinnamon and Interrupted Ferns—always come first, and are soon followed by the sterile leaves. Very few, if any, new leaves appear during the summer. Only sterile leaves appear on *Thelypteris palustris,* the Marsh Fern, until late June; generally all of the later leaves are fertile. The bright green of the early fragile fern changes to russet during the warm days of summer; new green leaves appear when cooler, damp weather returns. Some ferns, like the Rattlesnake Fern, normally produce only a single leaf each year. If this leaf is destroyed, it is usually not replaced until the following year.

## *Learning the Names*

To avoid confusion, learn a few simple names first, associating them with living plants and their features. Learning the basic characteristics of genera, and observing how one fern differs from a related fern can be of much value.

In studying the leaf, first consider its form, whether simple or compound. There are very few ferns that have simple leaves like the Walking Fern or Bird's-nest Fern. All of the ferns with compound leaves have distinctive silhouettes, and reference to their photographic patterns in Chapter 10 will help narrow the search. If the leaf is compound, determine whether it is pinnate or pinnatifid, 2-pinnate or 3-pinnate. Where strongly dimorphic leaves are present, the problem is simplified. Sharply defined sori will often indicate the genus, and identification of the species will follow as other diagnostic features are discovered.

In teaching identification, I have found that a comparative approach is best. Here somewhat similar leaves of different genera are selected and their diagnostic features compared. As an example, see how this method works with some pairs of species.

21

## Some Examples

Walking Fern—Bird's-nest Fern: The Walking Fern has a long, slender, tapering leaf with lobed base and short petiole. In contrast, the leaf of the Bird's-nest Fern is long and double-tapering. It is narrow at the base and reaches its maximum width near the middle and again narrows as the apex is reached, a shape referred to as *elliptical.* This leaf is *sessile,* joining the rhizome without a petiole. While the leaf pattern is particularly definitive, also examine the nature of the sori, if present. Both of these plants have sori of the straight line or *linear* type. Notice that the sori on the Walking Fern are haphazardly arranged, whereas those on the Bird's-nest Fern are parallel to each other and slightly oblique to the costa or midrib.

Christmas Fern—Common Polypody: This pair has deeply cut leaves which will require more careful observation. From their silhouettes, these leaves appear strikingly similar. First analyze their pinnae. The Christmas Fern has two obvious characteristics, an *auricle* or little upturned thumb-like projection on each pinna, and a little stalk connecting the pinna to the rachis.

The Polypody, instead of being pinnate like the Christmas Fern, is deeply segmented or pinnatifid, and the auricles are lacking. Comparison of the margins of the pinnae of these two species shows that the serrations of the pinnae of the Christmas Fern terminate in sharp bristles while the margin of the Common Polypody is *entire* or smooth.

The comparison can be carried further with the fertile leaves. The Common Polypody when young has many greenish-white sori, all geometrically spaced with great uniformity. As the leaf approaches maturity, the sori develop into little golden brown, well-defined mounds. Another characteristic of the Common Polypody is the lack of indusia; the sori of this fern are exindusiate or naked.

In this respect the Christmas Fern is markedly different with its indusia-covered sporangia, and only the upper pairs of pinnae are fertile. Immature leaves have sori appearing as small, light green discs, with indusia round and centrally attached. At maturity the indusia are *evanescent* or shriveled, or lacking entirely and the enlarged sori are *confluent.*

Another feature for comparison is the rhizome. The Christmas Fern has a stout underground rhizome, with the leaves growing from a crown. The crown, partly exposed above the surface, is visible at any time of the year as a group of compacted crosiers. As the first crosiers uncoil, more are formed. A few of these newly formed crosiers will be released later in the summer, but most will be stored and develop as leaves for next year's plant.

The rhizome of the Polypody is a creeping-branching system. The plant sends up single leaves at intervals instead of several from a crown. An effect of denseness is achieved by the ever criss-crossing of the rhizomes. Thus two ferns that appear somewhat alike are entirely different in pinnae, sori, and rhizomes.

Consider now a group of three somewhat similar ferns—*Dennstaedtia punctilobula,* the Hay-scented Fern; *Dryopteris spinulosa,* the Spinulose Shield-fern; and *Athyrium filix-femina,* the Lady Fern. In this group three genera are represented, each having its own characteristics. To simplify this comparison, here is a tabular analysis of the dominant features.

## COMPARISON OF HAY-SCENTED FERN, SPINULOSE SHIELD-FERN, AND LADY FERN

| Species | Leaf Division | Rhizome | Sorus | Indusium | Petiole | Pinnae |
|---|---|---|---|---|---|---|
| *Dennstaedtia punctilobula* (Hay-scented Fern) | 2-pinnate, pinnules lobed | Hairy. Rapidly spreading and branching, forming dense network near surface | At the margin | Cupshaped, open at the top | Covered with many segmented white hairs | Opposite or sub-opposite. Thin, pale green. Covered with fine white hairs. |
| *Dryopteris spinulosa* (Spinulose Shield-fern) | 2-, 3-pinnate | Scaly, bearing leaves in a symmetrical crown | On the under surface | Kidney-shaped | Occasional brown scales | Opposite or sub-opposite. Deep green, firm |
| *Anthyrium filix-femina* (Lady Fern) | 2-pinnate, pinnules lobed to pinnatifid | Spreading, bearing compact groups of leaves | On the under surface | Elongate, straight or curved | Many long, dark brown scales | Alternate. Yellow-green to medium green |

Eight additional pairs of ferns are grouped in the following list. Although each pair has similarities, you might find it interesting to supply the diagnostic features that make identification certain.

*Thelypteris phegopteris,* Long Beech-fern—
    *Thelypteris hexagonoptera,* Broad Beech-fern

*Thelypteris noveboracensis,* New York Fern—
    *Thelypteris palustris,* Marsh Fern

*Dryopteris goldiana,* Goldie's Fern—
    *Dryopteris marginalis,* Marginal Shield-fern

*Pellaea atropurpurea,* Purple Cliff-brake—
    *Pellaea rotundifolia,* Button Fern

*Cystopteris fragilis,* Fragile Bladder-fern—
    *Woodsia obtusa,* Blunt-lobed Woodsia

*Osmunda claytoniana,* Interrupted Fern—
    *Osmunda cinnamomea,* Cinnamon Fern

*Adiantum pedatum,* Common Maidenhair—
    *Adiantum capillus-veneris,* Southern Maidenhair

*Onoclea sensiblis,* Sensitive Fern—
    *Woodwardia areolata,* Narrow-leaved Chain-fern

# 5. The Culture of Hardy Ferns

In fern culture, first consider three growing essentials—light, soil, and moisture. Ferns will thrive in the garden if native conditions are reasonably simulated. This does not necessitate a critical pH test for every plant as long as the approximate acid, neutral, or basic soil conditions are met. But if it is known that the Walking Fern is at home on the face of a limestone outcropping, it would be foolish to attempt to grow it in a sour, marshy area. Cinnamon Fern is somewhat indifferent and will survive in almost any soil, but given its native acid, marshy soil, a tall, luxuriant stand will develop. Some ferns will survive for a year or two where incorrectly placed, only to gradually weaken and disappear. The presence of fertile leaves on a fern usually indicates a strong plant that will be successful.

Most ferns prefer shade although nearly all will grow in a limited amount of sunshine, especially if filtered through tree foliage. A few species like the New York Fern, Sensitive Fern, and Ostrich Fern can tolerate full sun exposure throughout the day if given ample moisture to balance the loss of shade. In their habitat, ferns sometimes depart from growing conditions considered normal for a given species. They seem to break all rules of reason and knowledge found in the literature. In one instance I photographed a beautiful stand of Marsh Ferns growing on a sunny Vermont hilltop.

## Planting

Although fern planting can be done at any time of the year, it is generally less disturbing to both plant and garden in early fall. Whether planting a new garden or making additions to an existing one, follow a definite plan. In spacing plants, use the "1, 2, 3 rule" as a minimum; that is, 1 foot between small Spleenworts, 2 feet between medium-sized plants like the Shield Ferns, and 3 feet between the large ones like Goldie's Fern. What seems ample spacing in early spring will often look crowded by late June. Different species can be used in group plantings providing all have similar growing requirements.

There is little concern about the crown-forming ferns staying in their original position. For the slow-spreading species, use a sharp knife to divide the plants. Pull out the ferns prone to spread rapidly until the proper boundaries are again established; maintain these boundaries by sinking 12-inch corrugated aluminum stripping around the planting.

Before moving ferns from their habitat or transplanting in the garden, learn something about the structure of their rhizomes. Some plants, like the Shield Ferns, grow in deep humus and have shallow roots. They are dug best with bare hands. Others with deep, clumpy roots, like the Virginia Chain-fern and Silvery Glade-fern, will require a sharp garden spade to cut the branching rhizomes before the plants can be lifted. Use a spade to divide the clump if smaller sections are desired.

In transporting ferns a long distance, I use plastic bags for the small species—plants up to 15 inches. To prevent wilting, add a little water to the bag and tie the top. Leaves of larger plants need more protection. For these, use several thicknesses of newspaper and roll the plant, leaves and rhizomes, into a cylinder. Stand these units in a box or basket and sprinkle lightly to supply moisture. When transporting material during hot weather, determine the coolest place in the car. Using this method, I have carried ferns over 300 miles in July without a wilted or broken leaf.

Good planting requires care and soil preparation. All ferns except those that are at home in rock crevices will grow best in loose soil. Dig a hole large enough to spread the rhizomes in a natural position. Hold the plant vertically until the crown or partially concealed crosiers are just at ground level. Gradually fill the hole with soil and small stones. Stones as large as potatoes are best for Shield Ferns, Ostrich Ferns, and Osmundas. Plants obtained from mail-order nurseries will have their roots washed of all soil and wrapped in sphagnum. If they cannot be planted immediately, keep them damp but do not stand them in water.

There is no hope of recovering broken leaves or crosiers. Remove all damaged structure by cutting with shears at the base. All newly transplanted specimens must be kept wet until the roots have become well established. Inverted baskets or large water-soaked clay flower pots will protect new plants from strong wind and sun.

## Autumn—Winter Care

Following nature's pattern, fall and winter care need only consist of a good covering of leaves. Leaf mulch will protect the shallow-rooted plants from heaving during alternate freezes and thaws of early and late winter. Where leaf coverings might be blown away in windy passages, especially between houses, salt hay held in place by an old screen or lattice is beneficial. Since next year's crosiers of many species are formed in the fall, keep plants well watered during a dry fall period.

## Spring Preparation

Late in March, when last year's tree-leaf covering is dry, is the time to prepare the fern bed for the coming season. Never use any kind of rake as the soft, tender crosiers will be damaged or destroyed. Carefully lift and crumble the dried tree leaves, letting the shreds loosely cover the plants. By following this practice each spring, the fern bed is relieved of its choking blanket and some life-giving elements are returned to the soil. Oak leaves are difficult to shred; it is better to place these on the compost heap for a year or two. Remember, garden tools—rakes and hoes, forks and cultivators—are *never* used on a fern planting.

## Fertilizing and Watering

Some commercial fertilizers are too strong for ferns and will kill or severely damage them. No supplementary feeding is necessary other than shredded tree leaves, humus or compost, and perhaps a light sprinkling of bone meal in the fall. If ferns naturally growing on limestone have been planted near an acid-soil area where leaching may occur, increase the alkalinity by occasionally adding a small amount of ground limestone or cracked oyster shells.

There is usually no watering problem in spring or fall when the air is damp and the soil cool. During prolonged dry periods, water frequently enough to keep the roots damp at all times. As with a lawn, guard against superficial watering which moistens only a thin top layer. Three evenings a week devoted to deep watering will thoroughly charge a well-mulched soil. Most ferns cannot tolerate standing in water or saturated ground, but a good mulch of compost, shredded leaves, and peat moss will assure drainage and also the retention of moisture around the roots.

## Weeds and Other Pests

Each spring many unwanted plants will appear in the well-mulched fern garden. These are not limited to the herbaceous weeds, but include myriads of young trees growing from wind-blown or bird- or squirrel-carried maple wings, wild cherries, acorns, walnuts, and buckeyes. All take over quickly in the loose woodland soil if not promptly pulled out. A covering of peat moss will discourage many of these pests. Buckwheat hulls, slow to disintegrate, will give a fern bed an attractive carpet-like foundation.

Fortunately the ferns do not have many enemies. Slugs are nocturnal prowlers confining most of their forages to near-ground-level attacks. Commercially available slug and snail bait, in either pellet or meal form, will keep them under control if applied liberally.

Fungi, although not a problem with older and stronger plants, can cause trouble with younger plants, particularly those being grown from spores. The succulent Rattle-snake Fern is one that is often destroyed by a fungous attack just above the soil line. Ample ventilation and a well-kept ground surface will allay but not completely prevent attack.

# 6. Growing Ferns in the Home Garden

In planning a fern garden, consider the plants to be used and the space they will occupy. Ferns differ greatly in size, pattern, and shades of green, allowing a wide variety of plants for selection. Group the plants by size, the large ones like Goldie's Fern, the intermediates like the Marginal Shield-fern, and the miniatures of the size of the Maidenhair Spleenwort. Carefully arranged, ferns can be both useful and beautiful in many landscape plans. Large ferns can soften the lines of a fence or hedge, relate a high porch to the ground, or bring interest to a foundation line. In front of older laurel and rhododendron, Cinnamon and Interrupted Ferns serve to conceal awkward leafless growth. Ferns of intermediate size make artistic groupings alone or with flowering plants. Miniature ferns grow best in the protective crevices of large, weathered stones in a rock garden or rock border.

*Planning the Garden*

Plan first on paper. A well-considered drawing produces an orderly layout and saves replanting. Make the drawing to a convenient scale, as 1/8 inch or 1/4 inch to the foot; on it indicate house and garage, driveway, large trees, a brook, and any other permanent features. Include those of adjoining properties, as nearby trees and buildings may greatly influence the final plan. Actually, a lot may be deeply shaded without a tree on it. Drainage from higher land can cause flooding and erosion, problems that must be solved.

Study the plot plan in Figure 8; it is a typical suburban property with a centrally located house, breezeway, and garage. Adjoining is the Kings' house on the west, the Browns' house on the south, and a vacant lot on the east. Shade for the heat of the day comes from a stately tulip tree in the south corner of the lot, the Browns' colorful maple, the Kings' magnificent oak. Pine trees on the vacant lot are attractive but offer little shade. The house faces north and with open shade all day on this exposure, the area is ideal for most ferns. Here, before ferns were considered, attempts to grow flowers in the shaded areas had been frustrating. But now, where there had been failure, a new opportunity presented itself—a fern garden.

## Soil Preparation

Since many ferns are found in cool, moist woodland, it is necessary to approximate these conditions. Topsoil, with the exception of a superficial layer, is often stripped from a property. To get a good start, remove poor soil and clay to a depth of 10 inches and refill with a natural soil mixture, principally of leaf mold or compost. Good topsoil, humus, peat moss, and sand in fairly equal quantities also provide conditions suitable for most ferns. Work in oak leaves, wood chips or sawdust for species that require acid soil, such as the Beech, Chain, and Lady Ferns. To provide alkalinity for species like Maidenhair Spleenwort and Bulblet Bladder-fern, add ground limestone or ground oyster shells. The alkaline release of the oyster shells is slower and they also improve drainage. Since this soil mixture is light and fluffy, allow for settling by using enough to let the bed stand 6 to 8 inches above the existing level of the soil.

Where the garden is to have a background of a fence or hedge, raise the bed about a foot and edge the area with large, weathered stones. This adds to its attractiveness and the elevation assures good drainage, while the stones provide many pockets and crevices for miniature ferns. To emphasize a woodland appearance, place a few rocks at random throughout the area.

## Uses for Larger Species

Ferns can make effective backgrounds that gracefully outline the boundaries of a garden. It is here that bold woodland monarchs can be used. Plant these against a rail fence or in front of evergreens, as shown in the plot layout. In fairness to neighbors, select a non-spreading species like *Dryopteris goldiana*, Goldie's Fern. The crosiers grow from a crown-like formation rather than a wandering rhizome and the plant grows tall, 50 to 60 inches, with a wide leaf and unusually strong petiole.

The three commonly found species of *Osmunda* are also good for background. *O. cinnamomea*, the Cinnamon Fern, *O. claytoniana*, the Interrupted Fern, with similar sterile leaves, and *O. regalis*, var. *spectabilis*, the Royal Fern, spread slowly and are handsome from early spring to killing frost. Alternating groups of species gives interest to a planting and produces a strong, stately effect, while random use of many kinds makes a spotty picture.

For transition from planted property to vacant land, there is nothing better than *Matteuccia struthiopteris*, the Ostrich Fern, with its tall, dark green, wax-like leaves. Although it is also a crown-former, it spreads rapidly by underground runners that soon make dense growth. Used properly and given space to spread, the Ostrich Fern is most effective. When planting any of the large species, avoid crowding by allowing each plant a minimum of 3 feet. Remember that sparse spring growth can become a jungle by July, spoiling the beauty of both plant and rockwork.

## Ferns in the Intermediate Group

Ferns of intermediate height are pleasing on slopes or in borders along walks and drives. Lady Ferns of many varieties with their delicate lacy leaves of yellow-green are a first choice. In good soil and with ample moisture, they grow 30 to 36 inches high. They are not crown-formers, but instead form an expanding clump of rhizomes and they require division every three or four years. This is a simple operation, beneficial to the plant.

Plant some of the *Dryopteris* group among the Lady Ferns. All of the Shield Ferns have heavy, dark foliage offering contrast of color and form. This is particularly true of *D. marginalis*, the Marginal Shield-fern. The Marginal Shield-fern is often found growing with *D. spinulosa,* the Spinulose Shield-fern, and the *D. intermedia,* Intermediate Shield-fern. These three are crown-formers and will stay where placed. Plant them next to large stones and they will soon give the appearance of a woodland even in a small home garden.

Be sure to include *Polystichum acrostichoides,* the Christmas Fern, in your garden. Hardy and definitely evergreen, it slowly forms a spreading crown that does not readily encroach on neighboring plants. It is often found growing with the Shield Ferns. Among the first to appear in the spring, this plant droops its heavy, fast uncurling crosiers backward until the rachises have sufficient strength to grow erect.

For daintiness, the Maidenhair Ferns have no equal. *Adiantum pedatum,* the Common Maidenhair, grows in cooler areas and *A. capillus-veneris,* the Southern Maidenhair, in warmer regions. Both do best in a shady, moist garden spot. While there is similarity in their pinnules, the leaf pattern of the Southern Maidenhair is more delicate than that of the northern species. The Maidenhair Ferns complete the planting shown in the plot drawing. To include more on such a property would cause crowding.

In larger gardens, include other plants of the intermediate group. When using such notorious spreaders as the Hay-scented and New York Ferns, control them with natural barriers. *Dennstaedtia punctilobula,* the yellow-green Hay-scented Fern, is soft in color and texture and grows well in full sun or deep shade. Placed next to a house, its spreading can be checked as the lawn is mowed. Control *Thelypteris noveboracensis,* the New York Fern, in the same way. Both are excellent for broad plantings as ground covers, particularly on slopes. In front of these intermediates, *T. hexagonoptera,* and *T. phegopteris,* Broad and Long Beech-ferns, give variety with their outstretched basal pinnae.

For a garden with both sun and shade, a hardy exotic, *Athyrium niponicum,* the Japanese Painted-fern, is colorful in shades of green, gray, and wine. The leaves are gracefully tapered; some varieties are low and spreading, others are more erect.

## Miniatures for the Rock Garden

By all means have a rock garden. In the plan there are two, one in front of the breezeway on the shady north side, the other at the rear where there is alternate light and shade throughout the day. My preference for a rock garden border is weathered limestone, particularly stones full of niches for miniature growers. Soft brown sandstone and hard igneous rocks can be introduced in a random manner where flowers and ferns will look well among them. Select rocks that are large enough not to settle out of sight or be completely hidden as plants develop.

To insure good growth, work in among the rocks a cubic yard or two of screened topsoil mixed with equal amounts of commercial humus or well-aged compost, peat moss, and sand. Guard against termites if the rock garden is next to a house by keeping the soil at least 10 inches away from the wood. A slight slope is good for drainage, but excessive pitch invites erosion that destroys small growers.

Plant *Asplenium trichomanes,* the Maidenhair Spleenwort, between the rocks at the front. In its habitat it often grows on steep faces of cliffs, which assures good drainage. *Camptosorus rhizophyllus,* Walking Ferns, are pleasing companions and require about the same conditions. Put a little humus in a crevice or pocket where roots will keep cool and damp. A slug repellent may be necessary when evenings are hot and humid.

*Polypodium virginianum,* the Common Polypody, will grow in a crevice between stones. It spreads slowly but eventually makes an evergreen covering. Like the rhododendron, its leaves curl in cold weather.

*Pellaea atropurpurea,* the Purple Cliff-brake, requires a limestone niche. It tolerates considerable sun once it gets its roots far into the crevices.

Where the rockwork is 3 or 4 feet high, plant *Cystopteris bulbifera,* the Bulblet Bladder-fern, either beside or between the stones. Keep both soil and rocks damp and the long, tapered leaves will flow down over the stones. In time, little ferns will grow from the bulblets.

*Cystopteris fragilis,* Fragile Bladder-ferns, are prettiest growing at the base of stones. The leaves are bright green in early spring and turn russet in hot weather. Later, a new growth of green leaves keeps the plant looking fresh until frost.

Woodsias grow well in the garden. *Woodsia obtusa,* the Blunt-lobed Woodsia, somewhat like the Fragile Bladder-fern, does best on the cool, shaded side of a large stone. *W. ilvensis,* little Rusty Woodsia, prefers a sunny, windy exposure.

*Botrychium virginianum,* Rattlesnake Ferns, are pleasing for a well-shaded spot. They come up in early spring with a peculiar vernation, not the usual fiddleheads, and multiply very slowly—only by spores. The roots of *Botrychium* are odd and fleshy, and grow deeper in the soil than those of most ferns. The size of the plants and the near colorless petioles above the bud-sheath are guides to the depth at which they should be planted.

*Asplenium platyneuron,* the Ebony Spleenwort, is an erect little fern, usually 8 to 12 inches high, and it somewhat resembles a small Christmas Fern. For an artistic setting, plant a group of three in front of a piece of sandstone. This fern grows under widely different conditions of soil and moisture.

Where the rock garden is adjacent to a high porch, make a background planting of Shield Ferns. *Dryopteris cristata,* the Crested Shield-fern, more erect than the others, will look well at the ends with *D. marginalis,* Marginal Shield-ferns, and *D. spinulosa,* Spinulose Shield-ferns, planted between. *Athyrium niponicum,* the Japanese Painted-fern, is attractive for small clumps in front of the Shield Ferns. Divide the Painted Ferns every two or three years so small plants nearby will not be crowded. For the rock garden in front of the breezeway, limit the planting to ferns. On the south side, where there is alternate light and shade, mingle small annuals and biennials with the ferns for they complement each other.

## Wild Flowers and Ferns

Since most ferns appear early in the spring but do not attain full stature for nearly six weeks, it is possible to have many woodland flowers among them. Trilliums, Mayapples, Dutchman's Breeches, Wild Ginger, Bloodroot, and wild Geraniums all grow well in the deeply mulched areas. These have about ten days of beautiful early color—yellow, lavender, or white—and then a total retreat. Eastern Columbines and Jack-in-the-pulpit are attractive and quickly take hold among ferns. Violets in a wide range of species, and planted in front of ferns, are pretty both in flower and long-lasting foliage. If the proper ferns are selected, the flowers will not be crowded. Varieties of narcissus also make ideal companions, their long yellowing leaves will hardly be noticeable as handsome Osmundas, Christmas, and Shield Ferns mature.

Many wild flowers grow under the same conditions as ferns, but some cannot be grown away from their natural environment. The Lady Slipper and Trailing Arbutus, and other fast disappearing plants, should never be taken from the woods unless it is to save them from destruction where a road or development is about to be built. Some wild flowers can be bought from growers either as plants or seeds. Observe the law of conservation whether written or unwritten—protect our natural heritage. In fairness to future generations, protect both flowers and ferns.

When ferns are planted only 2 to 3 feet apart, there will be little room for flowers after mid-June; by that time spaces will be filled by the growth of the ferns. With occasional deep watering, the beautiful foliage of many species lasts until frost, while the hardy evergreen ferns remain throughout most winters.

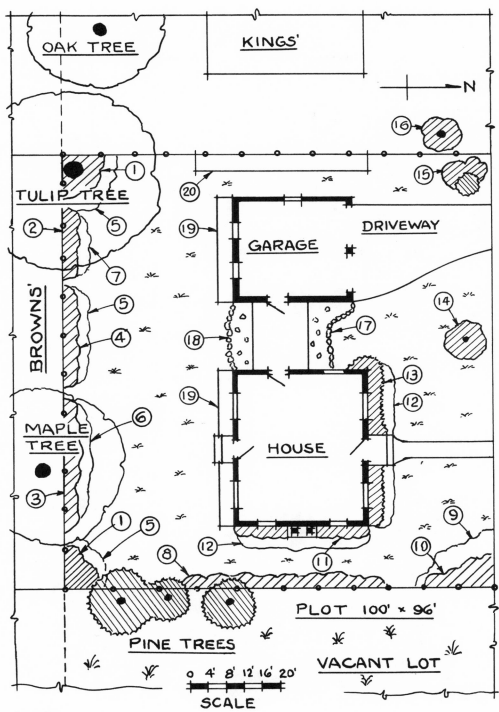

8. Garden Plan

1. **Goldie's Fern**
2. **Interrupted Fern**
3. **Cinnamon Fern**
4. **Royal Fern**
5. **Marginal Shield-fern**
6. **Spinulose Shield-fern**
7. **Intermediate Shield-fern**
8. **Ostrich Fern**

9. **Maidenhair Fern**
10. **Christmas Fern**
11. Dwarf evergreens
12. Assorted medium-sized ferns
13. Mixed evergreens
14. Holly tree
15. Rhododendron and spreading yew

16. Magnolia
17. Rock garden with miniature ferns
18. Rock garden with ferns and flowers
19. Annuals
20. Rose garden

33

9. **Foundation plantings**

Above: **Lady Ferns** and **Spinulose Shield-ferns** conceal a garage foundation. Below: **Christmas** and **Broad Beech Ferns, Silvery Glade-ferns,** and **Marginal Shield-ferns** among sandstone rocks lower appearance of foundation line.

*J. Horace MacFarland*

10. **Ostrich Ferns,** tall and stately, border a flagstone walk joining porch and garden.

*Jeannette Grossman*

11. **Maidenhair Ferns** and mossy saxifrage like cool crevices between mossy rocks above garden path.

*Roche*

12. Colorful, low spreading **Japanese Painted-ferns,** with a background of **Interrupted Ferns,** border a garden.

*Gottscho-Scheisner*

13. Tall **Cinnamon Ferns** with a background of white birch and a birdbath of native sandstone for a feature.

14. Suggested Miniature Ferns for the Rock Garden

Upper left: *Asplenium trichomanes*, **Maidenhair Spleenwort.** Upper right: *Woodsia ilvensis*, **Rusty Woodsia.** Lower left: *Pellaea glabella*, **Smooth-stemmed Cliff-brake.** Lower right: *Asplenium platyneuron*, **Ebony Spleenwort.**

**15. Hardy Ferns for Today's Garden**

Here are four medium-large hardy species that may be used as focal points in the garden. They appear best when widely spaced and growing from a well-mulched ground cover. Upper left: *Polysticum acrostichoides,* **Christmas Fern.** Upper right: *Blecknum spicant,* **Deer Fern** (Hard Fern). Lower left: *Osmunda claytoniana,* **Interrupted Fern.** Lower right: *Matteuccia struthiopteris,* **Ostrich Fern.**

# 7. Woodland Plantings That Feature Ferns

A country place with land offers a wonderful opportunity for large, natural fern gardens. Where there is a composite of woods and meadows with variations in soil, moisture, and light, ideal conditions exist for many species. Before anything can be done with a woodland planting, it will be necessary to clear away undergrowth and lay out new paths and trails. Here are some suggestions for transforming a woodland tract into a natural garden.

## For Woodland Roads and Trails

Long trail-like driveways cutting through uneven ground sometimes have sloping banks that are likely to erode with heavy rains. Christmas Ferns will be helpful where slopes are not too steep, as their prostrate leaves form dense, soil-retaining mats. These ferns are evergreen and remain erect until late fall or early winter.

Other trail-driveways that traverse level ground can have more artistic plantings. Take advantage of large stones and boulders near the roadside. Christmas Ferns and Marginal Shield-ferns, both dark and evergreen, can be naturalized beside the stones. Arrange the ferns in groups of three, with 3 feet between the plants. Groups look better when widely spaced. Where the drive traverses moist but not really swampy land, plant *Athyrium thelypterioides*, the Silvery Glade-fern, which is most attractive when the sun shines on its soft green silvery-backed leaves. Allow ample room as it spreads rapidly.

The tall and vigorous Goldie's Fern is excellent for an area approaching deep woods. Again plant in groups of three with 4 feet between these giants. In between widely spaced groups use *Athyrium pycnocarpon*, the Glade Fern (not Silvery Glade); it will spread slowly. Both species are deciduous.

## Paths and Byways

Make the little foot-trail plantings the most interesting section of the garden, for along these byways visitors will be less hurried and more observing. Clear away last year's leaves and debris so that paths can be easily followed and create curves, both sharp and gradual, to conceal the next planting until that station is reached.

Paths covered with 2 or 3 inches of wood chips are preferred. Chips are natural to the woodlands; they retain moisture, are soft under foot, and gradually darken with age.

Cinder trails have no place in woodland gardens. They look unnatural, are dusty when dry, and easily erode in heavy rains. Avoid edging the path with small stones; their appearance is not pleasing and they can be hazardous when out of place.

Choose smaller ferns for locations near the path. Try to simulate the natural conditions for each variety. For instance, the Rattlesnake Fern may grow alone or in a colony, while the common Maidenhair tends to form patches. Avoid rampant growers that will choke out more delicate plants. The Bracken, Hay-scented, and Sensitive Ferns are definitely to be kept away from a path.

Find a place for the two Beech Ferns with their broad basal pinnae. Although both spread quickly, they have shallow rhizomes and are easily controlled. Lady Ferns, beautiful and lacy, belong in a woodland garden. Again, as along the roadway, plant the Christmas Fern and all the Shield Ferns in groups beside large stones or decaying logs and stumps. For the utmost in beauty, do not crowd.

Close to the path set limestone rocks, either native or transported, for the Maidenhair Spleenwort and Walking Fern. They are not always easy to start, but are attractive when established. In circumneutral soil, small stands of the Hairy Lip-fern and Ebony Spleenwort will do well.

Delicate spring flowers show to advantage among the smaller ferns—long-stemmed Wood Violets, Bluets, Bloodroot, Trout Lilies, Saxifrage, and Wild Ginger. Many of these can be obtained from nurseries specializing in wild flowers.

## Stone Walls, Ledges, and Steps

Make use of old stone walls. Between a wall and roadway is a good place for spreading species. With reasonable moisture, New York, Hay-scented, and Lady Ferns will tolerate full sun for several hours. If the stones are laid in mortar, the Purple Cliff-brake may be found growing in tiny crevices. This fern is difficult to start on walls but if carefully tended the first season, it gains a foothold. Where a wall is high and massive, place in front of it a stand of Cinnamon and Interrupted Ferns. Start a covering of the Common Polypody, especially on a low rambling wall, by planting a few rhizomes in humus pockets.

Geological formations of ledges, cliffs, and outcroppings existed long before plant life and are of various compositions. Some are hard igneous rock, some are metamorphic sandstone, others are soft, porous limestone. Use the humus-filled pockets and faults for adaptable plants; be guided by the natural requirements of each species. The Walking Fern, Maidenhair Spleenwort, Common Polypody, and Bulblet Bladder-fern all do well on limestone. Near other rocks, plant the Woodsias, Ebony Spleenwort, Fragile Bladder-fern, and Hairy Lip-fern. For background on large and distant ledges, plant Christmas and Shield Ferns.

Interrupt the path with a step or two to create a place for a special planting. Railroad ties and service poles, cut to proper length, make sturdy and pleasing steps. Massive limestone chunks are attractive and improve as they weather.

Arrange the plants artistically at the sides of steps, the tall ones to the rear and small ones in front. Braun's Holly-fern, with dark green, bristled pinnules and shaggy, brown petioles, and the low spreading, green-gray-wine-colored Japanese Painted-fern are pleasing together. If the steps are limestone, plant Walking Ferns and Maidenhair Spleenwort in crevices between the treads and risers. To complete this garden setting, place a rustic bench near the foot of the steps.

## Possibilities of a Brook

Racing over moss-covered stones, resting in quiet pools, or lapping the edges of alluvial flats, a brook suggests a fern planting at each turn. To lessen erosion, use the strong, bold Ostrich Fern with its dense, intertwining runners. It grows well in wet areas and is not harmed by prolonged spring floods.

Beside the brook or in nearby marshy areas the Royal Fern makes a luxuriant stand. The Virginia Chain-fern, although not as tall, is also at home in boggy places. It has strong spreading tendencies and forms an unusually heavy, intertwining rhizome. Locate it with care; once established it is difficult to eradicate.

Marsh marigolds planted within sight of a path or a bridge add a touch of gold to early spring foliage. Pitcher plants and Sundews, with their odd structures and carnivorous habits, grow well in open, sunny areas where the soil is wet and highly acid.

Plant the Bulblet Bladder-fern on high rock ledges beside the brook; its exceptionally long tapering leaves will flow over the cool mossy stones. Lady Ferns, Marsh Ferns, and Crested Shield-ferns suggested for other woodland garden areas can be repeated near the brook.

## Old Foundations

There may be unsightly foundations, ruins of old farm houses and barns, along the trail-driveway. Rather than remove them, transform them into a beautiful formal or sunken garden. Fill the foundation almost to grade level with rubble and nearby loose stones. For access to the foundation, neatly open the wall in one or more places, keeping in mind the location of the path. Cover the stone-fill with at least a foot of good woodland soil for the plants.

If the fern monarchs are already represented in the wooded area, confine this foundation-planting to ferns of intermediate size. Select plants such as the Marginal, Intermediate, Spinulose, and Crested Shield-ferns for the inside wall. Put smaller plants in front of these with the Spleenworts, Cliff-brakes, and Woodsias among the stones in the border. Arrange the house ferns—Japanese Holly-fern, the Davallias, and Boston ferns—in this garden for the summer months.

A layer of brown buckwheat hulls over the central area will harmonize with the green foliage and mottled colors of the stones, and will give a carpet-like finish. A rustic bench or two may be added if there is room.

## Bird Baths and Feeders

Birds belong to the woods, some as residents, others migratory, stopping only for food, drink, and lodging for a night. Make the woodland garden attractive for them with appropriate feeders and baths. Rustic bark feeders in off-path locations will be attractive. A large stone with a basin-like cavity makes an excellent bird bath. One can be made by chipping out a hollow in a piece of soft sandstone. Place it on the ground with a nearby planting of small ferns—Fragile Ferns and Blunt-lobed Woodsias. Where a brook or spring is near and on a higher level, plastic or soft copper tubing bent to follow the ground contour will assure a supply of fresh, cool water.

## Transitional Plants

Between the house garden and the woodland tract lies the transitional zone, a region neither garden nor woods. Plant this to blend rather than divide the two areas. Set medium and large ferns among the lower varieties of shrubs. Use the slower spreading Christmas Ferns and Shield Ferns in random clusters. Farther into the woods where the soil is damper, use stands of Osmundas to complete the transition.

Spreading yews, laurels, various viburnums, and andromedas look well on the garden side. Slope the planting toward the woodland trees with rhododendrons and conifers. Tamaracks are attractive and, although not evergreen, harmonize with spruces and hemlocks. Plant the English Crested Male-fern at the base of any large stones or boulders that have been bulldozed to the edge of the garden.

*J. Horace MacFarland*

16. *Dryopteris filix-mas* cv.'**Cristata', English Crested Male-ferns,** in a transitional planting joining garden area with woodland tract. Rocks give a rugged sense of beauty.

*J. Horace MacFarland*

17. Barrier planting, composed of low border violets, *Matteuccia struthiopteris,* **Ostrich Ferns,** and wall of rhododendron and arborvitae.

*Gottscho-Schleisner*

18. **Interrupted Ferns,** like sentinels, seem to be guarding the smaller wild plants along a brook in the woodland garden.

*Gottscho-Schleisner*

19. **Cinnamon Ferns** with advanced fertile and sterile crosiers in foreground and a stand of **Christmas Ferns** at the right, amid a wild flower planting.

*Gottscho-Schleisner*

20. **Common Maidenhair Ferns** for a marginal planting along a woodland garden path.

*Coniogramme japonica,* **Japanese Evergreen Ferns,** between rocks bordering a brook. Ground cover is moss.

21. **Ferns in Gardens of Pacific Northwest**

*Polystichum munitum,* **Western Sword-fern,** next to flagstone step. *Skimmia japonica* is in the back ground.

# 8. *Growing Ferns Indoors*

Gardens indoors extend the fern grower's pleasure throughout the year, for many ferns grow well in the house. Some require less attention than others, but to say that ferns or any houseplants are carefree would only result in frustration for the inexperienced. As with all things, success is a measure of enthusiasm and effort.

## *Gardens at the Window*

Picture windows, with low sills and broad panes, offer opportunities for delightful indoor gardens. Here, with pebble trays, glass shelves, and hanging baskets, the soft colors of flowers will associate with the interesting leaf patterns of the ferns.

For limited space, there is nothing so effective and rewarding as a pebble tray. It is easily made of galvanized sheet iron by a handy gardener or local tinsmith, Figure 28. Make it about 2 inches deep and large enough to fit the windowsill snugly. If it is professionally made, have the edges rolled to improve the appearance and add stiffness. With fluorescent lights, a bookcase under a living-room window or in a hallway can be made into a beautiful little garden spot.

Cover the bottom of the tray with white seashore or roofing pebbles. These make a pleasing healthy base for the potted plants and insure drainage and ventilation. The galvanized coating of the tray will last for some time. If rust spots appear, sand them and then completely paint the tray with red oxide primer, followed by a coat or two of enamel. Do not use black asphaltum waterproof paint directly on any iron surface.

Where the window faces north, almost any fern will do well, but flowering plants have different requirements of light. Control with curtains, draperies, or Venetian blinds the excessive light of a southern exposure. Guard against crowding the tray. Each plant needs ample room for both beauty and health. Limit the pot sizes to 2, 3, and 4 inches. Larger ferns are pleasing at the sides and for a background. Ferns with their different shades of green blend with each other and complement the colors of flowering plants.

## Ferns for the Tray Garden

Start the garden with several plants from a florist or nurseryman specializing in ferns. Select some of the *Pteris cretica* cultivars, all widely different and attractive. Get them in 2-inch pots; they cost only about two dollars each at this stage. Select small specimens; this makes it possible to study their growth habits and see how ferns harmonize with other plants. Some will grow faster and taller than others; some will be bushy. As they develop, notice how each succeeding leaf is larger, and how pattern and color change as muturity is reached. Some leaves grow long and tapered; others become crested, especially at their tips. Colors change from soft, light green to a deeper, bolder color; some become variegated with silver, others develop creamy-white central stripes. Perhaps a half-dozen of these plants will be sufficient.

Also obtain some of the "fuzzy-footed" ferns with scale-covered rhizomes. Include a *Polypodium aureum*, Golden Polypody; its wandering rhizome is as fascinating as its leaf structure. This plant grows fast and in the course of a year will need to be moved to a roomier location. Two or three different Davallias, also of the fuzzy-foot group, will add further interest to a tray garden. These have leaves more fern-like than the others and plants grow much more slowly. They can remain in the tray for about two years before their rhizomes will require dividing. Davallias in 2- or 3-inch pots cost about four dollars each.

A Staghorn Fern will be a showpiece. There are many available species in the genus *Platycerium,* and all are different at maturity. When small, the leaves are like green buttons. Plants are exceptionally slow growing, and are a delight when the first tiny "antlers" appear. Large Staghorn Ferns cost thirty dollars or more, the little button-sized plants about three dollars.

There are many others to choose, but stop before the tray is crowded. Reserve some tray space for young sporophytes that may be transplanted later from the spore tubs.

## Glass Shelves

Use these shelves for artistic window arrangements of both flowers and ferns. Almost any ferns while small are suitable. Little wire brackets bent to hold pots in a tilted position will display the foliage attractively. Make use of both hanging and climbing species. Some varieties of Boston ferns, faster growing than many others, eventually extend gracefully down. The pellaeas are not climbing ferns but do produce proportionately long, chestnut-brown to black, wiry rachises, and with their shiny green pinnae are attractive in the window. Their long leaves eventually need support. Put *Lygodium scandens,* the Climbing Fern, on a bottom shelf with a cord ladder or small trellis to guide the upward growth. Obtain heavy plate glass for the window shelves. Safety glass, somewhat more expensive, is worth the difference in view of the breakage hazard.

Do not leave tender plants next to a window during severe winter weather unless there is an outer storm sash. Most of these ferns grow best in a warm atmosphere during the day with a lower temperature at night.

## Window Casings

For this location use side brackets, hanging baskets, and cork-bark plaques. Sidewall brackets that hold one or several pots are available to accommodate small and medium-sized plants. Select some of the smaller Boston Ferns for this use, providing there is no direct sun. A suggestion for a multiple bracket includes a bushy specimen of *Adiantum hispidulum*, Rosy Maidenhair, on top, and, immediately below, two plants of *A. capillus-*

*veneris,* the Southern Maidenhair, with their flowing leaves.

Ferns like the Golden Polypody, Staghorns, Bear's-foot, and the Davallias are epiphytic, naturally making their homes in trees. Use hanging log-cabin baskets of redwood, shown in Figure 28, to simulate their growing conditions. Line the baskets with osmundine fibre and fill with humus and fir bark chips to assure proper moisture, good drainage, and ventilation.

## Planters and Room Dividers

These are plant boxes for ferns or flowers and are available from small table sizes to large wheeled models for a patio. They are made of plastic, brass, glass, rattan, ceramic, and wood.

Gardeners handy with tools, as well as ideas, can make their own planters, cut from transparent or colored plastic sheets, ⅛ inch thick and cemented with strong, lasting epoxy resin. Brass can be hammered to give an antique effect. Sheet copper formed to size and shape will be pleasing if allowed to develop a patina.

For a large wooden planter, use unpainted redwood. It weathers slowly and does not deteriorate for years. If the planter requires a paint finish, get ⅜-inch thick fir plywood. Both exterior and marine plywood are waterproof. Have the plywood cut at the lumber-yard unless the home shop is equipped to do this. Assemble the pieces with rustproof screws and "fill" or "seal" the grain with dilute white shellac or a special plywood sealer.

For a natural wood planter, select one of the beautiful veneer plywood finishes in mahogany, birch, maple, oak, or pine. Finish it with penetrating wax or hand-rubbed flat varnish for an attractive surface which quickly sheds water.

Fill small, table-sized planters with potting soil and use three ferns—*Pteris ensiformis* cv. 'Victoriae', an erect Victorian Brake, in the center and a small, bushy *Pteris cretica* on each side. Or, put the tall one at the end with a slope down to a flat, spreading species. In the large planters, keep the ferns in separate pots. This has many advantages, especially when occasionally changing arrangements of both ferns and potted flowers.

Consider growing the many varieties of Boston ferns with their long, flowing leaves or the more modern bushy types. Three or four closely spaced in a planter will give the appearance of a large, single plant.

Fall, winter, and spring suggest groupings of ferns with seasonal flowers for Thanksgiving, Christmas, and Easter. Potted chrysanthemums, poinsettias, and white lilies are best when placed among the low, thick ferns like *Pteris cretica* cv. 'Wilsonii' or cv. 'Rivertoniana'. Both cultivars have crested leaves and a dense spreading foliage.

When the Boston Fern with its long and flowing leaves comes to maturity, it will be attractive on a pedestal in a hall or an archway. *Cyrtomium falcatum,* the Japanese Holly-fern, and larger plants of *Polypodium aureum,* Golden Polypody, are also suitable for these locations. *Asplenium nidus,* the Bird's-nest Fern, with erect, brilliant green, simple leaves makes an excellent table fern.

Use the small ferns growing in a pebble tray as table decoration. Put a small flowering plant or potted bulb in the center of a shallow ceramic or wooden bowl with three or four small potted ferns around it. Then fill the bowl with enough dampened peat moss to conceal the pots. Try different combinations of flowers, ferns, and bowls; there seems to be no end of possibilities.

*Roche*

### 22. Exotic Ferns for the Indoor Garden

Top row, l to r: *Polystichum tsus simense, Polypodium aureum, Pteris ensiformis* cv. 'Victoriae', *Adiantum hispidulum*
2nd row, l to r: *Asplenium nidus*
3d   row, l to r: *Adiantum bellum, Pellaea viridis*
Bottom row:    *Nephrolepis exaltata* cv. 'Hillii'
               *Pellaea rotundifolia*

52

*Roche*

23. **Exotic Ferns for the Indoor Garden**

    Top row, l to r: *Platycerium grande, Humata tyermanii, Phyllitis scolopendrium* cv. **'Undu-**
                 **latum'**, *Phyllitis scolopendrium*
    2nd row, l to r: *Cyclophorus lingua, Blechnum gibbum, Platycerium lemoinei, Pteris cretica*
                 cv. **'Cristata'**
    3d  row, l to r: *Doryopteris pendata* var. *palmata, Cibotium schiedei*
    Bottom row:   *Pteris quadriaurita* cv. **'Argyraea'**, *Polypodium aureum*

53

## SOME CULTURAL SUGGESTIONS

### Light

Ferns require light, either natural or an artificial equivalent. The amount of light needed depends largely on the type of fern. Certainly a fern whose native home is a jungle, with only filtered sunlight, will not thrive in a solarium or on a windowsill with strong summer sun. Winter sun, which is of shorter duration and weaker intensity, is not too bright for most ferns.

### Soil, Potting and Fertilizing

Soil for potted plants can be prepared in advance and stored for later needs. A somewhat universal and circumneutral soil mixture is made by screening equal parts of good topsoil or compost, humus, sand, and milled sphagnum, with a little bone meal added. After screening, the material is baked in an oven at 250° F. for about one hour to kill any harmful organisms. Moisten this mixture before using it by spraying with water and stirring until it is sufficiently damp.

In planting a fern in a clay pot, cover the bottom with *crocks*, small pieces of broken flower pot, and add sufficient soil to form a base for the fern. Center the plant and pour soil evenly around and over the spreading roots. Add more soil and smaller crocks until the pot is filled to within ½ inch of the top; if there is less space, watering is difficult. A test of good potting is whether rapid drainage of excess water is possible. Remember that roots require oxygen as well as moisture, and that most ferns should never stand in water or have soggy soil.

Transplanting a fern from a 2-inch pot to a 6-inch pot can be injurious. An increase in pot-size of 1 inch in diameter is proper and assures better drainage and ventilation.

If a plant is already in a large pot and further increase in the size of the pot is not feasible, carefully remove the old soil from the roots, clip and thin them, and repot. Also thin the foliage by removing all dead and old leaves. Spray freshly potted ferns several times daily until their roots become adjusted.

Feeding ferns with prepared chemical plant foods is an artificial stimulant to growth. These foods contain a balance of nutrients required by the plants and are helpful when used according to manufacturers' directions. Some gardeners claim good results with natural fertilizers on both indoor and outdoor ferns. In any case, supplementary feeding should not be considered a substitute for repotting before the soil becomes exhausted. I limit the fertilizing of my indoor plants to a small amount of bone meal in the potting soil, and a monthly application of dilute emulsified fish oil.

### Watering

Some ferns require more moisture than others. Size and type of pot, glazed or porous, and the humidity of a room all influence water intake. When watering plants, supply enough to thoroughly penetrate the soil, and allow the excess to drain off; to moisten the surface only can mean nothing less than slow death. Over-watering, particularly when there is poor drainage, will also eventually kill a plant. Leaf wilting, unless disease is present, is a symptom of lack of water; yellowing, other than that of natural aging or disease, is generally caused by excessive moisture or poor drainage. Large ferns, difficult to water from the top, should be placed in tubs with water up to the pot rim and left long enough for all the soil to be moistened. When the top soil *feels* damp, the plant has had enough.

Roots are not the only means by which ferns receive moisture. To encourage healthy growth and luxuriant foliage, give a mist-spray or fogging occasionally. Where there are many plants, a 2-gallon pressure-type sprayer is effective and makes the task easier.

## Temperature

Temperature requirements depend on the origin of the species. Most warm-climate ferns grow well in the average winter warmth of the home—a day temperature of 68°–72° F., a night temperature of 62° to 65° F. While plants are reasonably tolerant of variations, a uniform day-night cycle gives best results.

## Parasites

The most insidious trouble is caused by fungi, for the early stages of infection are almost invisible. Attacks are generally limited to succulent parts, particularly delicate petioles of young sporophytes near ground level. While fungous spores are ever present, their growth can be accelerated by over-moist conditions. A mercurial solution such as Semesan is a useful control.

Scale can cause serious damage or even destroy a plant if it gets out of control. Leathery leaves like those of the pellaeas and cyrtomiums are especially susceptible. The parasite appears as a brown scale, actually a small shell-like covering of a sucking mite. If there are only a few scales they can be picked from the leaf, but if the attack is advanced it is best to destroy the plant. Be cautious about introducing new plants; if doubt exists as to the health of a plant isolate the plant for a quarantine period.

Mealy bugs, because of their size and whiteness, are easy to see and readily removed with a small artist's paint brush soaked in Black Flag-40, 1 teaspoonful to a gallon of water to which a few Ivory soap flakes have been added. Avoid harsh commercial spray compounds for these are harmful to the delicate foliage of many ferns.

Slugs and snails hide or bury themselves during the day and are hard to find, but their nocturnal damage is evidence of activity. A few moistened pellets of snail bait placed on the surface of each pot will be effective. Another nuisance, millipeds, can be found by early morning inspection and destroyed. During the day, they are found hiding under moist pots.

# 9. How to Propagate Ferns

For the serious gardener, the propagation of ferns can be one of the most fascinating phases of their culture. In addition to reproducing themselves by spores, ferns also propagate by vegetative budding or by division of the rhizome. Of these methods, propagation by spores provides more intimate knowledge of the fern and its life cycle. Each method has merits; for some ferns, one method may be more desirable than another.

## Growing from Spores

In nature, old farmhouse wells are sometimes found lined with Ebony Spleenwort, and limestone abutments of bridges are dotted with Purple Cliff-brake, which makes one wonder why man's attempts at spore growing are not always successful. But remember, a myriad of spores has been expended for each one that has become established. Many spores never germinate, as they fall or drift to places unfavorable for growth. Spores that reach the prothallial state still have much to endure during their first two years; excessive rains wash away their feeble footholds, sustained dry periods parch their delicate tissues, and fungi damp out the lives of many.

To add interest to the spore growing project, gather a number of mature fertile leaves of different species. Examine the sori with a 10-power magnifier; immature sori are generally light green; those that have ripe spores will be very dark green, dark brown, or black and are now ready for collection. After dehiscence only empty sporangia remain.

Collect the spores by laying the leaves, sori side down, on a piece of hard-finish white paper. Cover the leaves with a newspaper or blotter to prevent the spores from blowing away. This absorbent covering also aids in removing moisture from the leaves. Within a day or two, when the sporangia have discharged their contents, carefully lift both paper covering and leaf. Remove the chaff—particles of indusia and sporangia—by tilting the paper at a sharp angle and tapping lightly. In this operation the larger particles will be winnowed away, leaving the spores. Fold the paper along the center, and with more vigorous tapping the spores will roll toward the crease. Guide them into a small bottle, then cap and label with the name of the species, the location where found, and the date of the collection. Store spores not needed for immediate use in a cool, dark place.

Viability varies with the species, time, and conditions of storage. Spores of the

*Osmundas,* containing chlorophyll, are usable for only a few days; some spores from other genera have been known to germinate many years later. I have had spores of *Dryopteris marginalis* germinate in five days after storage at 40° F. for eighteen months.

For spore growing, I use wide-mouth glass jars or small plastic refrigerator containers with tight fitting covers. Sterile conditions are important. Jars are best sterilized in a pressure cooker; for the plastic containers soaking in a 10 percent Clorox solution is sufficient to kill any harmful organisms that might later "damp-off" the delicate prothallia.

The growing medium can be a mixture of humus, peat moss, and coarse sand, or a commercially prepared soil such as Swiss Farms or Black Magic African-violet mix. Sterilize all growing mixtures by thoroughly baking at 250° F. for one hour, or steaming in a pressure cooker. A layer of ½ inch in the bottom of each container is sufficient. On top of the soil spread a thin layer of finely divided "crocks" or broken flower pots previously soaked in the Clorox solution. Lightly tamp to an even surface and thoroughly dampen with sterile water.

Spores are sown by tapping them from a sheet of paper. Careful spreading will give even distribution; overconcentration will induce crowding and will be injurious later. Replace the plastic covers or cover the glass jars with cellophane wrap secured with a rubber band, and a miniature greenhouse is now ready.

For germinating and growing the spores, place the containers on a windowsill having a northern exposure, or 12 inches under cool fluorescent lamps burning 14 hours daily. Room temperature ranges from 65° to 70° F. are best.

Spores differ in germinating time. The first cell division of some species occurs within three or four days; others take as many weeks. As the prothallia start to form, a light green cast is noticed on the surface of the growing medium. It is difficult to see much detail at this time with the 10-power magnifier. A student's microscope can be used to study the structures which develop during this phase of the life cycle, and much of interest can be observed through weekly surveys.

If growing conditions are favorable, the prothallia will become flat, green heart-shaped organisms after about three months; they will then be about ¼ inch in their largest dimension. Occasional gentle spraying of the prothallia at this time will supply moisture necessary for the spermatozoids to swim to the archegonia and fertilize the egg cells. Before long, young leaves of the new sporophytes will be visible to the naked eye, but details can only be seen through a magnifier. A new gardening thrill is the reward of those seeing these tiny plants for the first time.

Where prothallia are too close to allow the young sporophytes to develop, transplant little clumps of three or four to accelerate further growth. When the plants are about 1 inch high, transplant them again into 2-inch clay pots. To prevent their delicate structure from drying, put them in a plastic covered propagating box (Figure 28) half filled with damp peat moss or vermiculite. Since it is almost impossible to identify young ferns, carefully mark both the growing containers and the newly transplanted sporophytes. By the end of the second year they can be used as houseplants or added to the hardy garden collection.

Damping off of the young ferns by fungi is frequent and discouraging. Fungous cells are everywhere and their growth is accelerated by warmth and moisture. Fungi can be controlled by reducing the amount of moisture and occasionally spraying with a fungicide. If there are only a few plants, paint the first leaves and petioles, using an artist's brush and a mercurial solution.* The solution is a deadly poison; label and store it in a safe place.

---

*Semesan, a product of DuPont, diluted 1 teaspoonful to 1 quart of water, can be applied at intervals of ten days.

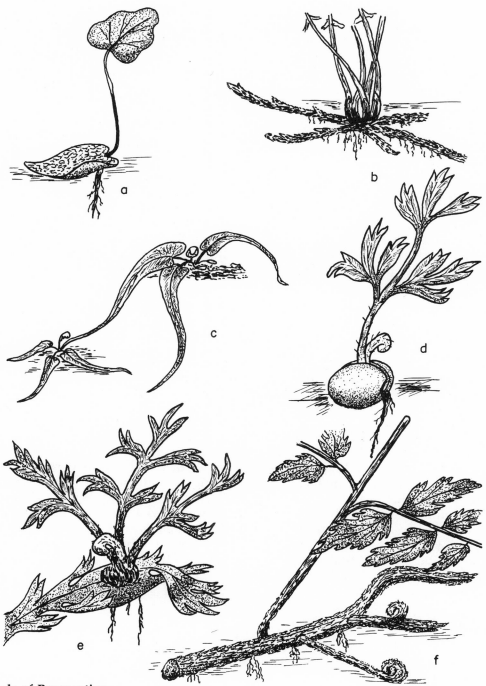

24. **Methods of Propagation**

    a. Young sporophyte growing from prothallium of *Pellaea atropurpurea,* **Purple Cliff-brake.**

    b. Stolons growing from rhizome of *Matteuccia struthiopteris,* **Ostrich Fern.**

    c. New plant growing from apex of mature leaf of *Camptosorus rhizophyllus,* **Walking Fern.**

    d. Juvenile leaf growing from bulblet of *Cystoperis bulbifera,* **Bulblet Bladder-fern.**

    e. Young sporophyte growing from vegetative bud on parent leaf of *Asplenium bulbiferum,* **Mother Fern.**

    f. New leaf and croziers growing from surface-rhizome of *Humata tyermannii,* **Bear's-foot Fern.**

## Rhizome Division

Propagation by this method is the easiest and quickest way to start additional plants, and is certain to be satisfactory. Division can be performed at any time but early fall is least disrupting to the garden and best suited for adjusting the rhizomes. In dividing large clumps, dig up the whole plant and cut it in half, or as desired. Plant the divisions quickly in their new locations, and water. If final planting must be delayed, temporarily "heel in" the plants and keep them moist.

Ferns that form crowns rather than intertwining rhizomes require greater care in dividing. With a small, sharp knife, divide the rhizomes carefully, disturbing as few as possible of the present leaves and the closely spaced dormant crosiers. Some ferns, particularly those of the epiphytic davallias, have rhizomes growing on the surface or hanging over the edge of the pots. New plants can be started by placing the overhanging rhizome on a small pot containing moist soil and sphagnum. In time, roots will reach into the soil and the new plant can be severed from the parent. Other rhizome sections cut from the parent plant can be placed on the damp surface of the growing medium. To prevent rotting, do not cover the rhizomes. Several cuttings can be rooted in one pot and repotted when small leaves appear. Keep the cuttings moist at all times, but never allow them to become soggy.

## Leaf Buds

This asexual method, either by *buds* or *bulblets,* is a way that nature has devised to bypass the usual time-consuming method of the spore-prothallium-sporophyte cycle. Some ferns, an example being *Cystopteris bulbifera,* the Bulblet Bladder-fern, produce bulblets in addition to spores on the underside of the leaf. These bulblets look like small garden peas and fall to the ground at maturity. With proper conditions, the two sections composing the bulblet spread apart and a small root reaches down, while a tiny green leaf grows up. This little fern becomes established in a few months, but it is not until the second or third year that the plant assumes the characteristics of its parent.

Plants that reproduce by means of leaf budding are known as *viviparous* or "live-bearing" ferns, sometimes called *mother ferns.* Besides reproductive spores, they have tiny buds on the upper surface or edge of the pinnules which grow into small plants while still attached to the parent. The leaves of some plants are literally covered with these bud-plants, each crowding its neighbor for survival. When the young plants get larger and have three or four leaves, remove them with a portion of the parent pinna and plant them on the moist surface of vermiculite. Later, as roots appear, transfer them to a neutral growing soil.

25. **Fern nursery and neatly arranged window garden.**

Upper shelves: Germinating spores in covered glass dishes. Center: Mature plants of **Sword Fern, Maidenhair,** and **Hart's-tongue Fern.** Lower shelves: Additional spore dishes and juvenile plants growing under fluorescent lights.

Young sporophyte growing from prothallium of *Athyrium filix-femina,* **Lady Fern.**

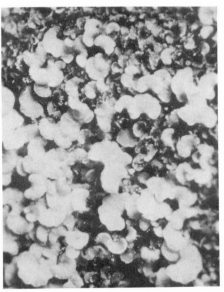

Group of young sporophytes growing from prothallia of *Onoclea sensibilis,* **Sensitive Fern.**

26. **Germinating Spores**

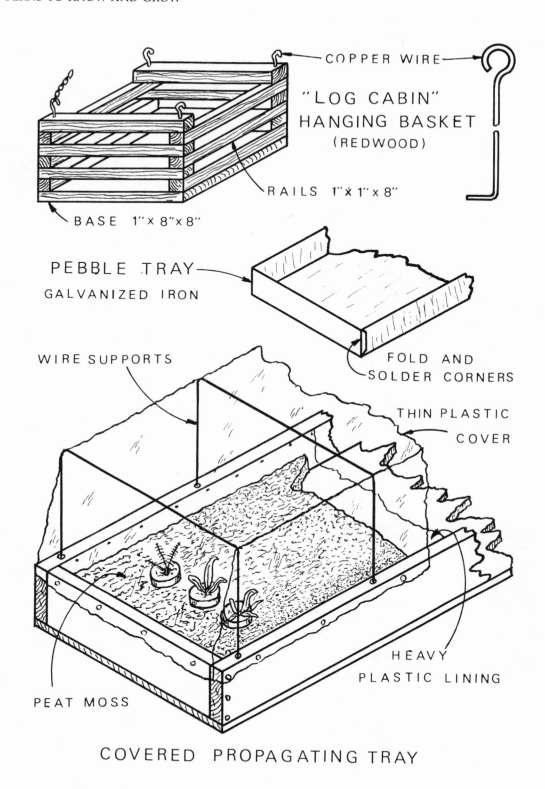

COPPER WIRE

"LOG CABIN"
HANGING BASKET
(REDWOOD)

RAILS 1" x 1" x 8"

BASE 1" x 8" x 8"

PEBBLE TRAY
GALVANIZED IRON

FOLD AND
SOLDER CORNERS

WIRE SUPPORTS

THIN PLASTIC
COVER

HEAVY
PLASTIC LINING

PEAT MOSS

COVERED PROPAGATING TRAY

27. **Hanging basket, pebble tray, and covered propagating tray**

# 10. Native and Exotic Ferns to Know and Grow

This chapter presents an encyclopedic reference of the most commonly found ferns, and many of the rare species, growing throughout the United States. A number of the more delicate exotic ferns suitable for house-growing are also included for reference and cultural guidance. All of the species included are markedly different. Those marked by only minor variations and uncommon hybrids have been intentionally omitted.

Some of the ferns included will not grow readily in a garden under ordinary conditions. Unless natural growing conditions can be simulated, it is very difficult to grow some of the Spleenworts of the genus *Asplenium.* Grape Ferns of the genus *Botrychium* are highly sensitive to ecological conditions and seldom survive after the second year when removed from their habitat. Thus, emphasis should be made on *growing* the ferns of simpler horticultural requirements, and *knowing* the remaining rare species.

A genus is a group of species having close resemblance in one or more characteristics. In this chapter several species of the genus *Dryopteris* are described. Most of these ferns are medium to large in size, and have brown-scaled petioles, round sori covered with kidney-shaped indusia, and grow from rhizomes terminating in a crown.

In some genera the species hybridize readily, and there seems to be an almost endless list of hybrids. As an example, *D. × bootii.* Boott's Shield-fern, is a natural but sterile hybrid between *D. cristata,* the Crested Shield-fern, and *D. intermedia,* the Intermediate Shield-fern, and as such carries some of the features of both parents.

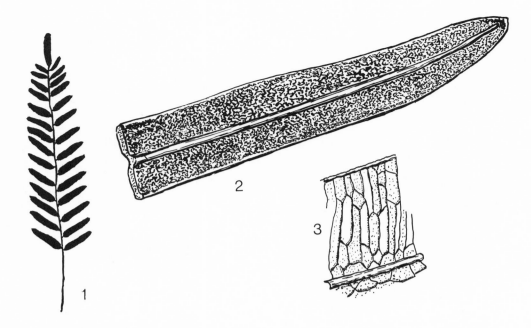

## Acrostichum aureum—Leather Fern
## Acrostichum danaeifolium—Giant Leather-fern

Leaves dark green, lanceolate, 1-pinnate, 6 to 12 or more feet long, up to 12 inches wide. Structure coarse, harsh to touch.

These ferns are native to tropical and subtropical areas, usually found growing along the fresh or brackish water edge of mango swamps and ditches. Their strong, spongy roots are of ecological value in protecting soil from erosion along the edge of inland waterways.

There is a marked similarity between these two ferns, but enough difference to give them individual species status. *A. aureum* may be identified by its uniformly spaced pinnae, the fertile pinnae being confined to the apical section of the blade. *A. danaeifolium* has crowded, papery, fertile pinnae extending to the base of the blade or nearly so. Both species form hexagonal areoles between somewhat parallel and slightly inclined veins extending from the midrib to the edge. Areoles of *A. aureum* are slightly larger.

SORI: Exindusiate sporangia have no definite soral pattern but grow independently from areoles. Sporangia eventually coalesce to form a heavy brown mat.

CULTURE: Because of their coarse and unattractive leaves and excessive size, these species are not recommended for horticultural application.

RANGE: *A. aureum* is of pantropic distribution; *A. danaeifolium* grows only in the American tropics.

---

1, Silhouette of leaf.  2, Fertile leaf at maturity.  3, Section of pinna showing typical structure of veins.

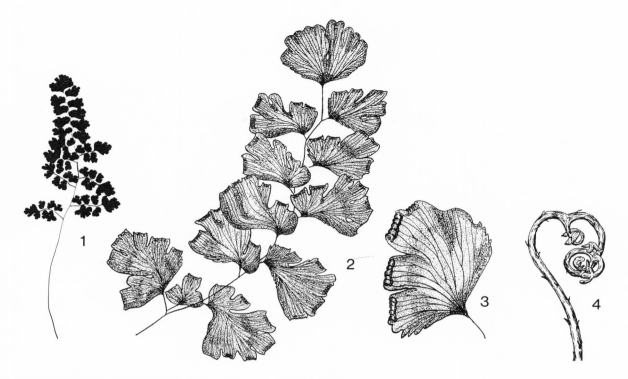

## *Adiantum capillus-veneris*—Southern Maidenhair

Leaves ovate-lanceolate, 1-pinnate above, 2-pinnate in lower half, with purple-black petioles rising at intervals from a creeping rhizome. Soft green, fan-like pinnules. Length from a few inches to nearly a foot.

The Southern Maidenhair or Venus'-hair Fern is one of the most delicate members of this genus. Although the petiole and rachis are dark and glossy, resembling black enameled wire, the slenderness of the leaf gives it a soft, flowing appearance. Like other members of its genus, this species has pinnules that follow a fan-shaped pattern, somewhat like the leaves of a ginkgo tree. Pinnules of membranous texture are marked with easily seen dichotomous veins, starting from the stalk and spreading to the outer edge.

This fern makes a good houseplant and can be individually potted for a glass window shelf or allowed to gracefully overflow the edge of a small planter. Horizontal rhizomes, from which grow a dense stand of leaves, quickly fill the pot. New crosiers, delicate in both structure and color, continually emerge among the older petioles. As the older leaves turn brown, carefully cut them close to the soil.

SORI: Sporangia are borne on the underside of the outer edge of deeply cleft pinnules; they are covered by the reflexed margin of the pinnule. The sori turn brown at maturity, adding a touch of color to the leaf.

CULTURE: Loose, moist woodland soil to which broken limestone pieces or cracked oyster shells have been added. Hardy in milder winter areas. Place in cool, shady location indoors. Divide plant often, prune severely, and repot.

RANGE: Subtropical parts of both hemispheres. Sporadically northward to British Columbia, South Dakota, Missouri, Virginia.

---

1, Silhouette of leaf. 2, Upper side of fertile pinna. 3, Underside of pinnule showing dichotomous venation leading to sori. 4, Crosier just prior to vertical and lateral expansion.

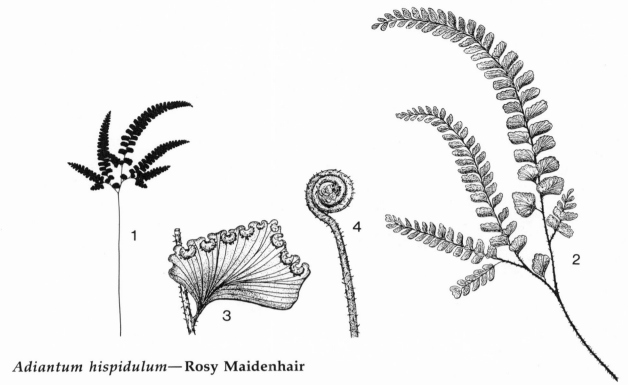

## *Adiantum hispidulum*— Rosy Maidenhair

> Leaf delicate, 2-pinnate, 6 to 12 inches long. Rose-color when young, changing to medium green. Petiole and rachises scale-covered, pinnules slightly hairy.

This is another of the many widespread maidenhair ferns. It is easy to grow and sufficiently different in color and leaf structure to add interest to the fern collection. New leaves continue to rise until their closely spaced petioles form a dense stand.

Like the Northern Maidenhair, its young, tightly wound crosiers are dull red-brown; in addition, they are covered with bristly hairs and scales. The leaves are exceptionally delicate when young, but later become stronger and heavier. Simultaneously, the pinnules increase in size and change to their final medium-green color. The division of the leaf is unusual in the genus; the basal pinnule of many pinnae is replaced by a small pinna. Characteristic of the genus *Adiantum*, venation is dichotomous, the veins radiating from the base of the pinnule.

Dense, dark brown scales remain on the petiole and rachises after the leaf reaches maturity and are easily seen. Light-colored or colorless scales and hairs are found on the surfaces of the pinnules and indusia.

SORI: Numerous and conspicuous, located on the underside of cleft pinnule; sporangia covered by the reflexed false indusium. Reddish-brown mature and exposed sori add to the beauty of the leaves.

CULTURE: Loose soil, rich in humus, to which broken or coarsely ground oyster shells have been added. Ample water to keep soil constantly moist. Avoid strong winter sunlight; place in full to open shade in summer. Divide plant and repot occasionally. Plant grows fast and will quickly fill larger pot. Keep plant neat by removing old, discolored leaves.

RANGE: Old World tropics.

---

1, Leaf silhouette. 2, Portion of blade. 3, Underside of pinnule showing prominent venation and kidney-shaped reflexed marginal covering of sporangia. 4, Young, tightly wound, scale-covered crosier.

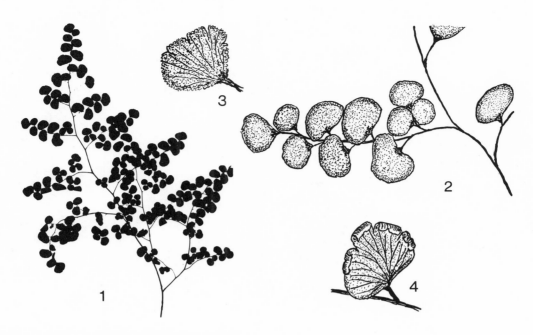

## *Adiantum jordanii*—California Maidenhair

Leaves ovate, 2-pinnate to 3-pinnate, up to 18 inches long. Dark, polished purple-brown stipes rising from a creeping rhizome. Pinnules strongly fan shaped, with prominent dichotomous veins.

Maidenhair Ferns grow throughout the world, with the vast majority being confined to the tropics or subtropic areas. *A. jordanii* is one of the few that grow farther north and may be found on ledges in cool, moist canyons of California. Pinnules vary in size from ⅜ inch to over 1 inch in width. Sterile pinnules have easily seen saw-tooth edges.

SORI: Sporangia are borne on underside of pinnules in one to four cleft divisions. Edges of pinnules reflex to protect sporangia by forming false indusia.

CULTURE: Well-drained, humus-rich soil or potting mix, constantly mildly damp. Prefers a slightly moist atmosphere.

RANGE: Western U.S. coastal States.

1, Leaf silhouette. 2, Portion of leaf. 3, Sterile pinnule. 4, Fertile pinnule showing cleft divisions and reflexed margin.

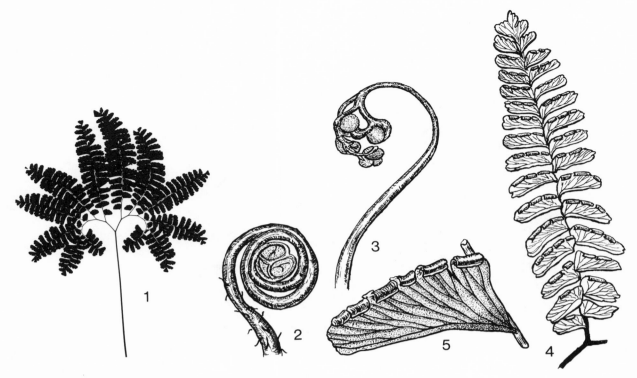

## *Adiantum pedatum*—Common Maidenhair

Leaf 12 to 26 inches long, petiole wiry, polished purple-brown to dark brown, continuing upward to divergent, spreading rachises having 5 to 7 pinnae forming fan pattern nearly parallel to ground. Pinnules alternate, light to medium green.

To many, the Maidenhair Fern is the daintiest and prettiest of all the northeastern species and should be included in all fern collections. Its early rising little crosiers, of earth-matching color, are seen only by the keenest observer. It is interesting to watch the petiole rise, then the pinnae uncoil, and finally the pinnules unfold.

In the silhouette of the leaf, the pinnae appear as arching branches. Actually, in the living plant the pinnae grow outward in a flat, fan-like position. There are many maidenhair ferns growing throughout the world and nearly all have these common features—leaflets, glossy petioles and rachises. These features quickly identify the different plants as members of the genus *Adiantum*.

The creeping-branching rhizome, with many wiry petioles at intervals of a few inches, grows just below the surface. In its habitat, this species may be found with three or four separated leaves or as large, lush patches.

SORI: Concealed sporangia at end of prominent, dichotomous veins. False indusium formed by deeply cleft reflexed margin of pinnule, darkening as sporangia mature.

CULTURE: Given a rich, loose, well-drained humus soil, this plant will remain attractive from early spring to fall. It must be kept moist at all times. While this plant is of the spreading variety, its outward growth is slow and causes no trouble.

RANGE: Nova Scotia and Quebec to Minnesota, south to central Georgia, eastern Oklahoma, and coastal Louisiana; California.

---

1, Leaf silhouette.  2, Early crosier showing compact arrangement of leaf parts.  3, Advanced crosier.  4, Underside of fertile pinna.  5, Enlarged sketch of pinnule, underside, showing venation and cleft indusium.

## *Aglaomorpha meyenianum*—Bear's-paw Fern

Strongly dimorphic. Leaves oblong-lanceolate, deep green, 12 to 24 inches long, 6 inches wide, pinnatifid, sessile. Rhizome stout, covered with rust-colored, elongate scales.

This is an epiphytic fern which grows as high as 36 inches in its native habitat. It has an unusually large, creeping, fleshy rhizome covered with slender rust-colored scales. Scales, which may grow ½ inch long, have straight or curved tooth-like projections.

Both fertile and sterile leaves are without petioles; the joining of the leaves to the rhizomes is completely obscured by the dense scale covering. A heavy costa, visible on both sides, gives stiffness to the leaves. Lower segments of both leaves are extremely short and blunt. On the sterile leaf the upper segments are opposite and larger than those of the fertile leaf, each ending in a sharp-pointed apex. The lower segments of the fertile leaf are similar but smaller than those of the sterile leaf and are without sori. Upper fertile pinnae are ribbon-like and about twice as long as the lower sterile segments. Each pinna consists of a firm midrib with alternately spaced, rounded lobes on each side, each lobe being nearly covered with a sorus. Broad-based leaves serve to catch and retain moisture and humus. Sterile segments of both types of leaves are leathery and marked with well-defined veins.

SORI: Round, exindusiate, numerous, one on each lobe of pinna.

CULTURE: Rich, damp humus. Plant in a porus clay pot or log-cabin basket lined with osmundine to insure good drainage and ventilation. Requires humid atmosphere or mist-spray at regular intervals.

RANGE: Philippines.

---

1, Leaf silhouettes (left) fertile, (right) sterile. 2, Base of leaves and crosier growing from heavily scale-covered rhizome. 3, Section of fertile leaf showing sori occupying center of small, rounded segments. 4, Rhizome scale with dentate edge.

69

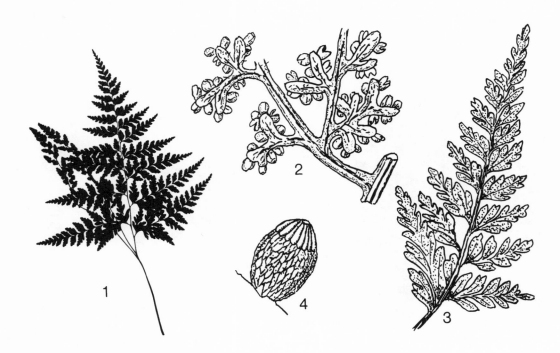

## Anemia adiantifolia—Pine Fern

Leaves triangular or nearly so, 2-pinnate-pinnatifid or 3-pinnate, medium green, 6 to 20 inches long. Segments of pinnae wedge-shaped, with prominent veins leading to coarsely toothed edges.

Pine Fern, with its odd fertile and sterile combination of pinnae, appears somewhat like *Botrychium virginianum,* the Rattlesnake Fern. It is one of a genus of over 60 species living almost entirely in the American tropics. Different species are able to adapt themselves to widely varying growing conditions. Some, like the Pine Fern, prefer the edges of lime sink-holes in the moist warm air of the Everglades; others live between rock crevices in the dry, cool air of the Inca ruins high in the Andes.

SORI: Sporangia borne on two parallel panicles arising vertically beneath basal pinnae. The *Anemia* genus is a member of the *Schizaeaceae* family and, in keeping with its characteristics, has a sporangium markedly similar to *Schizaea pusilla,* the Curly-grass Fern, and *Lygodium palmatum,* the Climbing Fern.

CULTURE: Makes a good houseplant where atmospheric moisture is sufficient. Use loose, humus-rich soil with old lime-cement chips. Keep moist but avoid excessive watering.

RANGE: American tropics.

1, Leaf silhouette. 2, Sporangia on upper area of fertile panicle. 3, Sterile pinna showing wedge-shaped segments. 4, Typical sporangium.

## *Arachniodes aristata*—**East Indian Holly-fern**

Leaves ovate-deltoid, 3-, 4-pinnate, 12 to 20 inches long, 9 to 12 inches wide, dark green, leathery, texture very harsh, spaced at intervals along a heavily brown-scaled rhizome. Petiole densely covered with brown scales which diminish on rachis.

*Arachniodes aristata*, a vigorous fern with broad leaves and long, tapering pinnae, is an exceptionally handsome plant and is best displayed in a hanging basket. Leaves terminating in spiny segments quickly relate to the "holly" common name. The brown-scaled rhizomes are unusually strong and invasive, penetrating a fiber hanging basket if necessary to gain their objective.

This fern may be quickly propagated by planting rhizome cuttings in the center of a basket and allowing them to grow to the edge and underside. Line the basket with coarse sphagnum moss and fill with a mixture of peat moss, humus, perlite, and chopped fir bark. To accelerate the growth of a large plant, start several cuttings in various areas of the basket. Do not bury the rhizomes, but rather pin them to the surface by means of heavy wire in the shape of hair pins. In this manner a dense root system will form on the underside of the rhizomes.

SORI: Small, round, in rows near midrib. Indusium circular, centrally attached, rarely kidney shape.

CULTURE: Grows rapidly from cuttings under fluorescent light 14 hours daily. Soil should be moist but not soggy.

RANGE: Japan and Himalayas to Sri Lanka, Norfolk Island, Fiji, Samoa, New South Wales, and Natal.

---

1, Leaf silhouette. 2, Basal pinna. 3, Fertile pinnule. 4, Sorus. 5, Rhizome-root system.

71

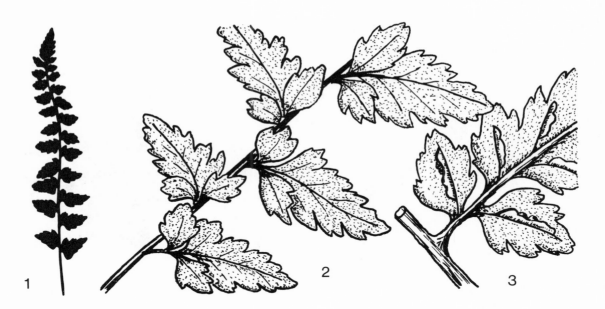

*Asplenium bradleyi*—Bradley's Spleenwort

Leaf medium green, oblong-lanceolate, pinnate, 4 to 7 inches long, with slender dark-brown petiole growing from a mat of old, denuded petioles. Pinnae numerous, oblong-ovate, toothed, petioles short.

Bradley's Spleenwort is a rare, naturally reproducing species, probably originating as a hybrid between *A. platyneuron* and *A. montanum*. Normally found growing in deep crevices of sandstone, gneiss, and other hard and noncalcareous rocks. Roots find moisture and nutrients in highly acid humus.

SORI: Linear. Short and numerous forming confluent patches at maturity, with delicate indusia opening away from veins.

CULTURE: Not available from commercial growers and difficult to find in natural habitat. Successful cultivation of this species is virtually impossible.

RANGE: Georgia to Oklahoma, north to New York and Kentucky.

---

1, Leaf silhouette.  2, Basal section of leaf.  3, Fertile pinna with mature sori.

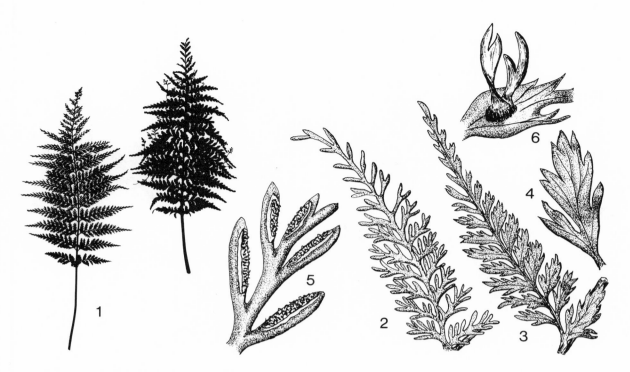

## *Asplenium bulbiferum*—Mother Fern

Leaf oblong-lanceolate, 2-, 3-pinnate, arching, medium soft-green, growing to 24 inches in length and 9 inches in width. Petiole black, scale-covered, the black continuing into rachis. Reproduces by spores or vegetative budding.

Fertile leaves have pinnules with narrow, linear segments, while the sterile leaves have pinnules with broader, multi-pointed segments. Intermixing of the two different leaves adds greatly to the beauty of the fern.

In addition to propagating by spores, this species has a second method of reproduction, that of "live-bearing" or "giving birth" to new plants. Tiny buds, like miniature crowns, develop on the upper surface of the pinnules of both the fertile and sterile leaves. At first, little leaves grow from these crowns; succeeding leaves become larger and more like the parent plant. Budding seems to be without limit, and eventually the mother-leaf becomes crowded with the growing young plants. Little rootlets are formed when the parent leaf contacts moist soil, and before long the little plants become independent.

SORI: Elongate, almost fully occupying the underside of the segment, covered by longitudinally opening indusium.

CULTURE: Rich, loose, neutral soil. Leaves wilt quickly if soil is not kept moist. Propagate new plants by cutting off several budding pinnules. Cover pinnules with moist mixture of soil and vermiculite, leaving small crowns and leaflets fully exposed. Cover with an inverted tumbler to insure higher humidity and prevent wilting. About two years are required to grow an 8-inch plant. Shortly after the first year, budding and tiny plants appear on the young mother-leaves. Spores will not develop until the fern becomes much larger.

RANGE: New Zealand, Australia, Malaysia.

---

1, Leaf silhouettes, (left) fertile leaf, (right) sterile leaf. 2, Fertile pinna. 3, Sterile pinna. 4, Enlarged sketch of sterile pinnule. 5, Enlarged fertile pinnule showing mature sori. 6, New plant growing from bud on sterile pinnule.

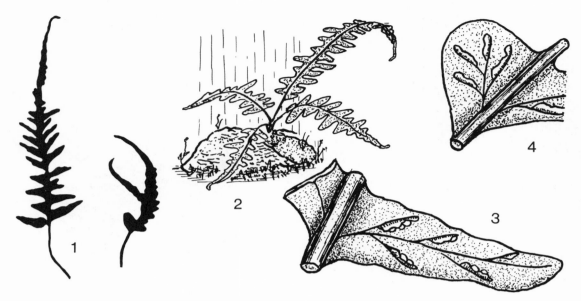

## *Asplenium* × *ebenoides*—Scott's Spleenwort

Leaves extremely variable, lanceolate, long tapering 4 to 9 inches long, pinnatifid, pinnate near base. Petiole dark brown, shiny, this color following rachis to middle of blade. Lower pinnae distinct. Evergreen.

Scott's Spleenwort is a rare, usually sterile hybrid between *A. platyneuron* and *Camptosorus rhizophyllus* found growing in the area of its parents. Leaves are variable, differing greatly on each plant. The hybrid is sterile, producing only aborted, inviable spores, except for one fertile population (colony). End of leaf proliferates by vegetative budding like Walking-fern parent. Grows as isolated plants on limestone cliffs or outcroppings.

SORI: Numerous, linear, with delicate indusium opening away from vein.

CULTURE: Not available from commercial growers. Difficult to maintain in cultivation and short-lived.

RANGE: Vermont to North Carolina, Alabama, Missouri.

1, Silhouettes of leaves showing extreme variations on one plant. 2, Habitat. 3, 4, Variations in leaf structure.

74

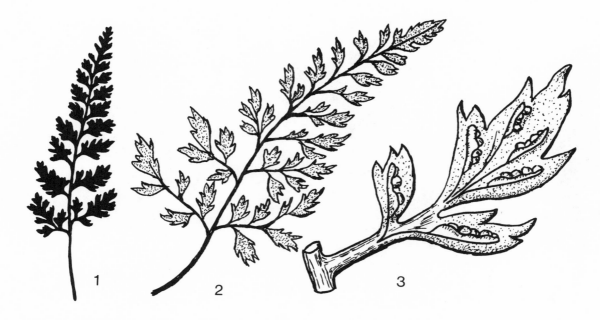

## *Asplenium montanum*—Mountain Spleenwort

Leaf 4 to 8 inches long. Blade bluish green, deltoid-ovate to lanceolate-oblong, 1-, 2-pinnate. Petiole slender, dark brown to ebony near base, changing to green above. Evergreen.

Mountain Spleenwort is not a common fern, and when found it is generally growing from a dense mat of dark brown dead leaves. It grows in damp crevices and beneath overhanging ledges of sandstone, gneiss, and other hard, noncalcareous rocks.

SORI: Linear, short, near midrib, covered by delicate indusium, appearing as confluent patches at maturity.

CULTURE: Since this fern is rare and virtually impossible to remove from its habitat without damage, it is suggested that only spores be collected and grown. When using this fern for a garden specimen, the native growing conditions must be closely simulated for successful culture.

RANGE: Georgia and Alabama to Ohio and New York; locally in Connecticut, Massachusetts, and Rhode Island.

---

1, Leaf silhouette.  2, Sterile leaf.  3, Fertile area.

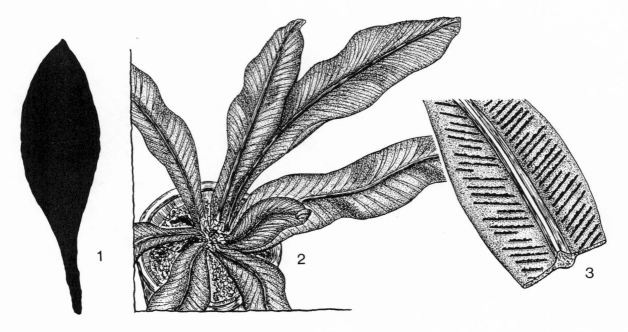

## *Asplenium nidus*—Bird's-nest Fern

Leaf simple, narrowly to broadly elliptical, leathery, glossy, brilliant green. Length about 12 inches.

This is another species that is not fern-like in appearance, and its "bird's-nest" arrangement of bold, brilliant, polished green leaves makes it a distinctive addition to the house plant collection. It is excellent for individual planting. In botanical gardens where ideal conditions of temperature and humidity are maintained, Bird's-nest Ferns grow to fully 4 feet. In the home, with cooler and especially drier atmosphere, this fern seldom exceeds 12 or 15 inches.

Leaves, simple though wavy-edged, bear no resemblance to native plants of the genus *Asplenium.* They are uniform in width for much of their length, except for a gradual taper to the rhizome and an abrupt apical taper. The costa resembles a polished ebony inlay and further enhances the beauty of the green leaf.

This fern has a dark scale-covered crown growing from an erect, stumpy rhizome. Leaves spread from the crown to form its characteristic "bird's-nest." New crosiers hidden under the dark scales unfold slowly, and as new central leaves grow, the older ones forming the exterior of the "nest" gradually darken and die.

SORI: Excellent example of linear sori. Here the herringbone pattern, typical of the genus *Asplenium,* is seen at its best. Rows are parallel to each other and oblique to the costa. Each row is covered with an elongate indusium which at maturity opens toward the apex. Fruiting occurs only on larger plants growing in greenhouses and botanical gardens.

CULTURE: Soil rich in humus, with constant moisture. Warm room, away from direct sunlight. Lack of humidity in a warm house may be compensated by spraying.

RANGE: Tropics of Eastern Hemisphere.

---

1, Leaf silhouette. 2, Wavy, forked-veined leaves forming "bird's-nest." Black tufted scales concealing dormant crosiers. 3, Underside of leaf showing parallel, oblique rows of sori.

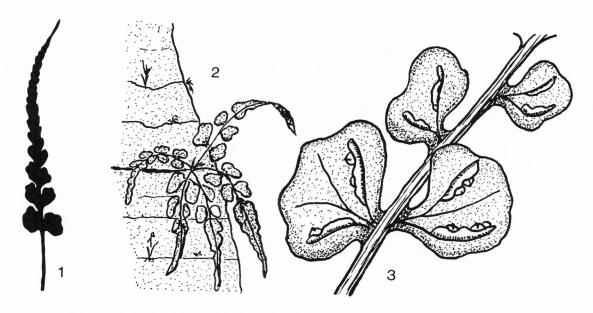

## *Asplenium pinnatifidum*—Lobed Spleenwort

Leaf 6 to 9 inches long, dark green, narrowly lanceolate, ending in long, slender tip. Blade pinnate below, continuously and deeply lobed above. Lower end of petiole brown, changing to green above. Evergreen.

Lobed Spleenwort is a rare, naturally reproducing species, probably originating as a hybrid between *A. montanum* and *Camptosorus rhizophyllus.* It grows in crevices of noncalcareous rock.

SORI: Few, linear, indusium opening away from vein.

CULTURE: Due to its critical growth requirements this fern is virtually impossible to grow in a garden.

RANGE: Pennsylvania and New Jersey, south to Georgia, and west to Oklahoma.

---

1, Leaf silhouette.  2, Habitat.  3, Basal area of fertile leaf.

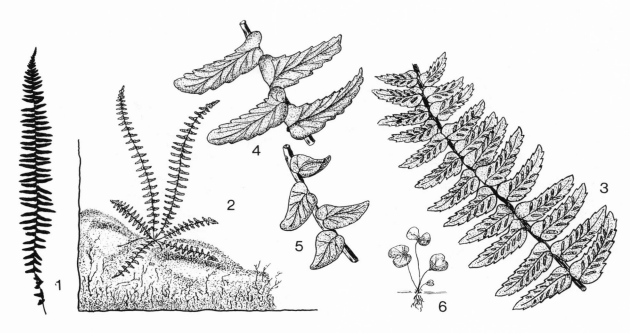

## *Asplenium platyneuron*—Ebony Spleenwort

Leaves slender and double-tapering, 1-pinnate, deep green, 6 to 20 inches long and 1 to 2 inches wide, having 20 to 50 pairs of alternately spaced pinnae, and dark, glossy, purple-brown petiole and rachis. Sterile leaves evergreen. Dimorphic.

This spleenwort resembles a small Christmas Fern, particularly from the erect position of the fertile leaves, and their auricled pinnae. Actually there is no relation as the plants represent two widely separated genera. Commonly 6 to 12 inches high, it is most desirable for a rock garden or stone ledge.

This fern grows luxuriantly on Vermont limestone ledges; it also thrives in the red sandy soil of New Jersey. Sometimes it grows on old mortar walls or crumbling foundations. It is not unusual to find it lining old farmhouse wells, where there is ample moisture and protection from the heat of summer and winter storms.

Like so many ferns, the Ebony Spleenwort develops the fertile leaves first. Sterile leaves soon follow, and more continue to develop throughout the summer. Usually the sterile leaves are shorter and broader, and spread out just above the ground. At first the petioles and rachises are delicate green, changing shortly to glossy purple-brown.

SORI: Elongate, straight, in herringbone pattern on opposite sides of midrib. Long indusia are attached on the vein side. Dehiscence occurs in early summer.

CULTURE: Requires loose woodland soil. May be planted in woodland garden beside large stones. Excellent in rock garden between limestone or sandstone rocks. Tolerates limited dry spells.

RANGE: Maine and southern Ontario to Georgia, west to Iowa and Texas, sporadically to Kansas and Colorado.

---

1, Leaf silhouette.  2, Plant with erect fertile leaves and prostrate sterile leaves growing among rocks.  3, 4, 5, Upper, central, and basal sections of leaf showing auricled pinnae.  6, Young sporophyte with light green leaflets and black petioles.

78

## *Asplenium pumilum*—Dwarf Spleenwort

Leaves 2½″ to 5″ or longer. Three-lobed blade composed of two basal pinnae and matching apical pinna, with possible additional pair of pinnae between the components forming a deltoid or pentagonal pattern. Stipe brown and scaly below, changing to green and glabrous upward. Blades slightly hairy on both sides.

Spleenworts form a large group of ferns growing throughout the world, mainly in the tropics or subtropical areas. Members of the genus have unusually diverse leaf patterns, ranging from the simple blade of *A. nidus,* the Bird's-nest Fern, to the multi-pinnate, *A. bulbiferum,* New Zealand Mother Fern. This little Spleenwort grows in northern Florida where it makes its home on the edge of lime sink-holes or on moss-covered limestone cliffs and outcroppings.

SORI: Many; elongate, indusia-covered, longitudinally attached to veins.

CULTURE: Because of the diminutive size and critical growing requirements of this species, it is not recommended for horticultural use.

RANGE: Florida, Central and South America, and West Indies.

---

1, Leaf silhouette.  2, Fertile leaf showing soral pattern.  3, View showing small plant growing from tufted root system.

## *Asplenium ruta-muraria*—**Wall-rue Spleenwort**

Leaf deltoid-ovate, 6 inches long, 2-, 3-pinnate, bluish green, growing from tufted mat of persistent old petioles. Petiole slender and fragile, brown at base, green above. Pinnae stalked, alternately and widely spaced. Evergreen.

Wall-rue Spleenwort is not common but when found it is generally growing on moist limestone cliffs and ledges. Often it may be seen among *A. platyneuron, Pellaea atropurpurea,* and *Camptosorus rhizophyllus.*

SORI: Linear, few. Indusium delicate, margin ciliate.

CULTURE: Can be grown on well-drained limestone but difficult to establish.

RANGE: Vermont to Michigan, south to Alabama and Arkansas. Common in southern England, central Europe and Italy.

---

1, Leaf silhouette.  2, Habitat.  3, Section of fertile pinna.

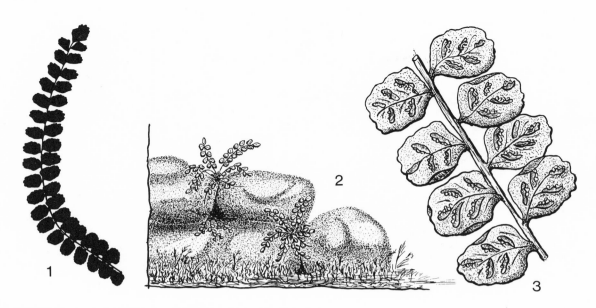

## *Asplenium trichomanes*—Maidenhair Spleenwort

Leaf slender, 1-pinnate, dark green, up to 6 inches long. Usually there are about 20 pairs of roundish-oblong, opposite to subopposite pinnae. Evergreen.

The Maidenhair Spleenwort is a small fern with spreading leaves. It is often found in company with the Walking Fern, growing out of crevices of moist, moss-covered limestone cliffs. Occasionally it is found growing on other large rocks in cool, damp wooded areas.

Although of the same genus, but of different species, the identification of the younger plants of Ebony Spleenwort and Maidenhair Spleenwort can cause confusion among beginners. In both species, the pinnae join the rachis by a short stalk, but the auricle found on the Ebony Spleenwort is lacking in the Maidenhair Spleenwort.

The sterile leaves are the first to appear in the spring; they grow in a prone position or nearly so. The fertile leaves appear later and grow in a more erect position. Both the rachises and petioles are shiny purple-brown, smooth and wiry. The green pinnae carry over to the following season but gradually drop off, leaving the stubble.

SORI: There are generally two or three, and occasionally four, pairs of alternately spaced, linear sori. Their elongate indusia are attached on the vein side. Just prior to dehiscence, the swelling sporangia change to rich, shiny dark-blue or black.

CULTURE: It is important to simulate natural growing conditions. A limestone rock with a carefully selected pocket, or two stones arranged to form a tight crevice, should be used. Humus with small pieces of limestone is used for the growing medium. The soil is best kept slightly moist at all times, always well drained. The plant tolerates alternate sunlight and some dry periods.

RANGE: Nova Scotia to Alaska, south to central Georgia and Arizona.

---

1, Leaf silhouette.  2, Plant growing on the surface or in crevices of calcareous rock.
3, Enlarged sketch of underside of leaf showing alternately spaced linear sori.

## *Asplenium viride*—Green Spleenwort

Leaf linear-lanceolate, 1-pinnate, 2 to 5 inches long, bright green, growing from tufted base. Petiole brown at base, changing to green above. Pinnae numerous, short-stalked, roundish-ovate, margins crenate, veins inconspicuous, and forking. Subevergreen.

Green Spleenwort is a small, delicate fern, most particular as to habitat, preferring cool, damp crevices and talus slopes of calcareous rocks. It is often found in association with *A. trichomanes,* to which there is some similarity.

SORI: Linear, few, covered with delicate indusium attached to vein side.

CULTURE: This is a rare fern and should not be taken from its natural habitat unless necessary to save it from destruction. Because of its critical growth habits it is not recommended for the ordinary garden.

RANGE: Newfoundland, Vermont, west to Alaska, and south to Colorado and Washington.

1, Leaf silhouette. 2, Underside of fertile leaf.

## *Athyrium alpestre*—**Alpine Lady-fern**

Leaves oblong-lanceolate, 2-pinnate-pinnatifid, 12 to 30 inches long, 3 to 6 inches wide, yellow-green when young, darkening with maturity. Pinnae numerous, becoming more widely spaced toward base. Leaves rise from crown terminal, short-creeping rhizome to form bushy, vase-like plant.

This species greatly resembles *A. filix-femina*, our Common Lady Fern. While over the years changes have been made in its generic name, its specific name, "alpestre," has survived. Most of the time the common name has been "Alpine Lady Fern," an exception being in "Alpine Polypody" when the botanical name was "*Polypodium alpestre.*"

SORI: Numerous, round, very small. Indusium lacking or rare, rudimentary if present.

CULTURE: Because of its vase-like appearance and soft feathery leaves, this plant is an excellent selection for the rock garden where the climate is cool and moist. Plant in humus-rich soil mixed with many small stones.

RANGE: Northwestern North America, eastern Canada, Eurasia.

---

1, Leaf silhouette. 2, Typical pinna. 3, Pinnule showing soral distribution. 4, Enlarged view of exindusiate sorus.

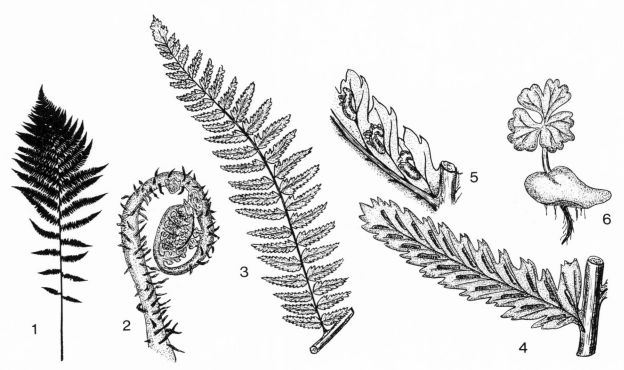

## *Athyrium filix-femina*—**Lady Fern**

Leaf lanceolate, 2-pinnate, the pinnules lobed to pinnatifid. Length 18 to 36 inches or more, 15 inches wide. Color differs widely with variants, age, and location, ranging from yellow-green to medium green. Maturing leaves are deeper green with a brownish cast.

Lady ferns are excellent species for either the woodland garden or for use among large flowering plants or shrubs. The blades are composed of many feathery pinnae, the upper pairs long-tapering and ascending. While some ferns send up most of their leaves early in the spring, the Lady Fern continues to release additional crosiers until late summer.

The opening crosier is an aid in identifying the plant. Unlike other ferns having flatly coiled or spheroidal crosiers, this fern has a rounded-oblong crosier heavily covered with dark brown, elongate scales. By looking into this little organ, now more yellow than green, the developing compact pinnae may be seen. Later, the fast growing crosiers droop backward until sufficient strength is gained for upward growth.

There are many lady ferns, the differences giving some species status and others variant status. These differences are in general morphology, color, and sori arrangement. The variety *rubellum* is another excellent fern and should be included in an expanding garden.

SORI: These are elongate, covered with straight, slightly curved or hooked indusia arranged obliquely along the pinnule midrib. With approaching maturity, the degree of curvature is increased until, in some varieties, the sori appear horseshoe-shaped and the indusia become small or disappear.

CULTURE: One of the easiest to grow and under favorable conditions will tend to spread slowly. Soil neutral to slightly acid. By keeping the fern constantly moist during dry seasons, its foliage may be prolonged until late summer.

RANGE: *A. filix-femina*—St. Lawrence valley region of Quebec to central Pennsylvania and Ohio. Var. *rubellum*—Newfoundland to Pennsylvania, in mountains to Virginia, west to Manitoba, the Black Hills of South Dakota, eastern Colorado, and northern Missouri.

---

1, Leaf silhouette. 2, Heavily dark-scaled oblong crosier. 3, Long, tapering pinna, upper side. 4, Fertile pinnule with straight sori. 5, Curved type sori nearing maturity. 6, Young sporophyte with first forked-veined leaflet.

## *Athyrium niponicum*—**Japanese Painted-fern**

Leaf lanceolate, colorful, 2-pinnate, 12 inches or more long and about 8 inches wide, the blade and the petiole of about equal length.

Most ferns limit their color to one of the many monochromatic variations of green. In the Japanese Painted-fern a great departure occurs for, in this unusual plant, wine-red has been subtly blended with the soft gray-green color of the leaves. Although this wine-red hue is mainly confined to the apical section of the rachis and midribs of the pinnae, the gradation is so delicate that the red appears to continue far into the pinnules.

The leaf silhouette shows several pairs of opposite pinnae, but other leaves on the same plant have their pinnae either alternate or subalternate. The long and gracefully tapering characteristic of the apical section of the leaf also appears in the individual pinnae. Planted in a fern garden, alone or among flowers, this fern with its quiet, yet colorful tones will receive admiration.

SORI: Characteristic of the genus *Athyrium,* the Painted Fern has its sori arranged in a herring-bone pattern. The sori are uniformly spaced and are adjacent to the veins of the pinnules. Light green at first, their color darkens to brown as the sporangia reach maturity. The elongate indusia are attached on the vein side.

CULTURE: Regardless of the origin of this deciduous fern, it is hardy in cold winters. Soil neutral to slightly acid. Watering this fern during dry seasons will prolong its beauty long into the fall. New crosiers continue to unfold until late summer.

RANGE: Native of Japan; readily available from most growers.

---

1, Leaf silhouette. 2, Sterile pinna. 3, Fertile pinnule showing soral pattern. 4, Early crosier. 5, Further growth of crosier.

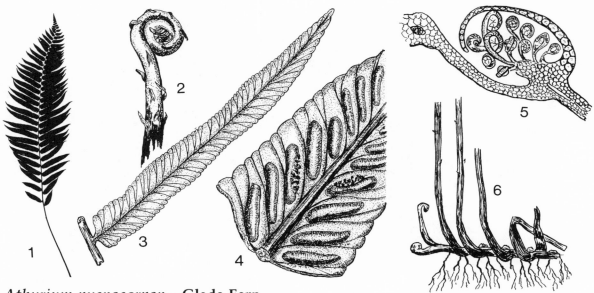

## *Athyrium pycnocarpon*—**Glade Fern**

Dimorphic. Leaves lanceolate, 1-pinnate, 30 to 48 inches long and 6 inches wide. Light, brilliant green, later changing to dark green, and finally becoming russet in late summer.

Also known as Narrow-leaved Athyrium and Narrow-leaved Spleenwort. Both the botanical and common names of this fern have been changed many times. Nineteenth century botanists named this species "narrow-leaved spleenwort" which was derived from its botanical name, *Asplenium angustifolium.* With its present classification, the preferred common name is Glade Fern or Narrow-leaved Athyrium.

Many ferns seem to grow in association with certain species. The Glade Fern often grows on the talus slopes among stands of Goldie's Fern.

Each leaf has as many as 20 to 40 pairs of long, tapering pinnae, joined obliquely to the rachis by well-defined stalks. Venation is free; the simple, forking, and reforking veins are easily seen. The leaves are dimorphic, although the dimorphism is not as obvious as in some species. Comparison will show that the fertile leaf, with its longer petiole, is taller, more erect and later appearing, and its pinnae are much narrower.

Similarity to the Christmas Fern is limited to the appearance of the 1-pinnate leaf. The sorus, crosier, shape of pinna, and the rhizome are helpful diagnostic features.

SORI: Sporangia covered by elongate indusium attached to the veins, obliquely arranged, forming a herringbone pattern. While the indusia are free on the upper side, they remain in contact until raised by expanding sporangia.

CULTURE: Prefers cool, deep humus mulch containing broken limestone pieces. Watering mulch each day during hot spells delays the tendency for the leaves to turn brown. New crosiers continue to uncurl until late summer. Slight spreading tendency.

RANGE: Maine and southern Quebec to Wisconsin, south to upland Georgia and eastern Kansas, and the coast of Louisiana.

---

1, Sterile leaf silhouette.  2, Crosier.  3, Sterile pinna showing forked veining. 4, Enlarged sketch showing sori arrangement.  5, Transverse microsection through maturing sorus, showing attached lower side and free upper side of indusium. 6, Progressive development of rhizome immediately below the surface.

86

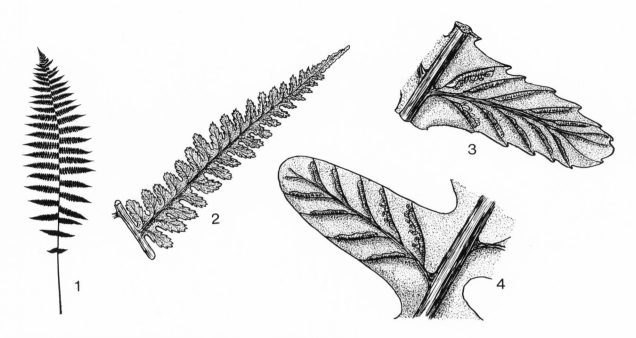

## *Athyrium thelypterioides*—Silvery Glade-fern

Dimorphic. Leaves elliptic-lanceolate, 1-pinnate-pinnatifid, 36 inches long, 7 inches wide. Yellow-green, changing to brilliant or deep green, depending on growing conditions. Russet-green in late summer.

Also known as Silvery Spleenwort. The name Silvery Spleenwort has been carried over from a previous botanical classification in the genus *Asplenium*. This species, commonly found along dusty roadsides, has found only restricted use as a garden fern. When moved to the garden and given proper care it becomes a beautiful fern. Its double-tapering leaves resemble somewhat those of the New York fern.

The leaves are dimorphic, but not strongly so. Fertile leaves are taller, more slender and upright than the later appearing sterile ones which are generally found growing on the outside of the clumpy base. Similar to other ferns in this genus, the Silvery Glade-fern continues to develop new leaves until late summer.

Pinnae, alternately spaced, are long and gracefully tapering. Lobes have varying lengths, sometimes giving the pinnae uneven edges. Variations exist among plants, and some may have the lobes serrate while others may have them entire.

SORI: Straight or slightly curved with heavy, well-arched, elongate indusia attached on the vein side and opening outward. Sori follow the herringbone pattern of the genus, and on strong plants are prominent from the apex to the lowest pair of pinnae. When young, sori are delicate silvery-green. Later, the underside of the lobe reflects a strong silvery sheen. As maturity is reached, the sori deepen to blue-gray.

CULTURE: Using a deep, mulched soil of rotted leaves and turned sod mixed with common sand, the fern quickly adapts itself to the garden. It will grow in considerable sun if the soil is always damp.

RANGE: Nova Scotia to Minnesota, south to Georgia and eastern Missouri.

---

1, Leaf silhouette.  2, Sterile pinna showing various lengths of serrate lobes. 3, Enlarged sketch of toothed lobe showing veins and elongate sori. 4, Same as 3 but showing entire edge.

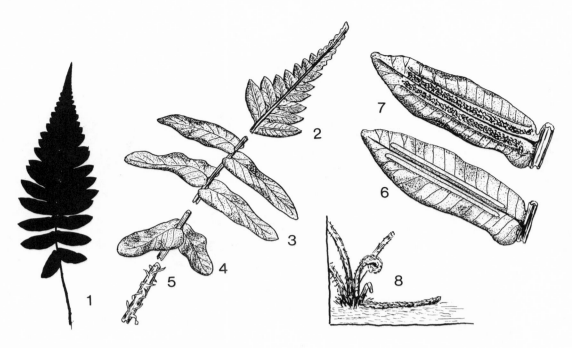

## *Blechnum occidentale*—**Hammock Fern**

Leaf ovate-lanceolate, 1-pinnate, 12 to 24 inches long, upper third gracefully tapering to apex. Terminal segments sessile, lower pinnae short-stalked. Petiole scaly.

The genus *Blechnum* includes a group of many tropical ferns throughout the world, as well as others in cooler areas. They range in size from this small one to *Blechnum brasiliense,* the large Brazilian Tree Fern, with its 4-foot leaves extending from a stumpy rhizome or caudex 3 feet high.

The upper part of the blade of the Hammock Fern has deeply cut, slightly overlapping segments. Lower pinnae are widely spaced and have their bases partly curved around the rachis; their surfaces are nearly parallel to the ground.

Crosiers when first observed are heavily covered with long, brown scales. As they advance, little coppery-green leaflets unfold. This color slowly changes, and by the time the leaf is nearly full grown it has become a blend of copper and green; it finally becomes deep green at maturity.

When this fern is potted for house use, its spreading rhizomes soon extend from rim to rim. New plants grow along the rhizome at short intervals. Their young coppery leaves mix with the older green leaves, making the plant a colorful addition to the fern collection.

SORI: Markedly linear, following both sides of the midrib almost the entire length. Elongate indusia open on midrib side. At maturity, the sporangia become confluent, giving the appearance of two narrow red-brown velvet strips separated by the midrib.

CULTURE: Potting mixture of loose humus or woodland soil and sand, with some limestone chips or ground oyster shells. Filtered sunlight in winter, open shade in summer. Keep moist but avoid overwatering.

RANGE: Limestone region of northwestern peninsular Florida, rare; West Indies; Mexico to Argentina.

---

1, Leaf silhouette. 2, Underside of tip showing overlapping of segments. 3, 4, 5, Lower and basal pinnae, and scaly petiole. 6, 7, Underside of fertile pinnae showing the two linear sori before and after dehiscence. 8, Scaly crosier, lower petioles, and stolon.

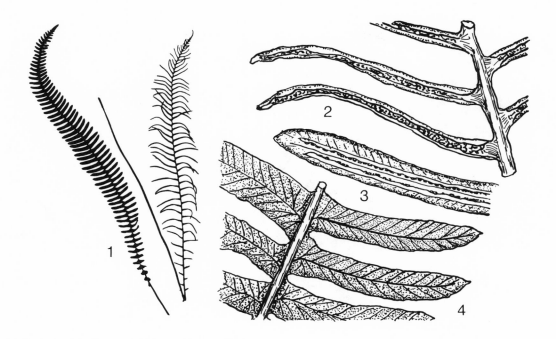

## *Blechnum spicant*—Deer Fern, Hard Fern

Leaves linear, tapering each way from middle, 1-pinnatifid, dimorphic. Fertile leaf much taller, reaching 30 inches in height and 1 to 3 inches in width. Leaves forming crown have close-set oblong or linear-oblong, apiculate segments gradually becoming rudimentary auricles at base.

*B. spicant* is commonly encountered by the traveler when in some regions of the cooler areas of the northern hemisphere. This fern forms dense patches at the edge of pine forests and woodland clearings. It has been a long-recognized species, having been mentioned in John Gerarde's Herbal of 1639. At that time it was known as the Hard Fern, and botanically classified as *Lomaria spicant.*

SORI: Continuous, indusium-covered, flanking both sides of midrib nearly full length of segment. Aging and drying segment reflexes to virtually cover sporangia.

CULTURE: Excellent selection for cool, moist-area rock garden. This fern, with its dark green leaves, can be used in borders with brilliant, shade-loving flowers. Prefers mulch-soil mixed with small stones.

RANGE: Northwestern North America south to California, Europe, Asia; especially well-established in northern British Isles and Norway.

---

1, Silhouette of leaves; left, sterile; right, fertile. 2, Fertile segments at maturity. 3, View of fertile segment before drying. 4, Mid-section of sterile leaf showing abrupt, sharply pointed ending of segments.

## *Bommeria hispida*—Copper Fern

Blade pentagonal, 1- to 2-pinnatifid, 1 to 3 inches broad. Leaf usually 4 to 6 inches long with occasional leaves reaching 10 inches. Fine bristly hairs cover the top surface, with heavily matted, rust-colored hairs on underside concealing veins and naked sori.

Few ferns can tolerate extreme dryness and heat for extended periods. This species is small, growing from a tufted rootstock-base, with roots penetrating crevices selected for its home. Somewhat indifferent to the rock composition, it limits its growing areas to the cool, shaded side of large desert boulders or the higher ledges of damp, canyon walls or outcroppings.

SORI: Naked, growing along veins near their marginal endings. Hair-covering of leaf makes sori virtually invisible.

CULTURE: Not advisable for horticultural application unless exact growing conditions can be simulated.

RANGE: Southwestern United States and Mexico.

---

1, Leaf silhouette. 2, Partial view of underside of leaf. 3, Ferns growing on rock ledge.

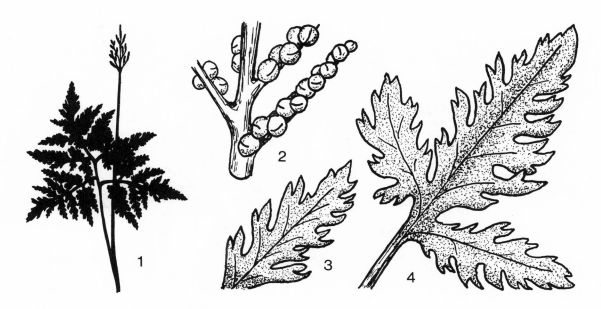

### *Botrychium dissectum* f. *dissectum*—Dissected Grape-fern

Fleshy plant, 4 to 12 inches long. Sterile blade triangular, 2-, 3-pinnate. Petioles of fertile and sterile portions join at or slightly below surface of ground. Degree of cutting of sterile blade extremely variable. Evergreen.

Plant appears in late June or early July in areas of moderately damp acid soil of open woodlands. Fertile portion of frond wilts and dies back after dehiscence of spores. Sterile portion quickly turns to bronze color after frost and remains upright until replaced by new leaf the following year.

SPORANGIA: Same as *B. virginianum.*

CULTURE: Soil condition very critical, making culture difficult. Pest control is important.

RANGE: Nova Scotia, New Brunswick, Quebec to Minnesota, south to Florida, Missouri.

1, Leaf silhouette. 2, Fertile area. 3, 4, Sterile pinna variations.

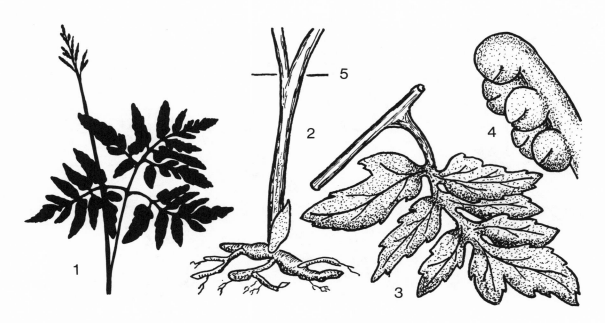

## *Botrychium dissectum* f. *obliquum*—Ternate Grape-fern

Similar in many respects to *B. dissectum* in leaf structure and growing conditions. Pinnules elongate, with edges having a lesser degree of incision. Evergreen.

This Grape-fern is apparently a minor variation of *B. dissectum*. The plant appears late in June, remaining erect throughout winter. It has fleshy roots situated 2 or more inches below the surface of the ground.

SPORANGIA: See *B. virginianum*.

CULTURE: As with all grape-ferns, the culture of this fern is very difficult. Snail, slug, and small rodent control is necessary.

RANGE: Nova Scotia and New Brunswick, west to Wisconsin and Iowa, south to Georgia and Louisiana.

---

1, Leaf silhouette.  2, Root and bud sheath.  3, Sterile pinna.  4, Portion of fertile area.
5, Indicates approximate ground line.

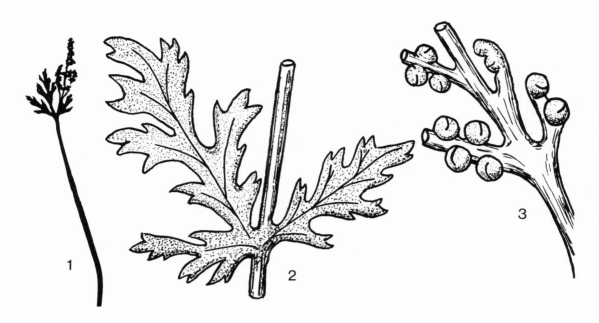

## *Botrychium lanceolatum*—Lance-leaved Grape-fern

Leaf somewhat fleshy, usually 5 to 7 inches long, with extremes 2 to 9 inches high. Sterile blade triangular, high on petiole, sessile or nearly so, 1-, 2-pinnatifid. Roots fleshy, spreading 2 or more inches below surface. Deciduous.

Lance-leaved Grape-fern, also known as Triangular Grape-fern, is one of the rare species of this genus. It is found growing in cool, humus-rich damp soil of woods and meadows.

SPORANGIA: Sessile, borne on panicle having short stalk, 2-, 3-pinnate.

CULTURE: Very difficult to grow in cultivation. Seldom appears after first or second year when transplanted.

RANGE: Labrador to Gaspé Peninsula, Quebec; Maine; Alaska to Washington, and in mountains to Colorado.

---

1, Leaf silhouette.  2, Sterile blade.  3, Fertile area.

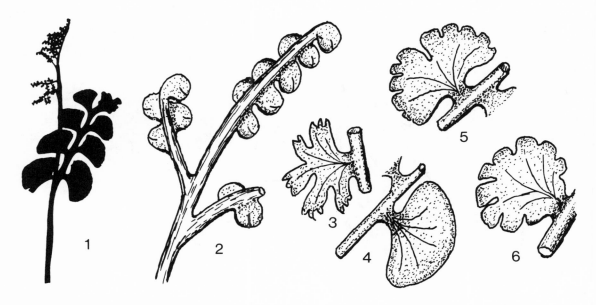

## *Botrychium lunaria*—**Moonwort**

Leaf light green, fleshy, up to 6 inches long, with 4 or more pairs of simple to variously incised pinnae. Pinnae nearly opposite, separated or overlapping. Bud sheath at base of petiole. Deciduous.

Moonwort, one of the smallest North American ferns, is a rare species found only in areas of cooler climate. It grows in dry elevated pastures, gravelly soil, and open wastelands, either as isolated plants or in colonies.

SPORANGIA: Spherical, sessile, growing on fertile panicle, 1-, 2-pinnate.

CULTURE: Not possible under ordinary horticultural conditions.

RANGE: Labrador and Newfoundland to Alaska, northern Minnesota, northern Michigan, south in mountains to Colorado, Arizona, and California; Maine.

---

1, Leaf silhouette.  2, Fertile area.  3, 4, 5, 6, Sterile pinna variations.

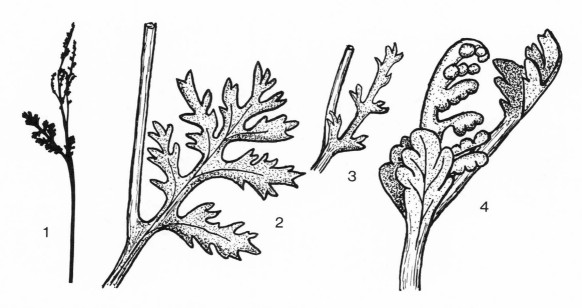

## *Botrychium matricariifolium*—**Matricary Grape-fern**

Leaf fleshy, 2 to 12 inches long, emerging from ground with straight-rising sterile blade tightly clenching fertile 1-, 2-pinnate panicle. Sterile blade high on common stalk, may be petioled to nearly sessile. Blade varies in size and shape, with lobes having sharp or blunt endings. Sterile blades occasionally have fertile edges or small fertile panicles. Deciduous.

Matricary Grape-fern, sometimes called Daisy-leaf Grape-fern, is among the first of the ferns to appear in spring. Isolated plants to colonies grow in dry to moist thickets.

SPORANGIA: Spherical, sessile, borne on 1-, 2-pinnate panicle.

CULTURE: Virtually impossible except in woodland garden having similar soil conditions. Readily devoured by snails and slugs.

RANGE: Labrador and Newfoundland, to Alberta, south to Maryland; Ohio, South Dakota, Nebraska, and Idaho.

1, Leaf silhouette.  2, 3, Sterile blade variations.  4, Young leaf unfolding.

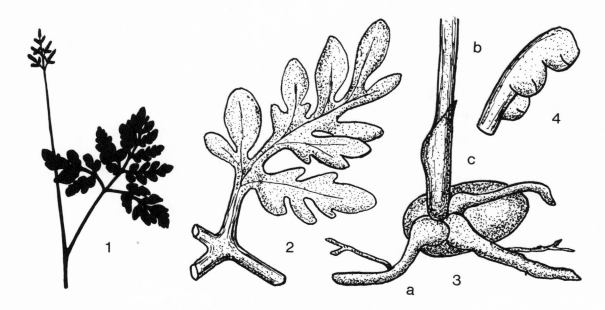

## *Botrychium multifidum*—**Multifid Grape-fern**

Leaf leathery, brilliant green, 4 to 15 inches long, appearing in June or July; later darkening in color but remaining erect throughout winter and following spring. Sterile blade deltoid, variable in cutting, appearing as 3 divisions each, bipinnate or pinnate-pinnatifid. Fertile panicle 2-, 3-pinnate. Petioles of fertile and sterile portions join at surface of ground. Evergreen.

Also known as Leather-leaf Grape-fern. The sterile blade remains erect until almost overtaken by the new growth.

SPORANGIA: See *B. virginianum.*

CULTURE: Virtually impossible in ordinary garden due to critical soil requirements.

RANGE: Labrador and Newfoundland, New England and New York, west to Wisconsin, Minnesota.

---

1, Leaf silhouette. 2, Pinna. 3, (a) Roots, (b) Vertically ascending steam, (c) Prothallium. 4, Sporangia.

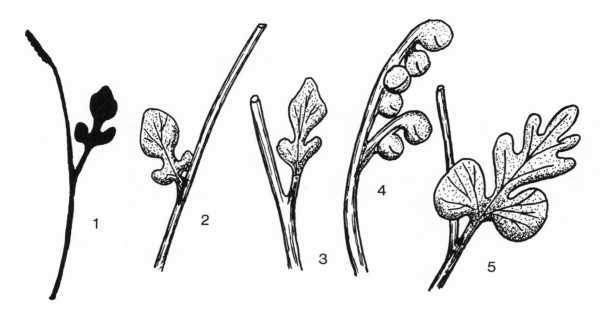

## *Botrychium simplex*—**Simple Grape-fern**

Leaf light green, fleshy, 1 to 6 inches long. Blades variable, ranging from simple triangular-ovate to deeply roundish-lobed. Petiole bears a sheath above fleshy root system. Deciduous.

Simple Grape-fern grows in woods and open slopes, invading pastures. Appears in early spring, disappearing in early summer. Many plants so small they can only be found by removing leaf-mulch covering.

SPORANGIA: Spherical, sessile on fertile panicle, occasionally appearing on blade.

CULTURE: Too small and too difficult to maintain in horticulture.

RANGE: Newfoundland to New Jersey, Pennsylvania, west to British Columbia, Wyoming, Colorado, and California.

1, Leaf silhouette.  2, 3, 5, Sterile leaf variations.  4, Fertile area.

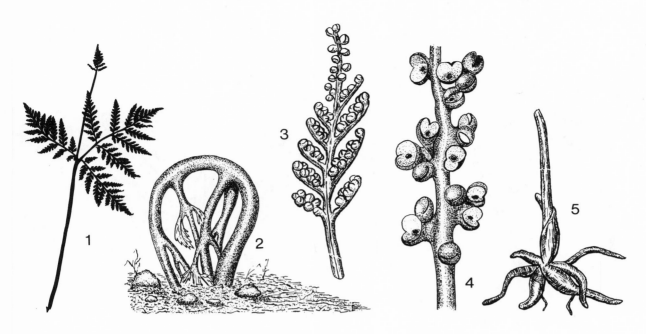

## Botrychium virginianum—Rattlesnake Fern

Leaf 6 to 30 inches long. Sterile part of the blade triangular, somewhat horizontal, yellow-green to rich green, formed by 2 large opposite basal pinnae and 4 or 5 pairs of opposite or subopposite smaller pinnae above. Fertile part of blade rises from base of sterile part. Sterile part approximately equidistant between ground and fertile tip.

This is a succulent fern with soft, juicy tissue above the ground rising from a small, deep, erect stem with spreading, fleshy roots. The base of the petiole is expanded into a sheath that encloses three or four leaf buds, one for each succeeding year.

Rattlesnake Ferns do not have crosiers, but instead form their leaves underground during late winter and early spring. When ready, virtually full grown, compactly folded leaves push upward and open only when completely above ground.

As the blades unfold, the fertile part, if present, can be seen immediately. During the first years, plants are always sterile, but it does not follow that older plants are invariably fertile each year. This fern, one of the earliest to appear, will under favorable conditions remain green all summer. The fertile part, however, withers shortly after dehiscence, giving the plant a sterile appearance.

SPORANGIA: Sessile, spherical capsules appear as tiny balls pressed into branches of panicle. Examination shows an equatorial line girdling each sporangium on immature plants. Dehiscence occurs along this line, discharging cream-colored spores into the air.

CULTURE: Provide a rich, loose, moist woodland soil, neutral or slightly acid, and open shade. In transplanting, replace roots and stem at their natural depth. Size and depth of roots will vary according to plant size. An inverted wire basket and snail repellent are helpful protection against rabbits and slugs.

RANGE: Prince Edward Island and New Brunswick to southern British Columbia, south to central Florida and California.

---

1, Leaf silhouette. 2, Plant unfolding by means of straight or erect vernation. 3, Panicle, showing arrangement of sporangia. 4, Enlarged sketch of panicle, showing opened sessile sporangia. 5, Fleshy roots, and sheath around petiole.

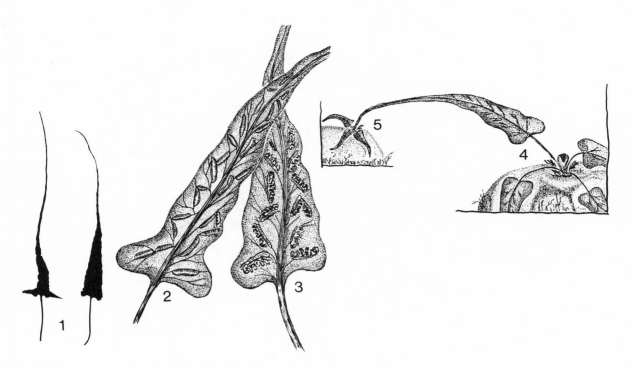

## *Camptosorus rhizophyllus*—**Walking Fern**

Leaf simple, slender, tapering, 4 to 12 inches long, usually roundish or rarely pointed lobes at base. Evergreen.

This fern extends its long, tapering leaves to other locations where the tips become rooted and start new, independent plants. Thus, in addition to propagating itself through the conventional life cycle, it has an additional method known as vegetative reproduction.

In nature, the Walking Fern is usually found on bare or moss-covered limestone ledges and cliffs, with its roots extending into crevices. It grows as a solitary plant or in large, leaf-tangled mats covering boulders. The plant endures dry spells of reasonable duration; prolonged droughts leave nothing but the dry tangled masses of the long leaves. Occasionally the plant grows in unusual locations. One botanist has reported it growing on a tree trunk.

Leaves vary at the base. While the usual fern has very slight or well-defined roundish lobes, others have long tapered basil points.

SORI: Haphazardly arranged along veins on underside of leaf in the broader area. Combinations of linear sori make patterns of V, N, M, or W in addition to the simple form of I. The elongate indusia are attached to the vein and virtually disappear as maturity is reached. As the brown, swelling sporangia increase in size, the original linear configuration is nearly lost.

CULTURE: Excellent miniature fern for the rock garden or limestone ledge. Take advantage of natural pockets in weathered limestone or create openings between stones for planting. A circumneutral soil is best. Keep the roots moist after planting, but avoid overwatering. Slugs are devastating, particularly on hot, humid nights; control them with commercial repellants.

RANGE: Southern Quebec to Minnesota, south to central Georgia and eastern Oklahoma.

---

1, Leaf silhouettes showing different basal lobes. 2, Underside of leaf with maturing sori. 3, Underside of leaf after dehiscence of sporangia. 4, 5, Plant growing on rock surface with leaf extending to new location.

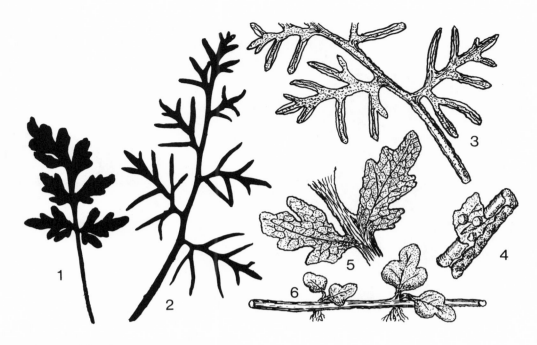

## *Ceratopteris pteridoides*—Water Fern

Leaves with thick, inflated stipes, strongly dimorphic, generally aquatic, growing under, on, or above the surface of still, shallow ponds, free-floating or rooting in mud. Sterile leaf triangular, much smaller than fertile leaf, having 3 or more pairs of deltoid, succulent pinnae. Fertile leaf triangular to triangular-lanceolate, 5 to 10 or more inches long, with pinnae having distinctive, horn-like segments encasing sporangia.

This species, under normal conditions, is a fast growing and spreading annual or short-lived plant. In addition to reproducing sexually from its spores, it also reproduces vegetatively from adventitious buds growing along the marginal sinuses of the sterile leaves.

SORI: Sporangia large and sessile, growing individually at intervals along wide-spreading, anastimosing veins, and protected by a continuous, marginal indusium.

CULTURE: Easy to grow in warm, partially to fully sunlit pool or aquarium.

RANGE: Southern Florida, Louisiana, tropical America.

---

1, Silhouette of sterile leaf. 2, Silhouette of fertile leaf. 3, Section of fertile leaf with horn-like segments. 4, Enlarged view of fertile area. 5, Section of sterile leaf showing coarse, anastimosing veins. 6, Section of rachis of old leaf showing juvenile plants at intervals.

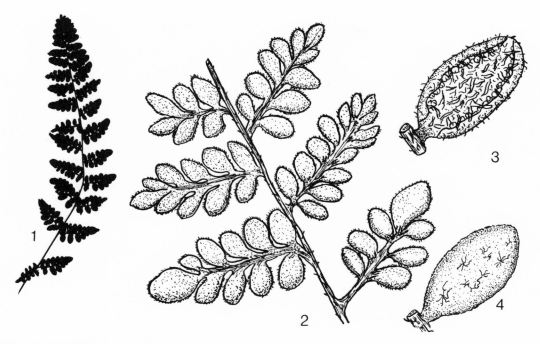

## *Cheilanthes gracillima*—Lace Fern

Leaves, 3 to 10 inches long, grow in clusters from tufted, short, creeping rhizome. Stipe 1 to 4 inches long, dark brown, either naked or nearly so. Blade linear-lanceolate, 2-pinnate with lower pinnae lanceolate-oblong, pinnately divided. Pinnules dark green, underside densely covered with white to cinnamon-colored, matted hair; upper surface with occasional white stellate hairs.

Lace Fern is one of the so-called "lip" ferns of the large *Cheilanthes* genus. In general, these are small to medium rupestral (growing on rocks) ferns with dull green or gray-green to bluish-green leaves, having reflexed margins essentially covering the sporangia. Many of these species grow in crevices or between large igneous or calcareous boulders. While a large number of lip ferns are native to the southwestern United States, others may be found growing throughout the country and extending into Canada.

SORI: Sporangia in continuous row around edge of pinnules, tightly covered by reflexed margin, becoming confluent at maturity.

CULTURE: Difficult unless natural growing conditions are carefully simulated.

RANGE: Southern British Columbia, western United States.

---

1, Leaf silhouette. 2, Portion of leaf showing 2-pinnate structure. 3, Enlarged view of pinnule, underside, showing reflexed margin and protective hair covering. 4, Upper surface of pinnule with occasional white stellate hairs.

101

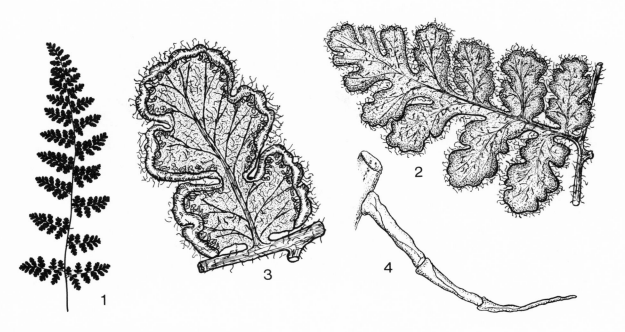

## *Cheilanthes lanosa*—Hairy Lip-fern

Leaf lanceolate, 6 to 8 inches long, medium yellow-green. Petiole and rachis purplish-brown to black, covered with many segmented hairs.

Leaves have opposite or nearly opposite pinnae and, depending on their size, are 2- or 3-pinnate. Although not readily seen, many fine white or light brown hairs are revealed by a magnifying glass. These hairs are on the petiole and rachis as well as on both sides of the pinnules; they are especially dense on the underside of the pinnules. Unlike the long, filamentous hairs found on some ferns, these hairs are composed of three to six long, jointed, cells.

Dense mats are formed by the creeping rhizomes, and in winter this fern may be recognized by the stubble of the deciduous leaves. Leaves continue to appear through the summer if moisture is sufficient. During dry spells the leaves disappear, but the plant revives with the coming of rain.

In studying this fern, compare its silhouette with those of other small ferns, especially those of the Fragile Bladder-fern and Blunt-lobed Woodsia.

SORI: As the fertile pinnules grow, the lobes appear to have rolled or reflexed margins. By looking at the underside of the pinnules, some of the young sporangia may be seen at the edge of the indusium. Toward maturity, the sporangia, bulging with their ripening contents, force the indusial margin back, giving the pinnule a more flattened edge than that seen earlier in the season.

CULTURE: Grows best in protected areas, preferably at the base of a large stone. Somewhat indifferent to the type of stone or soil used. It tolerates short dry periods, but can be kept green by occasional watering.

RANGE: New Haven County, Connecticut, and southeastern New York to Georgia, Kansas and Texas.

---

1, Leaf silhouette. 2, Upper side of pinna, showing hairy covering and rolled edge. 3, Enlarged view of pinnule from lower pinna, showing sporangia forcing their way from under the reflexed indusium. 4, Segmented hair from rachis.

## *Cheilanthes siloquosa*—**Indian's Dream**

Leaves, 3 to 10 inches long, with triangular-oblong to pentagonal blades 2 to 3 inches long, grow in dense circular clusters. Stipes slender, brittle, chestnut-brown, either dull or moderately polished. Leaves 2-pinnate to 3-pinnate with segments long and slender, terminating in sharp points.

Indian's dream, at one time designated "Oregon cliff-fern", normally grows in exposed areas of talus slopes and crevices of calcareous or serpentine rocks. It differs greatly from conventional ferns having feather-like leaves, in that almost all of its odd-shaped leaves are fertile, with virtually all segments throughout the entire leaf bearing spores along their edges.

SORI: Sporangia continuous beneath reflexed margin of segment, protected by an inconspicuous indusium, below margin, having irregular edge.

CULTURE: An interesting plant for rock garden application, but native growing conditions must be closely simulated.

RANGE: South of British Columbia to California, east to Montana, Wyoming and Utah; Gaspé Peninsula, Quebec.

---

1, Leaf silhouette.  2, Lower portion of fertile leaf.  3, Enlarged view of fertile segment showing reflexed edge and maturing sporangia.

103

*Cryptogramma acrostichoides*—**Parsley Fern**

Leaves ovate, strongly dimorphic, 1- to 3-pinnate, 3 to 6 inches long, growing from a clustered rootstock. Fertile leaf much taller, with straw colored, polished stipe 2 or 3 times the length of the blade, spore-bearing segments long and narrow. Sterile leaf, blade smaller with ovate segments, growing on much shorter stipe. Evergreen.

Parsley Fern is a rupestral plant preferring the crevices of granitic type rocks for its habitat. In the montane areas, where growth conditions are most favorable, the fern will form dense patches and cover the underlying boulders. This fern has long been known, having been mentioned in 1696 by Ray in his herbal, *Synopsis Methodica Sturpium Britannicarum.*

SORI: Sporangia grow from veinlets near margin of segment. Reflexed edges, forming continuous indusia, nearly meet the midrib, thus concealing the immature sporangia. As maturity is reached, the growing spores force back the covering to allow dehiscence.

CULTURE: Excellent rock garden plant. Growth is assured when all of the natural habitat requirements are met.

RANGE: Northern North America, Michigan, New Mexico, southern California.

1, Silhouette of fertile leaf. 2, Silhouette of sterile leaf. 3, Enlarged area of fertile leaf. 4, Enlarged section of sterile leaf.

## *Cryptogramma stelleri*—Slender Cliff-brake

Dimorphic leaves, ovate to ovate-deltoid, 2-, 3-pinnate or pinnatifid, 2 to 6 inches long, yellow-green, delicate soft texture. Fertile leaf taller than sterile, pinnules linear-oblong to linear-lanceolate. Pinnules of sterile leaf ovate, margin crenate. Petiole yellowish pale-brown, growing from creeping rhizome. Deciduous.

Appears early in spring, quickly disappearing during dry summer weather. Very partial to damp limestone outcroppings or strongly calcareous conditions.

SORI: Marginal; indusium formed by broad reflexed and continuous margin.

CULTURE: Growth requirements too critical to be considered as garden specimen.

RANGE: Labrador to Alaska, south to New Jersey, Pennsylvania, Iowa, Colorado, Utah, Washington, West Virginia.

---

1, Leaf silhouettes; fertile (left), sterile (right).   2, Section of fertile leaf.   3, Sterile pinnule.

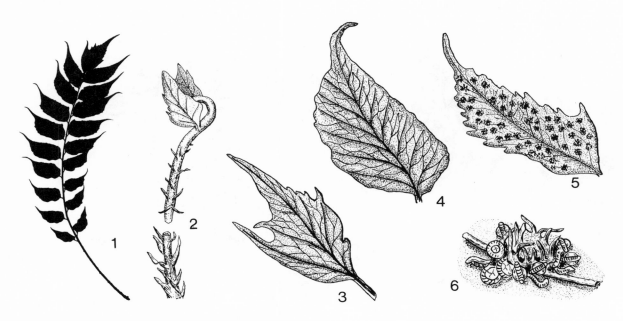

## *Cyrtomium falcatum*—**Japanese Holly-fern**

Leaf oblong-lanceolate, 1-pinnate, 12 to 24 inches long and 6 to 9 inches wide, with 10 to 14 pairs of random-spaced pinnae. Pinnae shiny, dark green, leathery. Petiole heavily covered with long, brown scales. Occasional scales on rachis.

A leaf of this fern resembles a sterile branch of an Oregon Holly. The genus *Cyrtomium* has several interesting and different species, most of which have a strong holly-like appearance. The species *falcatum* and its cultivar, 'Rochefordianum', are more commonly known. *C. falcatum* is native of warmer regions and is hardy only where the winters are less severe; it is fully evergreen in milder climates. In Bermuda it grows wild, choosing crevices in quarried coral block walls as its habitat. Both the natural species and its cultivar make excellent houseplants.

Leaves, when first seen, have silvery scale-covered crosiers partially concealed between the upturned basal pinnae. Pinnae are distinctly *falcate,* or scythe-shaped, with long, tapered, upward-pointing tips. Apical pinnae are usually more ornate. Edges of the pinnae of this fern are relatively smooth in comparison with those of its variant cv. 'Rochefordianum'. The deeply incised lower pinnae and more elaborate apical pinna of the cultivar convey a still stronger holly resemblance.

SORI: Irregularly spaced, distributed over all of the underside of pinnae. First noticed as small, light green dots with centrally attached indusia. A magnifier will reveal irregularly fringed edges on the indusia.

CULTURE: Loose, woodland soil with sand and large pebbles to insure good drainage. Prefers a cool room beyond the direct rays of the sun. Keep moist.

RANGE: Old World tropics and subtropics.

---

1, Leaf silhouette. 2, Crosier unfolding between the basal pinnae. 3, Apical pinna. 4, Typical sterile pinna. 5, Fertile falcate pinna, cv. 'Rochefordianum.' 6, Enlarged sketch of maturing sori.

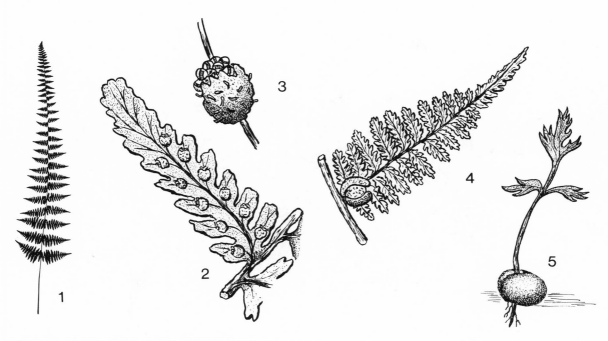

*Cystopteris bulbifera*—**Bulblet Bladder-fern**

Leaf tapering, 2-pinnate, yellow-green, about 24 to 36 inches long, 3 to 4 inches wide. Rachis and petiole pinkish-green when young, the color persisting or darkening with age.

This fern, with its long, tapering leaves, is one of the most graceful northeastern species. Where conditions are favorable, it will grow over 4 feet long. Although this fern is usually found on the shaded side of damp limestone cliffs and outcroppings, it also grows in moist, wooded areas.

In addition to reproducing through spores, it also reproduces by means of *bulblets.* These bulblets are similar to small green garden peas in size and color, and grow at the pinna-rachis junction or along the pinna midrib. There are from two to a dozen bulblets on one leaf. At maturity, the bulblets drop from the parent leaf and in time small plants appear, later developing the full and true characteristics of the parent.

SORI: Numerous and uniformly spaced, found on underside of pinnules of fertile leaves from leaf apex to basal pinnae. The arching indusium covers the sporangia by forming a tiny pocket or bladder. Open side of covering faces the tip of segment.

CULTURE: Although slightly indifferent to soil conditions, this fern does best with its rhizome closely packed in a limestone pocket or crevice. For the most natural appearance, have the rockwork in the garden sufficiently high to allow the leaves to arch gracefully downward. Keep cool and moist throughout the summer.

RANGE: Newfoundland to Manitoba, south to northern Georgia and central Arizona.

---

1, Leaf silhouette. 2, Arrangement of sori on underside of pinna. 3, Enlarged sketch of sorus showing indusial glands. 4, Pinna with bulblet at base. 5, Young plant growing from bulblet.

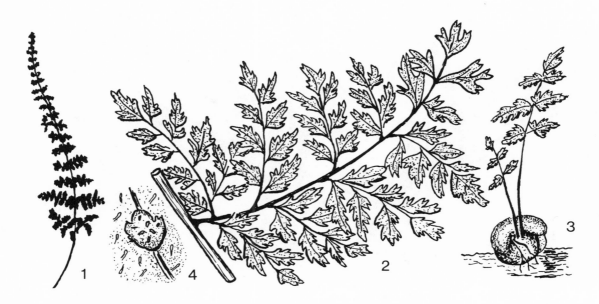

*Cystopteris bulbifera* var. *Crispa*—**Crested Bulblet Bladder-fern**

Leaves yellow-green, erect, tapering, 12 inches long, 2-, 3-pinnate. Pinna ovate, irregular, pinnules irregularly cut, fan-shaped. Stipe and lower rachis reddish, glandular.

This little plant was originally found growing in association with *C. bulbifera* on a limestone ledge overlooking the Housatonic River near Falls Village, Connecticut, ca. 1952. Numerous bulblets are formed on underside of leaf; these fall to ground either as bulblets or tiny plants, to start a new generation during the same season.

SORI: Numerous, with thin, bladder-like indusium. Indusium densely glandular.

CULTURE: Excellent for rock garden use when planted in limestone setting. Rapidly spreads by dropping bulblets.

RANGE: Connecticut.

---

1, Silhouette of leaf.  2, Basal pinna.  3, Juvenile plant growing from bulblet.  4, Sorus on vein.

## *Cystopteris fragilis*—**Fragile Bladder-fern**

Leaf lanceolate, 2-pinnate, medium green, about 10 inches long and 3 inches wide, with 8 to 12 pairs of opposite or nearly opposite pinnae. Leaf apex forms gracefully tapered tip. Lower pinnae widely spaced.

Also known as Brittle Fern, a name which is misleading. Actually the plant is less damaged during heavy storms than some of the sturdier species. The small, unprotected, brilliant green crosiers of this plant appear long in advance of true spring. Usually these early ones are found as tiny clusters beside a sheltering rock or as larger clumps in a ravine. More crosiers uncurl all summer; new light-green leaves replace the early ones which turn russet and die during warm, dry weather.

The Fragile Bladder-fern has variants, these variants in general being geographically and ecologically distinct. The variations are in the degree of taper of the lower pinnae, shape of the indusia, presence of minute indusial glands, and character of rhizome.

SORI: Few in number and irregularly spaced, growing on conspicuous veins. Sori covered with arching indusia, opening toward ends of lobes. Virtually transparent young indusia are pushed aside by growing sporangia and soon disappear entirely.

CULTURE: Easy to grow in open shade where soil is neutral or slightly acid. Keeping the plant moist will delay tendency to discolor early and also encourage fresh, green growth.

RANGE: Labrador and Newfoundland to Alaska, south to northern New England, Pike County, Pennsylvania, Missouri, western Texas and southern California.

---

1, Leaf silhouette. 2, Plant growing from rock crevice amid last year's stubble. 3, Upper pinna showing strong vein pattern. 4, Lower side of pinnule showing indusia covering sparse sori.

109

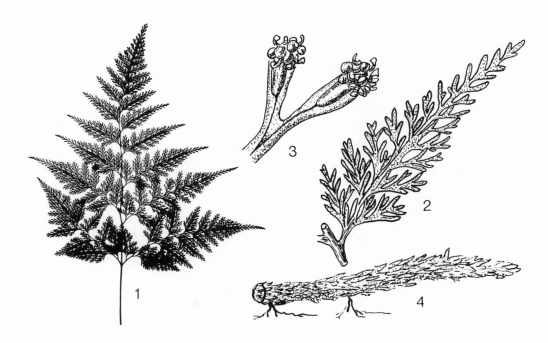

## *Davallia fejeensis* cv. 'Plumosa'—Plume Davallia

Leaves deltoid, 2-, 3-pinnate, segments needle-like, light green, very feathery, 12 to 20 inches long, growing at intervals of 2 to 3 inches from a heavily-scaled rhizome.

Many epiphytic ferns grow in the tropic-subtropic areas. Some of these species grow at ground level, entwining themselves on boulders or embankments; others prefer higher altitudes and become established anywhere between thatched roof-tops of native huts to the near-crown areas of palm trees.

Because of their beautiful leaf structures, colorful rhizomes, and adaptability to the home, various species of the *Davallia* genus are most attractive as houseplants. One, an exceptionally fine specimen, a horticultural variant, is *Davallia fejeensis* cv. 'Plumosa'.

SORI: At maturity, sporangia will continue to grow out of a semi-cylindrical indusium on the terminal of needle-like segments.

CULTURE: Fern will be displayed best when grown in a fiber planter or hanging wire basket. Use humus-rich growing medium consisting mainly of sphagnum moss and chopped bark. Medium should be moist at all times, but never allowed to become soggy. For propagation, use growing rhizome cuttings for planting in 3″ pots with loose growing mix.

RANGE: A horticultural variant of South Pacific origin.

---

1, Leaf silhouette.  2, Sterile pinnule with needle-like segments.  3, Enlarged fertile segment showing characteristic sori.  4, Apical end of scale-covered rhizome.

110

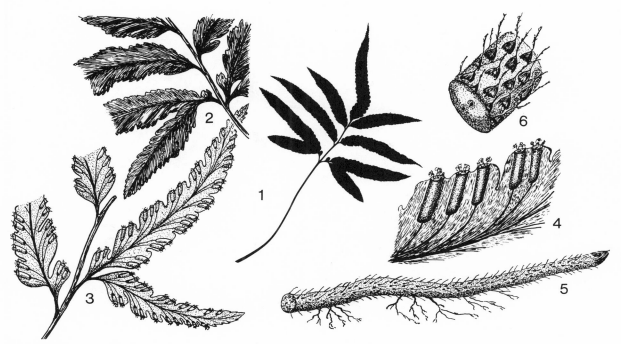

*Davallia pentaphylla*

Dimorphic. Leaves 4 to 6 inches long, 1-pinnate, with long tapering terminal pinna and 2 or 3 pairs of nearly opposite pinnae. Deep green. Exposed, horizontal and climbing rhizome covered with open-spaced brown, wiry scales.

The genus *Davallia* comprises a large group of epiphytic ferns. Their leaves range from the soft, delicate, lacy foliage of *D. fejeensis* cv. 'Plumosa' to the harsh, leathery texture of *D. solida*. In general, the species are characterized by their long, exposed, horizontal or climbing, scale-covered rhizomes. Some species have common names; often plants are indiscriminately called Rabbit's Foot, Hare's Foot, Squirrel's Foot, Ball Ferns, or just Davallias.

Rhizome scales of various species differ in size, shape, and color. In this species they are like little wiry bristles. When magnified, the scales appear elongate and branching, with shield-shaped bases; they are evenly arranged around the rhizome and point toward the growing end.

Leaves of *D. pentaphylla* depart from the general appearance of many species of this genus. The sterile leaves, with serrate edges and pinnately lobed basal pinnae, resemble those of some *Pteris cretica* ferns. Fertile leaves, deep green on upper surface and light green beneath, have wavy edges and are cleft between groups of sori. Petioles are articulate.

SORI: Like others of this genus, this fern has many sori with their open ends at the edge of the pinna. Each sorus is at the end of a prominent vein.

CULTURE: Grow in either pot or hanging basket. Being epiphytic, it should have a neutral humus soil and plenty of moisture. Place in warm, shaded spot. A long piece of cork bark for climbing is desirable.

RANGE: Malaysia, Polynesia.

---

1, Leaf silhouette (sterile). 2, Lower portion of sterile leaf. 3, Underside, lower portion of fertile leaf showing sori. 4, Enlarged sketch of mature sori. 5, Scale-covered, creeping rhizome. 6, Enlarged section of rhizome showing shield-shaped base of scales.

111

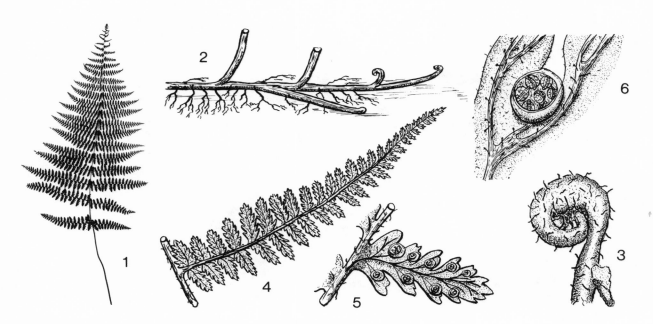

## *Dennstaedtia punctilobula*—**Hay-scented Fern**

Leaf lanceolate, 2-pinnate, pinnules lobed, feathery, yellow-green, 20 to 32 inches long, 11 inches wide. Slender rhizome, growing immediately below the surface.

Because this fern spreads rapidly, it is sometimes classified as undesirable. This bad feature is outweighed by its ease of adaptability in most gardens; it thrives in a wide range of soil conditions, tolerates prolonged wet or dry seasons, and grows in deep shade or full sunlight. Leaves are closely spaced and grow from a creeping-branching rhizome that soon becomes matted. The plant makes a dense stand and is an excellent ground cover for a slope. It is deciduous and turns brown early.

The crosiers are like little coils, and when they break through the soil are covered with silvery-white hair-like glands. When the blade is fully opened, these elongate, transparent *trichomes* will be found on the petiole and rachis as well as on the pinnules, especially along the midrib. It is from these little glands that the fragrance of freshly cut hay originates.

SORI: Small, with cup-shaped indusia containing few sporangia, situated in the *sinuses* of the segments. Part of the indusium is formed by reflexed margin of segment.

CULTURE: Indifferent to soil requirements, but grows best in slightly acid, damp, woodland mulch. Where the soil is soft, unwanted portions of the plant are easily removed by pulling out shallow rhizomes. Tiny snails denude the soft foliage in some locations; control them with commercial snail repellent. Wilting of individual leaves may indicate thrips.

RANGE: Nova Scotia to Minnesota, south to Georgia and Missouri, also isolated in Logan County, Arkansas.

---

1, Leaf silhouette. 2, Spreading rhizome. 3, Silvery-hair-covered crosier. 4, Upper side of pinna. 5, Pinnule with sori. 6, Details of sorus, showing cup-shaped indusium, reflexing of segment, veining, and glands.

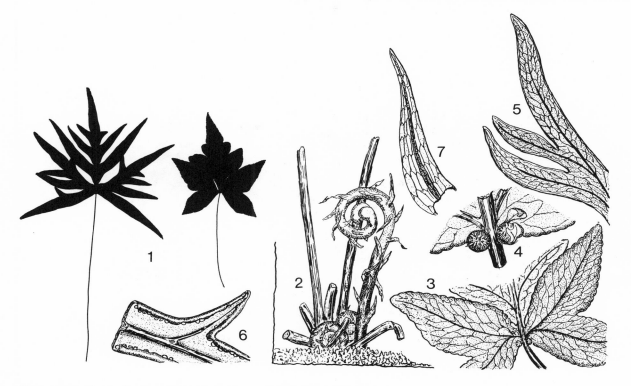

*Doryopteris pedata* **var.** *palmata*—**Spear-leaved Fern**

Strongly dimorphic. Leaves 9 to 12 inches long. Blades brilliant green, 4 to 6 inches each way, pedately divided. Petioles slender, polished, chestnut-brown.

This is one of the prettiest tender ferns, resembling some of the species of the genera *Pellaea* and *Pteris*. The leaves grow in tufts from a short rhizome; the dormant crosiers are barely visible beneath their heavy scale-covering. As the crosiers uncurl, the tiny leaf segments and first inch or two of the petiole are light green, covered with closely spaced scales. As the leaf reaches maturity, the petiole, darkening from the base upward, changes to chestnut-brown and is highly polished.

Sterile and fertile leaves follow a similar basic pattern but differ greatly in degree of slenderness. In addition to the beauty of the segments of the fertile leaf, the continuous brown border of the sori and dark costae add much to its attractiveness. The sterile leaf is definitely smaller, with broader segments. Small vegetative buds at the junction of the petiole and basal segments are borne on both sterile and fertile leaves.

While the blade is leathery, the network of veins is visible in strong light. Scales on petiole are elongate and, at maturity, have a dark central stripe.

SORI: Marginal, continuous, with reflexed indusium. Conspicuous at maturity.

CULTURE: Requires moist, rich humus soil, and warm, humid atmosphere. Deep shade.

RANGE: Central America, south to Bolivia.

---

1, Leaf silhouettes (left) fertile (right) sterile. 2, Scale-covered crosiers. 3, Lobed basal segments of sterile leaf. 4, Enlarged sketch of vegetative buds. 5, Underside of immature fertile segment showing inconspicuous sori. 6, Section of fertile segment at maturity showing opening indusium and dark costa. 7, Scale with dark central stripe.

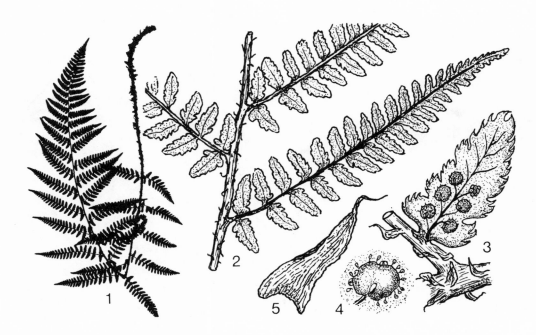

## *Dryopteris arguta*—Coastal Wood-fern

Blade dark green at maturity, ovate to deltoid-lanceolate, 2-pinnate-pinnatifid, up to 24 inches long and 14 inches wide, growing from a stout, heavy, chestnut-brown, scale-covered stipe up to 12 inches long. Pinnae long and upward spreading, with largest pinnae below the middle of blade. Lower pinnae become shorter and wider toward base. Pinnules blunt, with prominent, spreading veins ending in sharp, incurved, spiny teeth.

Coastal Wood-fern is strictly a western species growing mainly on rocky ledges and in wooded areas along the coast. Growing from a crown to form a beautiful vase-like pattern, this fern readily adapts itself to western gardens. It is excellent as a focal point or in group plantings. Unfortunately, this fern does not appear in eastern gardens.

SORI: Large, with shield-shaped indusium having a narrow sinus, arranged in single rows nearer to midrib than margin. Short-stalked glands growing on rim of indusium are easily seen with a magnifying glass.

CULTURE: Being a native of cool, damp woodland areas, a similar environment is best. Growing-medium high in humus, decomposed bark, and small stones, constantly moist, is suggested.

RANGE: British Columbia south through western states, rare in Arizona.

---

1, Leaf silhouette. 2, View of lower area of blade showing widely spaced pinnae. 3, Fertile pinnule. 4, Indusium with narrow sinus and glands along edge. 5, Typical chestnut brown scale.

114

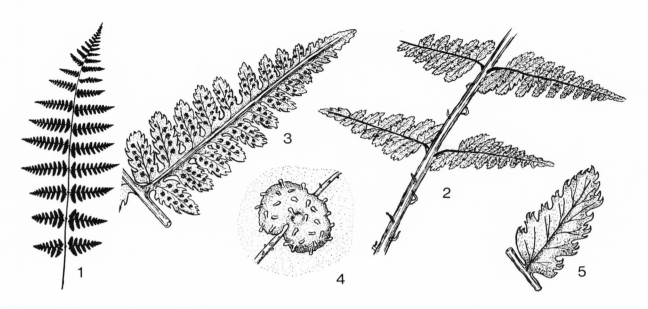

## Dryopteris × boottii—Boott's Shield-fern

Fertile leaf erect, deciduous, 36 inches long, 6 inches wide, narrowly oblong-lanceolate, 2-pinnate, deep green, leathery. Sterile leaf smaller, evergreen. Widely spaced horizontal-tilting pinnae are conspicuously spinulose.

D. × boottii grows in wet woods and swampy areas. It is a natural but sterile hybrid between D. cristata and D. intermedia and as such has several of the characteristics of both parents. Among the identification features from D. cristata are (1) relatively parallel sides of leaf, (2) widely spaced horizontal-tilting pinnae, (3) stubby triangular basal pinnae; and from D. intermedia (1) spinulose endings of pinnule segments, (2) glandular rachis, pinnae midribs and indusia.

Ordinarily this fern grows in very damp areas with both parents in close proximity and can be mistaken for its first named parent.

SORI: Small, numerous, mainly on upper pinnae, located near midribs, indusium kidney-shaped, glandular.

CULTURE: An excellent focal point plant for damp shady garden. Plant far enough from trees whose root systems might deprive the fern of moisture during dry season. Requires soil rich in humus.

RANGE: Nova Scotia to Virginia, Ohio, and Minnesota.

1, Leaf silhouette. 2, Basal area of leaf. 3, Fertile pinna after dehiscence. 4, Sorus with glandular indusium. 5, Sterile pinnule.

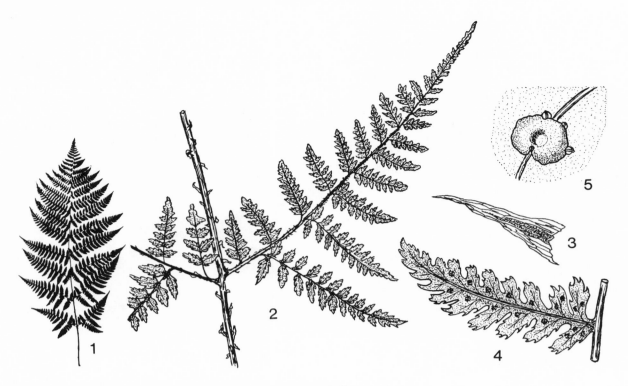

## *Dryopteris campyloptera*—**Mountain Shield-fern**

Leaf dark green, 24 to 36 inches long, 12 inches wide, ovate to nearly deltoid, 2-, 3-pinnate. Pinnae slightly ascending, with spinulose pinnules. Petiole covered with large broad scales.

*D. campyloptera* is one of the most beautiful spinulose ferns, with leaves growing from well-formed crown. Occasionally found growing on rocky slopes with other spinulose ferns.

In general, this fern is more featherlike and open than the others in the group. Particular attention should be given to the basal pinnae, which are strongly obliquely-triangular. Here the lower, innermost pinnule is sufficiently broad to span the two short upper ones, the three in combination giving a "two over one" effect.

SORI: Sorus covered with shield-shaped indusium, the indusium shriveling and disappearing as spores mature. Indusium glabrous or with few glands.

CULTURE: Grows best in partial shade in loose, humus-rich soil kept constantly moist. A large stone placed at the rear of the plant will add to its beauty and give some protection from wind and animals.

RANGE: Alaska and western Canada to California; in Rocky Mountains from Montana to Colorado; Minnesota, Wisconsin, adjacent Canada, east to Gulf of St. Lawrence and mountains of New England.

---

1, Leaf silhouette. 2, Basal pinna. 3, Broad-based scale. 4, Fertile pinnule after dehiscence and loss of indusia. 5, Sorus with shield-shaped indusium.

## *Dryopteris clintoniana*—Clinton's Shield-fern

Leaf leathery, oblong-lanceolate, pinnate-pinnatifid, 24 to 36 inches long, 9 inches wide. Basal pinnae elongate-triangular. Upper pinnae oblong-lanceolate, gradually tapering to sharp tips, not horizontal-tilting like *D. cristata*. Segments oblong-obtuse with coarse serrations. Petiole covered with pale-brown scales. Sterile leaf evergreen.

This fern, now known as a naturally reproducing species of hybrid origin, was discovered in the nineteenth century by George William Clinton (1807-1885). Originally it was considered a variety of *D. cristata,* a designation shown as late as 1950 in Gray's *Manual of Botany* (8th Edition). More recent cytological study has shown this fern probably a hybrid between *D. cristata* and *D. goldiana.*

Although it appears at first to be very similar to *D. cristata,* both fertile and sterile leaves are essentially alike, the fertile one not being conspicuously narrowed toward the base and the pinnae not horizontal-tilting. Leaves of *D. clintoniana,* growing from a crown, are markedly erect and form a vase-like pattern. Like *D. cristata,* this fern is native in swamps, wet woods, and damp thickets.

SORI: Large, close to midrib with glabrous, kidney-shaped indusium.

CULTURE: Good specimen fern. Plant in well-mulched, humus-rich soil kept damp throughout summer months. Protect from high winds.

RANGE: Quebec and Wisconsin to Virginia.

---

1, Leaf silhouette. 2, Basal pinnae. 3, Fertile segment. 4, Sterile upper pinna. 5, Sorus.

117

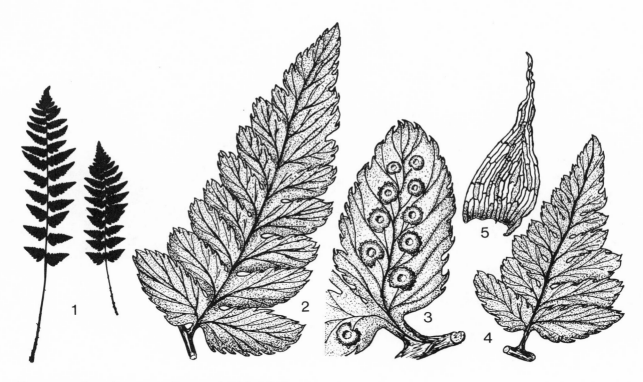

## *Dryopteris cristata*—**Crested Shield-fern**

Dimorphic, leaves linear-lanceolate, 1-pinnate-pinnatifid. Fertile leaves, narrow, up to 30 inches long. Sterile leaves shorter, broader, and tilting. Dark green, leathery.

Also known as Narrow Swamp Fern. This is a hardy but not fully evergreen fern, reflecting many of the genus *Dryopteris* characteristics. Brown-scaled crosiers rise from a crown formed during the previous year. The first crosiers develop into tall, stately fertile leaves; the later ones are sterile and shorter.

Pinnae, alternately and widely spaced along the rachis, have their surfaces in a horizontal plane, giving the leaf a step-like appearance. Double-forking veins are prominent in the large segments of these pinnae, while once-forked veins are found in the smaller areas. The basal pinnae are shorter than the higher pinnae and are nearly deltoid.

Like so many members of the genus *Dryopteris*, the Crested Shield-fern tends to hybridize with other *Dryopteris* species. When growing in its woodland habitat, it will often be found in close association with one or more of its crosses. The hybrids are sometimes quite similar and can only be recognized by fern specialists. Fortunately, dominant characteristics of both parents are present in the hybrids and aid in their classification.

SORI: Prominent on the upper pinnae midway between midrib and margin. Generally larger and flatter than others of this genus. At maturity, kidney-shaped indusia become much smaller and are difficult to see.

CULTURE: Requires cool, shady spot with moist, slightly acid, loose, mulched soil. Leaves are brittle and the fern should be kept out of windy passages and protected during storms. Excellent for woodland gardens and a good background plant for smaller gardens.

RANGE: Newfoundland to Idaho, south to the Dismal Swamp in southeastern Virginia and northern Arkansas.

---

1, Leaf silhouettes, (left) fertile, (right) sterile. 2, Upper side of fertile pinna. 3, Enlarged sketch of segment showing sori and veining. 4, Deltoid basal pinna, sterile leaf. 5, Enlarged sketch of scale from crosier.

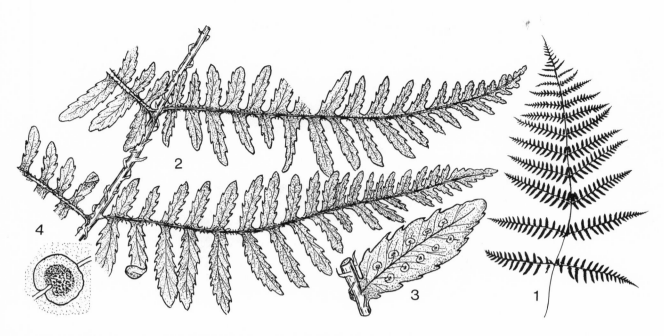

### *Dryopteris erythrosora*—**Japanese Red Shield-fern**

Leaf ovate-lanceolate, texture firm, 2-pinnate, up to 30 inches long and 15 inches wide. Crosiers first appear in copper-pink color, unfolding in delicate shades of bronze-green, and at maturity becoming a dark, shiny green. Petiole heavily clad with scales of dark brown or black. Pinnae lanceolate, 8 inches long and more than 1 inch wide. Pinnule segments terminating in sharp, incurved spines.

The common name, Japanese Red Shield-fern, alludes to the colorful array of red or magenta indusium-covered sori. This species is also known as Autumn Fern, so named due to the autumn-like display of color of its developing leaves.

The Japanese Red Shield-fern is unexcelled in the *Dryopteris* genus for its beauty of leaf structure and color. In a woodland garden setting or Japanese formal garden it is a most desirable plant.

While a native of Japan and China, this attractive fern is hardy in sheltered areas of the northeastern United States. In milder areas or with suitable protection it will remain green throughout the winter.

SORI: Circular, flat, up to 16 per pinnule, near midrib, arranged in pairs. Indusium kidney-shaped with colorful red central area.

CULTURE: Best grown as a feature plant with ample separation from other plants that might detract from its beauty. Planting it in front of a large stone will do much to enhance its character as well as protect its foliage. Requires loose, well-drained but constantly moist soil rich in humus. Open shade or alternating sunlight and shade.

RANGE: Japan and China.

---

1, Leaf silhouette.  2, Basal pinnae.  3, Fertile pinnule.  4, Sorus.

119

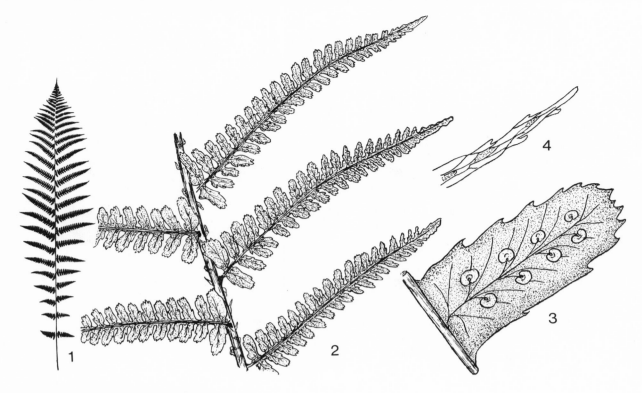

*Dryopteris filix-mas*—**Male Fern**

Leaf leathery, broadly lanceolate to oblong-lanceolate, 12 to 36 inches long, 8 or more inches wide, 1-, 2-pinnate, at first yellow-green, changing to deep green. Petiole chaffy, with long brown scales. Pinna long, acuminate, with blunt, deeply cut segments. Sterile leaf evergreen.

Male Fern is one of America's most stately ferns and long considered a rare species, its beauty only being exceeded by the even rarer Braun's Holly-fern. Because of extensive collecting these species have been endangered to a point where some stations have been completely destroyed. For a habitat this fern chooses cool, moist woodlands, glades, upland pastures and limestone slopes.

Fortunately, Male Fern is somewhat common in England where it is often seen along roadsides and in most home gardens. The relatively damper atmosphere and milder winters are beneficial to its survival.

SORI: Large, near midrib, with shield-shaped indusium. Indusium smooth or minutely glandular.

CULTURE: Where available this fern makes a strong focal point. Use soil composed of constantly damp humus and small stones. Planting beside a large rock will accentuate its beauty and add protection. Avoid natural wind passages.

RANGE: Newfoundland to Vermont and Michigan, British Columbia to California, South Dakota, Oklahoma, Texas.

NOTE: Since this fern is so rare and only thrives where native conditions can be simulated, it is suggested that it not be removed from the wild or purchased from commercial collectors.

1, Leaf silhouette.  2, Section of leaf.  3, Fertile segment.  4, Scale from petiole.

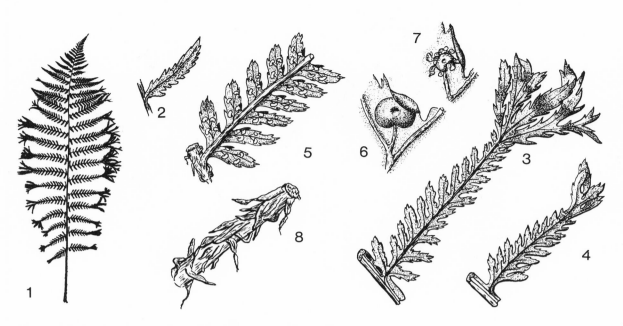

## *Dryopteris filix-mas* cv. 'Cristata'—English Crested Male-fern

Leaf ovate-lanceolate, 1-pinnate-pinnatifid, dark green, up to 36 inches long and 9 inches wide.

This fern, also known as the King of the Male Ferns, strongly resembles our exceedingly rare *Dryopteris filix-mas*, Male Fern. As a cultivar, it is typical of a large group of ferns developed by the English horticulturists during the early part of the nineteenth century.

Leaves are erect and grow from a crown of tightly spaced, densely scale-covered crosiers. Crowns for the following year are formed during the summer or early fall; they rest on the surface or slightly below the ground.

Characteristic of its genus, the petiole of this fern is stout and covered with long brown scales which gradually diminish as the rachis is reached. Pinnae terminate in uniformly divided finger-tip crests. Apex of blade is without any crests.

SORI: Round, with light-colored, kidney-shaped indusium, evenly spaced in single row each side of midrib. Indusium darkens and disappears as maturity is reached. Sorus at base of segment, on side toward apex of pinna, is partially covered with reflexed margin.

CULTURE: Moist, stony woodland-mulch. Complete shade or occasional short periods of filtered sunlight.

RANGE: Originated in England. Available from American growers.

---

1, Silhouette of leaf. 2, Pinna near apex. 3, Pinna at maximum width of leaf. 4, Basal pinna. 5, Underside of fertile pinna. 6, Sorus at base of segment showing reflexed margin. 7, Maturing sorus. 8, Base of petiole with heavy scale-covering.

121

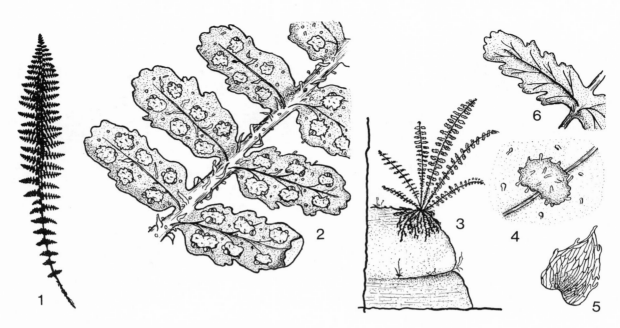

## *Dryopteris fragrans*—**Fragrant Shield-fern**

Leaf yellow-green, leathery, lanceolate, 4 to 12 inches long, 2½ to 3 inches wide, 2-pinnate. Pinnules blunt, with crenately-toothed lobes. Petiole densely covered with cinnamon-colored scales.

*D. fragrans* is a rare species generally found growing in the colder areas on north-facing cliffs or talus slopes. Leaves grow from center of spreading clump of an accumulation of two or three years of persistent dead leaves. Pinnae have distinctive curled-in edges, giving the plant a bushy appearance.

Many small glands are present on the underside of the pinnae and indusium, which give the strongly aromatic fragrance so characteristic of the species.

SORI: Round with large, irregular kidney-shaped, glandular-ciliate indusium.

CULTURE: A beautiful small plant but too critical in temperature, moisture, and soil requirements to be considered a garden plant.

RANGE: Arctic and subarctic regions; Labrador and Baffin Island to Alaska; south to Minnesota; Wisconsin, New York, and Vermont.

---

1, Leaf silhouette. 2, Section of fertile leaf. 3, Habitat showing plant arising from mat of dead leaves. 4, Sorus. 5, Scale. 6, Pinnule showing venation.

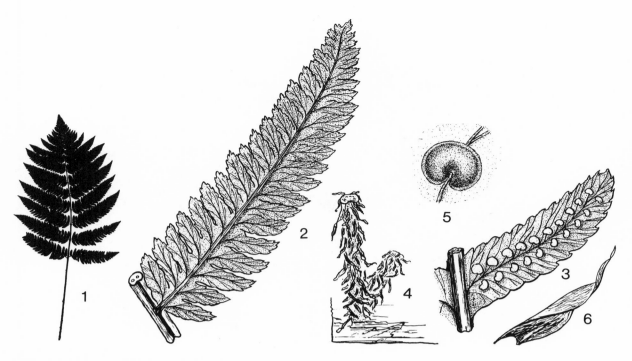

## *Dryopteris goldiana*—Goldie's Fern

Leaf ovate-oblong, 1-pinnate-pinnatifid, 48 inches long, 14 inches wide. Leathery, deep green. Under very favorable conditions, grows to 60 inches.

Also known as Giant Wood-fern. Although massive in shape and rugged in texture, this is a deciduous fern. Crowns of next spring's heavily-scaled crosiers form in late summer or early fall, and can be seen partially concealed in the dark leaf mold. These crosiers are the most shaggily clad of all the northeastern ferns. The covering is composed of many transparent, white and golden-brown elongate scales. These varicolored scales give the first inch or two of the petiole a mottled-striped effect.

Pinnae, when mature, are 7 to 8 inches long and slightly ascending. Their once-forked veins are sharply defined. While the silhouette of this leaf shows an opposite arrangement of pinnae, the same plant also had leaves with subopposite and alternately spaced pinnae.

SORI: Near midrib, spaced with almost geometrical accuracy. At first the sori are light green and covered with kidney-shaped translucent indusia. Maturing sporangia cause the sori to change to lead-gray, and finally dark brown. Indusia later shrivel or disappear entirely.

CULTURE: This fern requires a cool, shady location. Soil, rich in humus and rotting leaf mulch, with ample potato-sized stones around the roots. Keep the mulch moist at all times and give the leaves an occasional mist-spray during hot days.

RANGE: New Brunswick to Minnesota, south to southeastern Virginia, the mountains of North Carolina and Tennessee, and Iowa.

---

1, Silhouette of leaf. 2, Sterile pinna showing free veining. 3, Kidney-shaped indusia on lower surface of fertile pinna. 4, Heavily-scaled base of petiole. 5, Enlarged sketch of sorus. 6, Enlarged sketch of scale.

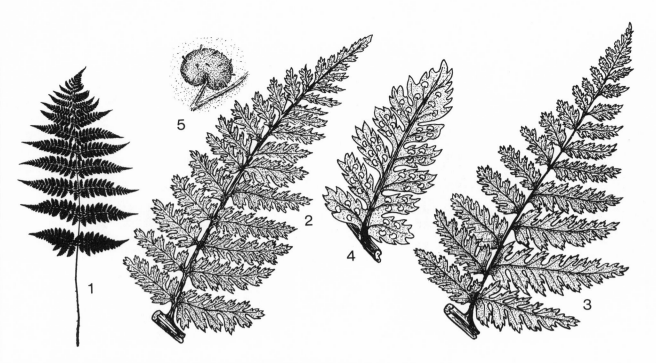

## *Dryopteris intermedia*—**Intermediate Shield-fern**

Leaf oblong-lanceolate, deep green, 30 inches long and nearly 10 inches wide, 2-pinnate, occasionally becoming 3-pinnate at basal pinnae. Crown-forming, does not spread. Evergreen or nearly so.

Also known as Fancy Fern or Intermediate Fern; it is one of the most common northeastern shield-ferns. Its combined beauty and sturdiness, with lasting leaves, make it an attractive addition to either the small garden or the larger woodland plan.

Following the *Dryopteris* pattern, the new brown-scaled crosiers rise from a crown that was formed during the previous season. As the days of spring become warmer, the leaves grow rapidly until their full height is reached. However, it is not until some time later, when the pinnae fill out, that the leaf attains its mature beauty.

The basal pinnae are of diagnostic value since they aid in distinguishing this species from the closely related Spinulose Shield-fern. In these pinnae the longest pinnule is second from the rachis on the lower side.

The fertile leaves are first to appear; the sterile leaves, which rise later, are similar in shape but somewhat smaller. In healthy plants the majority of the leaves are fertile, and most of the pinnae bear sori.

SORI: Round, with kidney-shaped indusia, uniformly spaced along midribs. Indusia have small glands visible only early in the season. By maturity, most of the indusia are very small or lacking.

CULTURE: Simulate native conditions by deep, rocky soil, rich in humus, neutral to slightly acid. Excellent plant for use with large boulders in woodland garden. Deep shade to alternate sunlight, but requires moisture at all times.

RANGE: Newfoundland to Wisconsin, south to Jackson County, Alabama, and eastern Missouri, southward restricted to high altitudes; isolated in Glacier National Park, Montana.

---

1, Leaf silhouette. 2, Large upper pinna showing sharply incised pinnules. 3, Basal pinna having longest pinnule (lower side) second from rachis. 4, Underside of fertile pinnule. 5, Kidney-shaped indusium with glands.

124

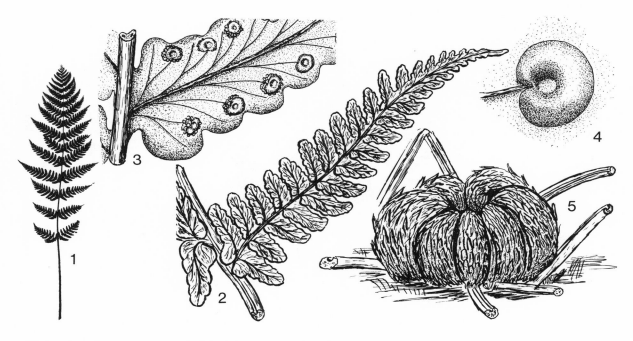

## *Dryopteris marginalis*—**Marginal Shield-fern**

Leaf lanceolate to ovate-oblong, 2-pinnate, dark blue-green, 15 to 20 inches long and 5 to 8 inches wide, having strong, leathery, heavily veined pinnules, and large, coarse, brown scales on petiole.

Also known as Marginal Wood-fern, Evergreen Wood-fern, and Leather Wood-fern. Leaves sturdy, remaining evergreen throughout the severe cold of the northern winters. During the late summer and early fall, the plant forms a crown of a dozen or more tightly closed crosiers at the base of the uniformly spread leaves. This crown is partially exposed above ground.

The early uncurling crosiers are heavily covered with coarse brown scales. Within a day or two the sori, far from full development, are well defined and easily seen on the unfolding apical pinnae. As the leaves continue to grow, their spring-like yellow-green changes to gray-green or blue-green by early summer. This fern does not spread, and makes a handsome, individual plant. In its woodland habitat, it is often found at the base of boulders. Its dead, matted leaves of the previous year assist in retaining soil on easily eroded slopes.

SORI: The entire fertile leaf, except a few of the lowest pinnae, is covered with sori uniformly spaced near the margin of the lobes. Thin, kidney- or shield-shaped indusia are attached at their centers and look like short-stemmed mushrooms. It is from the location of the sori and shape of indusium that the plant has received both its common and botanical names. At first, the indusia are nearly transparent or greenish-white. Later, as the sori grow, the apparent indusial color is influenced by the darkening contents of the sporangia, seemingly changing from lead-gray to brown at maturity.

CULTURE: Plant in deep, stony, well-rotted leaf compost, carefully observing crown position. Full shade to alternate sunlight or open shade. Keep mulch moist throughout summer.

RANGE: Nova Scotia to Minnesota, south to upland Alabama and Oklahoma.

---

1, Leaf silhouette.  2, Upper side of pinna showing leathery, deeply veined texture.
3, Mature and immature sori with kidney-shaped indusia on underside of pinnule.
4, Immature sorus.  5, Crown in late winter and early spring.

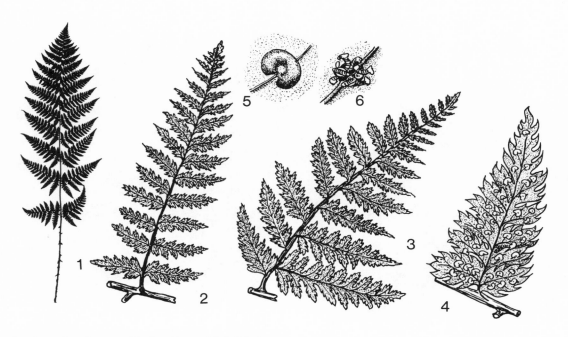

## *Dryopteris spinulosa*—**Spinulose Shield-fern**

Leaf oblong-lanceolate, 2- to 3-pinnate, 30 inches long and 7 inches wide, deep green. Crown-forming rhizome, non-spreading. Evergreen or nearly so.

Also known as Toothed Wood-fern, Fancy Fern, or Florist's Fern. Leaves of this fern and the other fancy fern, *Dryopteris intermedia,* are picked commercially by the thousands from the New England forests in mid-summer; they are held in cold storage and used in the floral trade throughout the country during the winter months.

The basal pinnae of this species are of particular importance diagnostically. These pinnae are obliquely triangular, with much longer pinnules on the lower side. Notice how the lower pinnule next to the rachis is longest. The other pinnules gradually become shorter as they approach the apex. Pinnules have deeply cut, serrate segments which end in bristles. Throughout the leaf, the bristle tips curve slightly inward.

Each spring the crosiers rise from amid the old, flattened leaves of the previous season. If the winter has not been too severe, these leaves on the ground will still be green. Although its rhizome is nearly horizontal, this plant forms a crown of heavily brown-scaled crosiers which are well advanced by early summer.

SORI: Covered by kidney-shaped indusia, centrally attached, situated on veins near pinnule midribs. Young sori appear as tiny dewdrops, uniformly spaced on pinnae of opening crosiers. Before long they become flattened, mushroom-shaped, light green dots. Sori darken to deep brown or black by maturity.

CULTURE: Neutral to slightly acid, deep, stony humus mulch. Keep mulch damp during hot weather. Makes beautiful planting along decaying log or in the hollow of a dead stump.

RANGE: Labrador and Newfoundland to Idaho, south to Virginia, or possibly North Carolina, and Missouri.

---

1, Leaf silhouette. 2, Upper side of pinna at broadest section of blade. 3, Basal pinna with broad triangular base. 4, Enlarged sketch of fertile pinnule showing sori and bristle tips. 5, Kidney-shaped indusium. 6, Sorus at maturity; indusium has disappeared and dehiscence of sporangia has occurred.

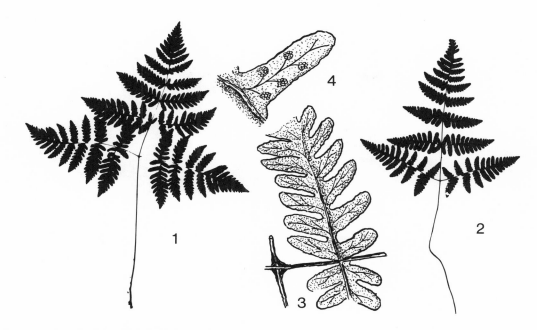

## *Gymnocarpium dryopteris* (1)—Oak Fern
## *Gymnnocarpium robertianum* (2)—Limestone Oak-fern

Oak Fern (1). Leaves 8 to 16 inches long with deltoid blades, ternately compound, growing at intervals from a slender, creeping rhizome. Basal pinnae broadly based, triangular, with long stalk, about equal in size to apical pinna. Rachis and blade without glands, or nearly so. A common species. Deciduous.

Limestone Oak-fern (2). Leaves 8 to 16 inches tall. Blade deltoid or nearly so, 2-pinnate-pinnatifid. Pinnae opposite, basal pair narrow-triangular, nearly symmetrical, with easily seen stalk. Upper pinnae sessile, oblong-ovate. Ultimate segments oblong with margin entire to crenate, often recurved. Rachis and blade densely glandular. A rare species. Deciduous.

A very slight difference exists between these two ferns, yet sufficient to warrant giving them species status. Study the architecture of the leaves by means of the silhouettes. Notice that the Oak Fern (1) appears markedly to be composed of three small, deltoid-blade ferns centrally attached. Limestone Oak-fern (2) appears to have its apical section over two outstretched, narrow pinnae.

SORI: Small, round or nearly so, naked, terminal on free veins somewhat evenly spaced in row medial to margin.

CULTURE: Easy to grow in medium of damp, stony mulch. Both species prefer alternate light and shade. As old rhizomes die, new plants come up in different areas.

RANGE: Northern United States, across Canada from Labrador to Alaska.

---

1, Leaf silhouette, oak fern. 2, Leaf silhouette, limestone oak-fern. 3, Pinnule on basal pinna. 4, Segment showing exindusiate sori.

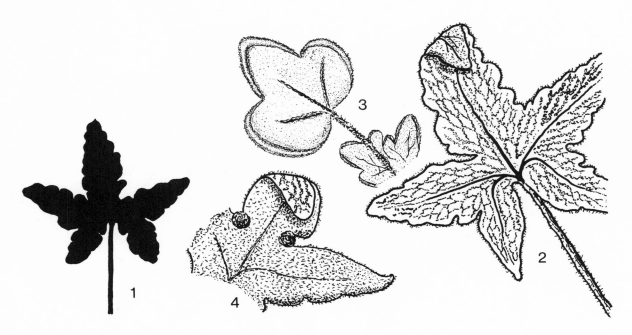

## *Hemionitis palmata*—Ivy-leaved Fern

Fertile and sterile leaves palmate, 2 to 5 inches across, composed of five divisions, light green. Divisions of fertile leaf more sharply defined, petiole dark chestnut-brown, 6 to 12 inches long. Sterile leaf smaller, blunter, petiole 2 to 4 inches long. Surface of blades and petioles covered with short white to rusty hairs.

In addition to the name Ivy-leaved Fern, other common names are Strawberry Fern, Star Fern, and Mule Fern.

Ivy-leaved fern, while still small, will do well in a terrarium when grown with suitable growing medium. Either subdued natural light or fluorescent light may be used. This species is a prolific spore producer and readily volunteers from spores; it can also be grown from its vegetative buds formed on the edge of the leaves. To propagate, pin a leaf to the growing medium and keep in a relatively high humidity. However, excessive humidity can induce fungal growth and be damaging to the younger leaves of the newly propagated plant.

SORI: Sporangia follow net-like vein pattern and at maturity become more or less confluent.

CULTURE: Use growing medium composed of peat moss, humus, perlite, and sand. Keep moist, but plant must have excellent drainage for survival.

RANGE: West Indies, Central America.

1, Silhouette of leaf.  2, Underside of fertile leaf showing reticulate vein pattern.
3, Crosier.  4, Vegetative budding occurring in sinuses of leaf.

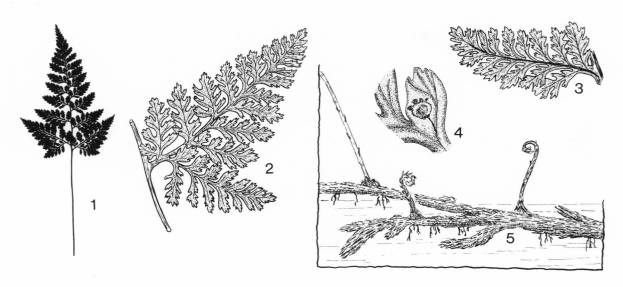

## *Humata tyermannii*—Bear's-foot Fern

Leaf 3-pinnate, 6 to 9 inches long, 4 to 5 inches wide. Blade elongate-triangular, dark green. Leaf grows at intervals from heavily white-scaled, horizontal and ascending rhizome.

Many ferns having rhizomes with white or colored scales carry names of animal feet. In the genera *Polypodium*, *Davallia*, and *Humata*, these names are overlapping and add confusion. While the "foot" structure or rhizomes differ greatly, they should not be considered the final diagnostic feature. Unfortunately the Bear's-foot Fern is frequently catalogued incorrectly as *Davallia griffithiana*.

"Bear's feet" or rhizomes, heavily clad in long snow-white scales, twine over the surface of the pot or hanging basket, reaching outward wherever an opportunity presents itself. Leaves are borne at 2- or 3-inch intervals. Initially, these are reddish-green, later becoming dark green. Color variation in foliage, in contrast with the snowy-white criss-crossed rhizomes, makes the fern an attractive houseplant. Petioles are articulate.

SORI: On segments covered by circular, flap-like indusia attached only at their bases.

CULTURE: Requires neutral soil rich in humus. Spreading of rhizomes should be anticipated, and a pot larger than ordinarily used is recommended. When the plant has rhizomes to spare, cut and start in a moss-lined, humus-filled hanging basket. "Feet" should not be buried but, rather, placed on the surface; in time newly formed roots will grow into the humus. When starting new plants, use a plastic bag as a moisture-retaining cover to avoid wilting of leaves. Rooting is slow. Keep soil moist but avoid overwatering. Healthy rhizome scales will remain silvery-white; when brown and soggy, it is a sign of overwatering. Restricted winter sunlight accelerates growth. Keep in open shade in summer.

RANGE: India, southern China.

---

1, Leaf silhouette. 2, Basal pinna. 3, Upper pinna. 4, Enlarged fertile segment with maturing sorus. 5, Surface-creeping rhizome showing spacing of leaves and crosiers.

129

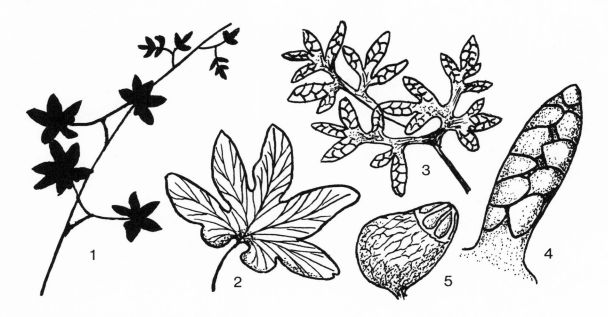

## *Lygodium palmatum*—Climbing Fern

Leaf light green, 24 to 60 inches long, slender, climbing and twining. Sterile pinnae confined to lower portion of rachis, fertile pinnae numerous, continuing to apex. Sterile pinna palmate, 1 to 3 inches wide, with 5 to 7 conspicuously veined blunt lobes; fertile pinna much smaller, with overlapping indusia, each covering solitary ovate sporangium. Sterile pinna evergreen.

Also known as Hartford Fern. The genus *Lygodium* comprises a small group of Climbing Ferns of worldwide distribution. Common to the genus is the imbricate covering of the sporangium. When established in favorable areas, the fern climbs on any nearby vegetation and can form dense bramble-like masses.

SPORANGIA: Instead of the spheroidal, capsule-type of sporangium with its annular band seen in so many ferns, this one has an egg-shaped capsule ending in an apical cap. Each sporangium is individually hidden beneath a pointed scale which acts as an indusium.

CULTURE: Climbing Fern can be grown in a garden providing the soil is constantly moist and highly acid. A trellis or equivalent will be necessary to support its vertical growth.

RANGE: Georgia to New Hampshire, Tennessee, West Virginia, Ohio, Florida, and Michigan.

---

1, Leaf silhouette. 2, Sterile palmate pinna. 3, Fertile pinna. 4, Enlarged fertile segment. 5, Sporangium.

## *Lygodium scandens*—Japanese Climbing-fern

An upward climbing, vine-like fern of indeterminate length, yellow-green to medium green, 3-, 4-pinnate.

Climbing Ferns twine around other plants and trellises, ultimately looking more like vines than true ferns. There are two well-known climbing ferns, *Lygodium palmatum,* the native Hartford Fern, and *Lygodium scandens,* the exotic Japanese Climbing-fern. Unfortunately, the Hartford Fern domesticates only with great difficulty and cannot be considered a good houseplant. The Japanese Climbing-fern readily adapts itself to the home and, given a trellis, makes an attractive addition for a window garden. Outgrowing the trellis, it will continue to climb to a nearby Venetian blind; it will even climb a lace curtain and pass through the open weave to gain greater light.

The petiole and rachis are extremely long and wiry and have oppositely paired pinnae growing at right angles. Both fertile and sterile pinnae grow from the same rachis. Sterile pinnae have long, tapered pinnules with deeply serrate edges. Fertile pinnae follow the same pattern but have coarser and fewer serrations which end in fertile lobes.

SPORANGIA: Instead of the spheroidal, capsule-type of sporangium with its annular band seen in so many ferns, this one has an egg-shaped capsule ending in an apical cap. Each sporangium is individually hidden beneath a pointed scale which acts as an indusium.

CULTURE: Loose, moist, but well-drained, slightly acid soil. Full winter sunlight, with open shade or alternate summer sunlight.

RANGE: Old World tropics.

---

1, Leaf silhouettes, (left) sterile, (right) fertile below, sterile above. 2, Sterile pinna. 3, 4, Fertile pinnae.  5, Enlarged sketch of fertile pinnule showing imbricated tips. 6, Enlarged imbricated fertile tip.  7, Enlarged egg-shaped sporangium.

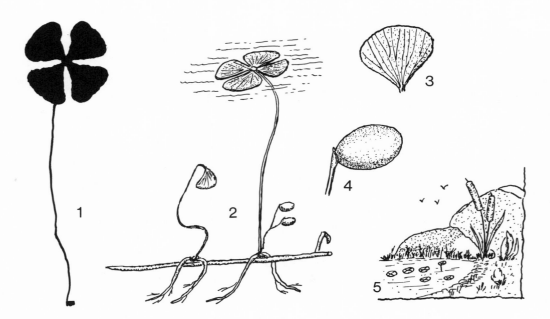

## *Marsilea quadrifolia*—**European Water-fern**

Blade, divided into four equal fan-shaped segments, appears like common four-leaf clover. Delicate, single leaves 4 to 8 inches long arise at intervals from continuously growing submerged stolon. Individual plants root in mud of shallow ponds and slow moving streams.

*M. quadrifolia* is not a native but, as its common name implies, is a European escapee which has become naturalized in New England, New York and New Jersey. In general, water ferns differ greatly from other ferns in that they are heterosporous. Instead of a single spore forming a prothallium or gametophyte, two different spores, a male microspore and a female macrospore which is much larger, are required to form the gametophyte from which the new plant grows.

SORI: Male and female spores are carried in hard-shelled, ovoid or clam-shaped sporocarps found on short peduncles at the base of the fern. While, as in other ferns, sexual reproduction is relatively slow, rapid growth and spreading of this species occur by means of its fast spreading stolons.

CULTURE: This plant, with its light-green leaves, some floating, others with their stems emerging 2 to 4 inches above the surface of the water, makes an interesting addition to a pool garden where it can be controlled.

RANGE: New England, New York and New Jersey.

---

1, Silhouette of leaf. 2, Plant with leaf on surface of water, and sporocarps at the base. Four-segment leaves are folded as they grow upward. 3, Segment showing distribution of veins. 4, Sporocarp. 5; Plants growing in shallow water and swampy edge of pond.

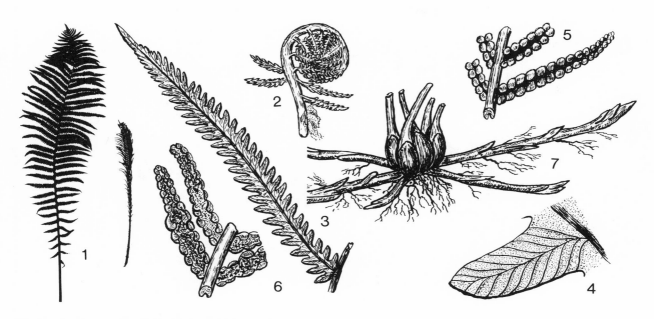

## *Matteuccia struthiopteris*—Ostrich Fern

Strongly dimorphic. Sterile leaf elliptic-lanceolate, reaching 60 inches in length, with maximum width one-quarter from apex. Deep green, leathery, 1-pinnate, deeply pinnatifid. Fertile leaf narrow and much shorter, with ascending pinnae.

The cultivated Ostrich Fern seldom attains its native height but with favorable garden conditions, especially plenty of moisture, it easily grows to 42 or more inches. With this height and its dark green, lustrous leaves, it is an excellent fern for a background planting. Leaves rise from a crown; dense underground runners, extending in all directions, reach out to establish new plants. Restrict planting to large areas or where spreading can be controlled.

Crosiers of sterile leaves appear much later than those of many ferns. When first seen, they are like small, emerald green balls. As they unfold, the lower pinnae stretch out at right angles from the rachis. The pinnae rapidly decrease in length near the apex, making the leaf appear blunt. These leaves become shabby late in the summer and die by early fall.

The fertile leaves appear in late June or early July and are about one-half the height of the sterile ones. The segments of the fertile pinnae tightly clasp the underlying sporangia, and it is only at maturity that the sporangia are revealed. These leaves, which change to shiny green-bronze and later to brown, remain erect all winter.

SORI: Sporangia, fully hidden throughout growing season, later bulge their pinna-wrapping and discharge the spores.

CULTURE: This fern is native in alluvial deposits, marshy areas, little islands and deltas of shallow streams and creeks. Although easy to grow almost anywhere, it reflects its care. Regularly watered plants will retain their grandeur into late summer.

RANGE: Newfoundland to Alaska, south to Fairfax County, Virginia, the mountains of eastern West Virginia, and central Missouri.

---

1, Leaf silhouettes, (left) sterile, (right) fertile. 2, Spheroidal crosier. 3, Sterile pinna. 4, Enlarged detail of sterile pinna segment showing simple veining. 5, Fertile pinnae approaching maturity. 6, Fertile pinnae after dehiscence of sporangia. 7, Crown with underground stolons.

133

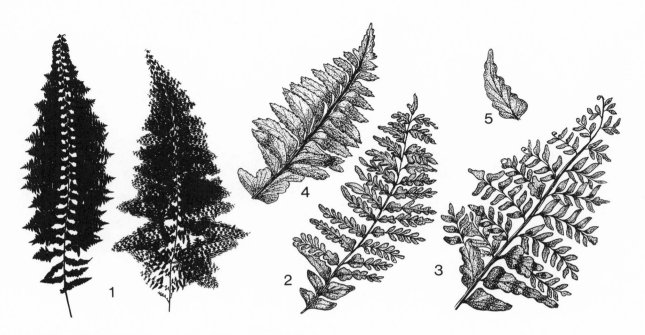

## *Nephrolepis exaltata* cultivars—Boston Fern

Luxuriant green leaves, length, width, and cutting differing with the variant. Leaves simple in appearance to extremely ornate, ranging between 1- and 5- pinnate.

The name "Boston Fern" is indicative of a single variant, and from this has originated the largest known group of fern cultivars. During the latter part of the nineteenth century, of all the potted ferns the Boston ferns were most popular; they could be seen in homes and public buildings almost everywhere. They were the most desired plants of growers and yearly sales soared in the hundred thousands.

The history of cv. 'Bostoniensis' has been carefully traced and recorded. It started with *Nephrolepis exaltata,* the Florida Wild Fern or Sword Fern. When potted for house use, the Sword Fern readily adapted itself and attained leaf lengths of four feet. While it could be propagated from spores, it reproduced more rapidly and conveniently from its far-traveling, scaly stolons which sent up new plants from closely spaced nodes. Easily produced and rugged, the fern soon became the houseplant of commerce.

Raising and selling these plants continued with growers until 1894 when a discovery was made. A shipment from a Philadelphia grower to a Boston distributor was different from the true *N. exaltata* so commonly used. At first it was considered another species, *N. davallioides,* and over 50,000 plants were sold before the error was discovered. In 1896 this newcomer was named *N. exaltata* cv. 'Bostoniensis', a name by which it has been known ever since. Cv. 'Bostoniensis', is a 1-pinnate fern and is in many respects similar to its progenitor *N. exaltata.* Today, the original cv. 'Bostoniensis' has largely been replaced by its more recent variants.

Some ferns hybridize readily. This occurs when two compatible prothallia of different species are near enough to allow cross-fertilization. However, hybridization is not the reason for the many variants of the Boston group. In the present case, changes

*Nephrolepis exaltata* cv. 'Elegantissima': 1, Leaf silhouettes showing wide variation on one plant. 2-6, Pinnate areas on different parts of same rachis. 7, Sori-bearing pinna. 8, Enlarged sketch of sorus.

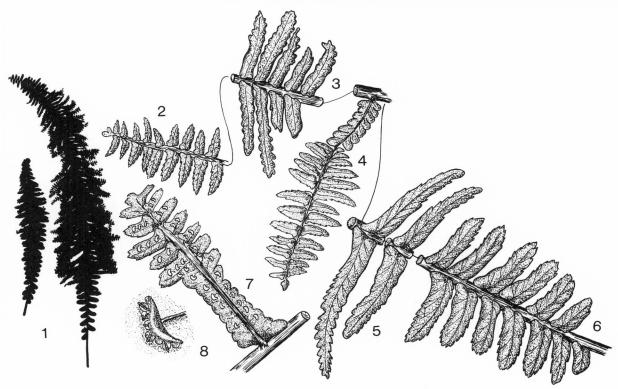

are attributable to *sports* or mutations. A sport involves a hereditary change caused in some other way than cross-fertilization. It is believed that an alteration of a gene has occurred, and when thousands of plants are studied a slight departure from normalcy may be seen in one. This is the way the first Boston Fern was discovered. From this original plant, others were propagated again from stolons and found stable. Usually the spores of these mutations are not viable and all future generations must come from stolons. Later, from this well-established fern other sports developed and a long hereditary chain was formed. From the original 1-pinnate Boston Fern came others that were 2-pinnate and, in turn, the beautiful present day 3-, 4-, and 5-pinnate ferns. With such a chain, botanical names became more complex as sport begat sport. Names such as *Nephrolepis exaltata* 'bostoniensis' 'piersoni elegantissima compacta' appeared and, though unwieldy, provided a family tree. Rather than continue this cumbersome taxonomy, Boston Fern growers now catalog them with the name of the last cultivar, as *Nephrolepis exaltata* cv. 'Compacta'.

Boston Ferns are, at times, not as stable as desired, and some have a tendency to revert to the wild *N. exaltata*. On a plant normally 3-pinnate, a 1-pinnate leaf of the ancestor will occasionally appear; this reversion should be removed immediately. A favorable feature is that as new mutations are developed the original long leaves become much shorter and broader, giving the plant a dwarfed, bushy appearance more suitable for many applications.

CULTURE: New plants are quickly started by detaching runner buds and potting in a mixture of good garden soil, sand, and humus to which a little bone meal has been added. It is a fast growing plant. Keep moist but avoid overwatering. Larger plants are best watered by immersing their pots in a pail of water for one hour. Do this twice a week or oftener, depending on the dryness of the house. Setting plant outside during winter rains when temperature is above 50° F. will be found refreshing and cleansing. It is better to start new plants than to continue to nurse old stock.

---

*Nephrolepis exaltata* cv. 'Whitmanii': 1, Leaf silhouettes showing variation on one plant. 2-5, Pinnae variations found on one plant.

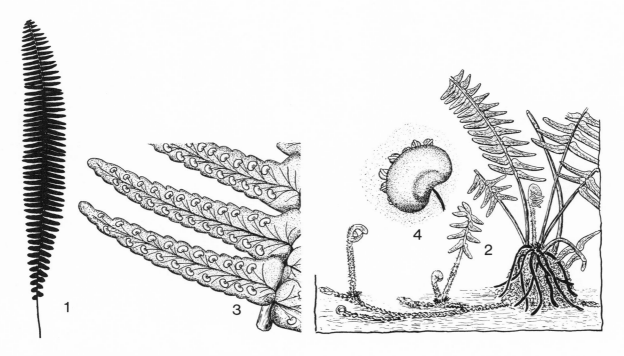

## *Nephrolepis exaltata*—Sword Fern

Leaf 1-pinnate, yellow-green to medium green, exceptionally long and narrow, slowly tapering toward apex and base. Length ranges from 2 to 6 feet.

Also known as wild Boston Fern. This is a fast growing, terrestrial or epiphytic fern, native of the American tropics and subtropics. It has the distinction of being the most prolific progenitor of all ferns; it is the sire of the long chain of Boston Fern horticultural mutations.

In the home, its pendulous leaves grow over 3 feet long when given reasonable care. Leaf growth occurs at the apex and, barring any injury, the leaves continue to lengthen for some time. While smaller plants are excellent for use in a planter, larger plants should be transferred to hanging baskets or pedestals where their long, flowing leaves will have greater freedom.

There is some resemblance in appearance between the Sword Fern and the Christmas Fern, although there is no generic relationship. Pinnae are articulate and closely attached to the rachis. Prominent auricles on the upper side of the pinnae cross the rachis and partially lap those on the other side. Edges are serrate on the upper pinnae, becoming more crenate in the lower pinnae. Venation is free, with either simple or forking veins reaching the sori or margins.

Older plants gradually raise their rhizomes, forming a heavy base. From this base, scale-covered stolons reach out along the surface in every direction. By encouraging these to root, new plants will rise at intervals.

SORI: Numerous, uniformly spaced. Orbicular to kidney-shaped indusia are attached on side toward midrib. Sporangia very dark when mature.

CULTURE: Loose garden soil with crocks. Full or filtered winter sunlight, open shade or alternate sunlight in summer. Keep moist, avoid overwatering. In spring, plant unpotted fern in garden for fast development of new plants from stolons. Remove all old leaves.

RANGE: Florida, Bahamas, Bermuda, West Indies, Mexico; Old World tropics.

---

1, Leaf silhouette. 2, Older plant growing from stump-like rhizome; young plants rising from stolons. 3, Underside of fertile pinnae showing uniformly spaced sori and overlapping auricles. 4, Enlarged sketch of sorus with sporangia bulging from free side of indusium.

## *Onoclea sensibilis*—**Sensitive Fern**

Strongly dimorphic. Sterile leaf deltoid-ovate, yellow-green to green, coarsely segmented, 12 to 30 inches long. Fertile leaf erect, persisting, 12 to 15 inches long.

Also known as the Bead Fern. The narrow, fertile "bead-stick" and broad sterile leaf make an unusual combination. Because of its prevalence and tendency to spread, this fern has at times been called the weed of the fern family. When carefully controlled, it will cause no more trouble than other spreading varieties. The leaves are not sensitive to the touch but are affected by climatic conditions, particularly cold weather. Often the sterile leaves turn brown after a very cool spring or fall night.

The sterile leaf is composed of several pairs of opposite pinna-like segments, all joined by a rachis-wing which widens toward the apex. The network venation is unlike many ferns; it can be studied by placing a small flashlight in back of the segments.

The bead-sticks or fertile leaves at first seem to have little relation to a fern, for the beads appear like small, distorted green balls with embossed brown lines. Actually, each green ball is a pinnule that has formed around several sori, and the brown line is a continuation of the vascular system. Thus the bead covering is not a capsule containing spores but a modified pinnule serving as a protective covering.

SORI: Composed of sporangia in cup-like indusia. Several sori enclosed in bead-like, closely spaced pinnules along numerous branches of fertile leaf. Beads first appear green, later changing to deep brown. Fertile leaf remains standing far into the second year.

CULTURE: Suggested only for the larger garden or where growth can be controlled. Grows in wet, marshy, subacid soil. Tolerates full sunlight where moisture is abundant.

RANGE: Newfoundland to Saskatchewan, south to northern Florida and Texas.

---

1, Leaf silhouettes, (left) sterile, (right) fertile. 2, Leaf segments with typical venation. 3, Branching bead-stick (fertile pinnae). 4, Fertile pinnule showing veins. 5, Enlarged section through fertile pinnule showing sporangia within indusia.

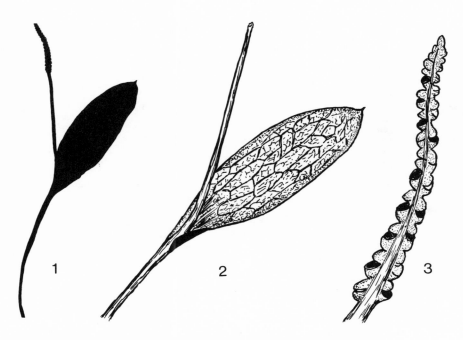

## *Ophioglossum engelmannii*—Engelmann's Adder's-tongue Fern

Leaf 2 to 8 inches long. Small elliptical sterile blade joining fertile stalk at approximate midpoint, the apical end terminating in a sharp, identifying point. Fertile stalk continues upward, terminating in synangium.

Several species of Adder's-tongue Fern grow throughout the United States. One, *Ophioglossum palmatum*, a very rare species, grows as an epiphyte on cabbage palmettos in Florida; others, more common, grow in damp meadows. Being relatively short and the same color as the grass that covers them, they may be easily passed by. *O. engelmannii* tends to grow in open, gravelly patches and is easily seen.

SPORANGIA: Sporangia fused to form characteristic synangium growing at apex of stalk arising from base of sterile blade. Individual sections of synangium split horizontally to allow dehiscence of spores.

CULTURE: Too small to be considered usable in horticulture.

RANGE: Southern United States, Mexico.

1, Leaf silhouette.  2, Sterile blade joining fertile stalk.  3, Synangium at maturity.

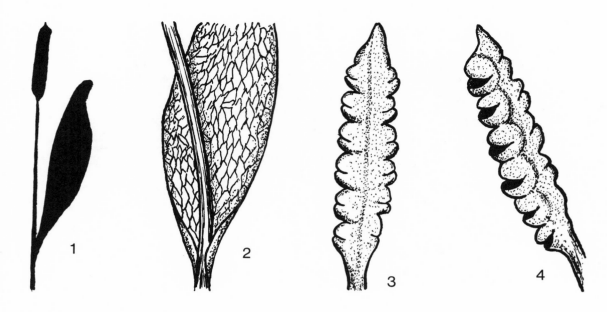

## *Ophioglossum vulgatum*—**Adder's-tongue Fern**

Leaf pale or yellowish green, 3 to 12 inches long. Sterile blade fleshy, ovate or elliptic, 1 to 3 inches long, sessile on stalk at approximately midheight. Veins anastomosing. Deciduous.

Grows in moist open woods, damp meadows, boggy thickets. Plants spread from fleshy roots. Leaf for succeeding year arises from bud within sheath at base.

SPORANGIA: Sporangia fused to form characteristic synangium growing at apex of stalk arising from base of sterile blade. Individual sections of synangium split horizontally to allow dehiscence of spores.

CULTURE: Can only be grown where natural growing conditions are critically duplicated. Too small to be of horticultural value.

RANGE: Prince Edward Island to Alaska, south to Florida and Arizona.

---

1, Leaf silhouette.  2, Sterile blade.  3, Synangium, immature.  4, Synangium after dehiscence.

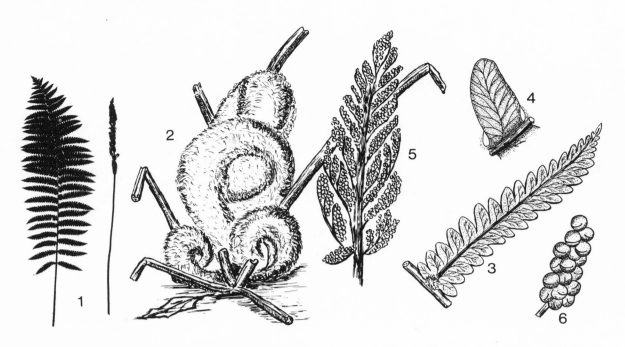

## *Osmunda cinnamomea*—**Cinnamon Fern**

Sterile leaf oblong-lanceolate, yellow-green to deep, waxy green, 1-pinnate, deeply pinnatifid; 24 to 36 inches long in gardens to over 60 inches long in native, swampy areas. Strongly dimorphic.

This fern, with its fertile "cinnamon stick" and lusty sterile leaf, is an excellent example of dimorphism. When first seen, a covering of white woolly hair conceals the crosiers. As the warm sunlight strikes through the leafless trees, the fertile crosiers soon uncurl and the woolly coverings are cast aside. At this time, tiny spherical spore capsules are easily seen with a magnifier. Groups of two, three, and four fertile crosiers unfold simultaneously far in advance of the slower growing sterile leaves.

Once the fertile leaf starts to uncoil, growth is rapid until the mature height is reached. Upward pointing fertile pinnae are spread along the upper section of the rachis or are closely grouped, giving the appearance of a solid mass. After dehiscence of the sporangia the leaf turns golden brown and withers. It remains on the ground and provides positive identification of the species throughout the summer.

Usually all of the sterile leaves to appear in a season are released immediately after the fertile ones. The sterile leaves are strong and erect; they remain green all summer. Brownish tufts of hair are found at the junction of the pinnae and rachis.

SPORANGIA: Spherical capsules growing on segments of opposite pinnae. Brilliant green when young, changing to deep green just prior to maturity. Dehiscence along equatorial line of sporangia scatters light green spores.

CULTURE: Excellent species for background or transitional planting of larger gardens. Grows best in constantly damp, acid soil. Indifferent to light if soil and moisture conditions are suitable. Spreads very slowly.

RANGE: Newfoundland to Minnesota, south to central Florida and New Mexico.

---

1, Leaf silhouettes. (left) sterile, (right) fertile. 2, White, woolly fertile crosiers in center, sterile crosiers at base. 3, Sterile pinna with woolly tuft at base. 4, Sterile segment showing venation. 5, Apical portion of fertile leaf. 6, Enlarged sporangia with equatorial lines of dehiscense.

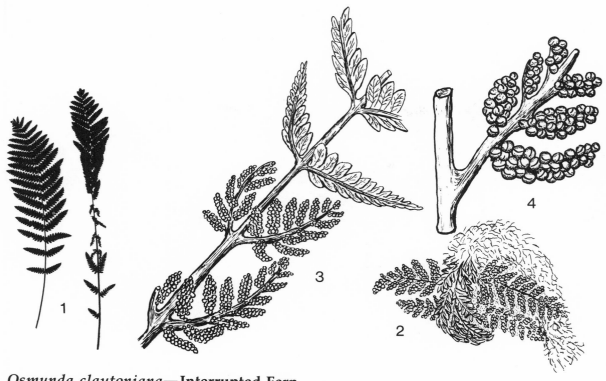

## *Osmunda claytoniana*—Interrupted Fern

Leaves dimorphic, oblong-lanceolate, coarse, leathery, yellow-green to dark green, 1-pinnate, deeply pinnatifid, over 5 feet long in native, swampy areas. Fruiting occurs on 2 to 5 pairs of pinnae in the lower half of an otherwise sterile leaf.

Also known as Clayton's Fern. This fern is one of the first to show its white cotton-ball crosiers in the spring. As the crosiers uncurl, the matted, hairy winter covering is broken, exposing the tender yellow-green pinnae. So much alike are the crosiers of the Interrupted Fern and the Cinnamon Fern that it is difficult to distinguish between them without evidence of last year's fertile leaves. However, before long two or more pairs of fertile pinnae, already covered with fast growing sporangia, will grow outward at right angles to the rachis. Still tightly wrapped around these fertile leaflets are the upper sterile pinnae which later uncoil and form the large leafy portion of the blade.

As the fertile leaves advance, the sterile ones quickly follow, forming the outer circle of the plant. Other than lacking fertile pinnae, the sterile leaves look somewhat similar, although they are usually shorter, broader, and less erect.

The interrupted fern does not spread rapidly. The plant, over many years, dies in the center and growth continues along the periphery, eventually forming a "ghost ring".

SPORANGIA: Naked sporangia outline the fertile pinnae, and at maturity become so confluent that the identity of the segments is lost. With approaching maturity, the early delicate green darkens until the sporangia appear nearly black. Sporangia, like little balls, have an equatorial slit along which dehiscence occurs. After spores are discharged, the empty sporangia look like tiny shells.

CULTURE: Highly acid, constantly damp, shaded area if large plants are desired. The fern adapts itself to less ideal conditions, although smaller plants must then be expected.

RANGE: Newfoundland to eastern Manitoba, south to Georgia and northern Arkansas.

---

1, Leaf silhouettes, (left) sterile, (right) fertile. 2, Unfolding crosier with fertile pinnae partially extended from rachis. 3, Fertile pinnae and upper sterile pinnae. 4, Enlarged sketch of sporangia showing equatorial slits.

141

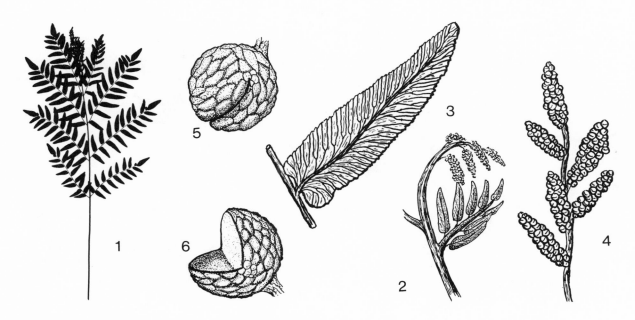

## *Osmunda regalis* var. *spectabilis*—**Royal Fern**

Leaf ovate-lanceolate, 2-pinnate, pinnae resembling locust tree leaves. Light reddish-green when young, changing to deep green . Leaves 3 to 4 feet long, some reaching 6 feet under ideal conditions. Fruiting at top of otherwise sterile leaf. Dimorphic.

The Royal Fern has many colloquial names; the Flowering Fern, Locust Fern, Buckthorn Fern, Ditch Fern, and Snake Fern are among the more popular. The plant lacks the delicate leaf pattern common to many ferns. In early spring when woolly white crosiers of the other *Osmundas* are so prominent, the reddish-brown hairy caps of the Royal Fern go unobserved by most people. While the advancing crosier is still partially closed, the soft green sporangia of the terminal pinnae appear from within.

The inflorescence-like fertile top of the Royal Fern gives the fern one of its com-common names—Flowering Fern. This top consists of hundreds of small spheroidal capsules or sporangia supported by groups of pinnules. At maturity the expanding capsules coalesce and conceal the pinnule structure.

In common with the other *Osmundas,* the Royal Fern spreads very slowly and individual plants do not lose their identity. Growth occurs circumferentially and after many years a ring of separate plants may be seen, all having their origin from the central plant.

SPORANGIA: Fertile terminal panicle composed of masses of exposed sporangia. Sporangia are spheroidal, discharging green spores by splitting along equatorial line. Young sporangia are brilliant green but after dehiscence become dark brown; the empty sporangia remain on the leaves until frost.

CULTURE: Requires highly acid, very wet soil for best growth. Light is not critical but open shade to alternate sunlight, depending on available moisture and soil, is recommended.

RANGE: Newfoundland to Saskatchewan, south to Florida and Texas.

----

1, Fertile leaf silhouette. 2, Sporangia forming on terminal pinnae. 3, Sterile pinnule with serrate margin. 4, Fertile pinna. 5, Sporangium approaching maturity. 6, Sporangium after dehiscence.

142

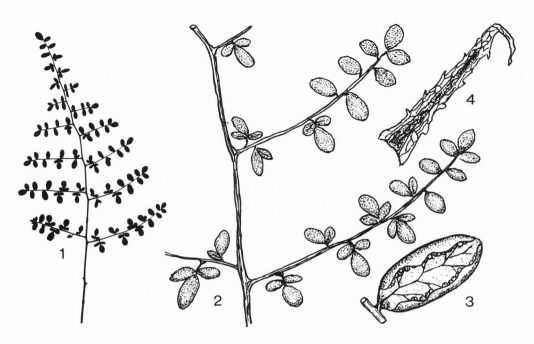

## *Pellaea andromedifolia*—Coffee Fern

Leaves, 4 to 18 inches long, grow at intervals from a scale-covered, long, creeping rhizome. Stipe, ½ the length of leaf, rachis flexuous. Blade triangular-ovate, 2-, 3-pinnate, basal pinnae rarely 4-pinnate. Pinnae, openly spaced on rachis, have several pairs of alternate, broadly ovate pinnules, either sessile or shortly stalked. Veins forking once are prominent on underside of pinnule.

The arid area of southwestern United States has many fascinating examples of American flora. These plants have adapted themselves to the extremely hot and dry climate, and are able to withstand sustained periods without water.

Coffee Fern is one of a large group of the Cliff Brakes and, in common with many others, has a hard, medium to dark-colored stipe and rachis, and pinnules with reflexed margins to protect the sporangia.

SORI: Sporangia are attached to end of forked veins. Protection is afforded by reflexed margin of pinnule.

CULTURE: Simulate natural growing conditions in garden by planting in elevated groups of calcareous rocks to provide good drainage. Avoid overwatering if used as a houseplant.

RANGE: California, Baja California.

---

1, Leaf silhouette. 2, Lower area, upper side of fertile leaf. 3, Enlarged view of fertile pinnule showing reflexed margin of pinnule partially covering sporangia, and prominent forked veining. 4, Enlarged typical scale from base of stipe.

143

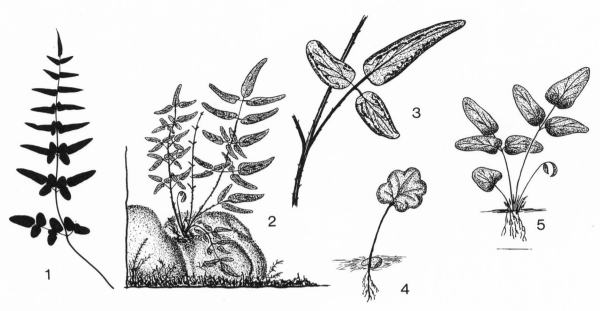

*Pellaea atropurpurea*—**Purple Cliff-brake**

Leaf lanceolate, 1-pinnate above, 2-pinnate below, usually 6 to 8 inches long, 15 inches long in more favorable locations. Delicate green changing to gray-powder-green, finally becoming leathery blue-green.

Also known as Hairy Cliff-brake. The Purple Cliff-brake grows on limestone, and with its roots impacted in the smallest crevice it appears to live on a minimum of soil nutrients and moisture. Plants growing under these adverse conditions are an easy prey for prolonged dry weather, but the leaves return the following year.

Each spring the plant appears much later than many ferns. At first, only two or three light green crosiers appear among last year's wiry stubble. As growth continues, usually eight to ten opposite pinnae form lanceolate leaves. Fertile pinnules are much more elongate and sometimes *hastate* (halberd-shaped) while the sterile ones are more rounded or elliptical. The leaves will often remain evergreen where the winter is not severe.

Young leaves have petioles of light green, darkening with age to purple-brown. Hairs are present on both the petiole and rachis.

SORI: Sporangia develop beneath the reflexed edge of fertile pinnules. At maturity, the enlarged sporangia push this margin back and discharge their spores.

CULTURE: Tolerates considerable sunlight where native conditions are simulated. Grows best when planted in limestone pockets which lead to moist earth. An occasional watering in dry seasons is important.

RANGE: Northwestern Florida to Arizona, north to northern Vermont, northern Michigan, and western South Dakota.

---

1, Leaf silhouette. 2, Plant growing in humus-filled limestone pocket. 3, Marginal fruiting on underside of pinna. 4, First leaf growing from prothallium. At this time the leaf is nearly circular. 5, Advanced sporophyte with elongating pinnules and tufted rhizome.

144

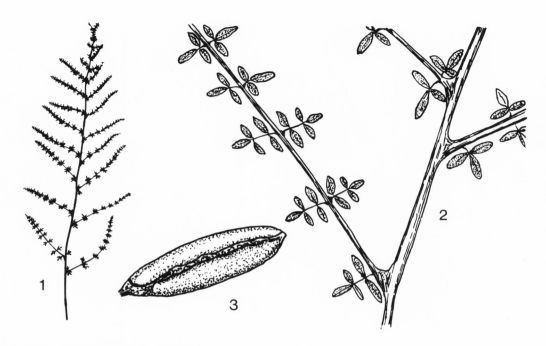

## *Pellaea mucronata*—Bird's-foot Fern

Erect, soft gray-green, leaves 6 to 20 inches long, broadly ovate-lanceolate, 2- or 3-pinnate, grow in clusters from a thick, short creeping rhizome densely covered with brown scales. Stipe wiry and without scales, brittle, smooth, dark brown. Pinnae alternate, long and ascending, with 6 to 15 opposite pairs of 3- to 5-foliate pinnules. Evergreen.

Bird's-foot Fern is one of a large group of terrestrial or rupestral ferns of the worldwide genus, *Pellaea.* Nearly all of the leaves of this species are fertile and remain evergreen. The plant has adapted itself to sustained periods of dry, hot weather, and is more or less restricted to our southwest.

SORI: Continuous row of sporangia follows the underside of margin, with margin reflexed to form a nearly closed pod-like segment.

CULTURE: Can be grown if natural conditions are closely simulated. For garden use, an elevated rocky mound will help provide needed drainage. Where the plant is grown in a greenhouse, a low humidity should be maintained.

RANGE: California, Baja California.

---

1, Leaf silhouette. 2, Lower portion of leaf. 3, Segment with reflexed margins nearly joining over midrib.

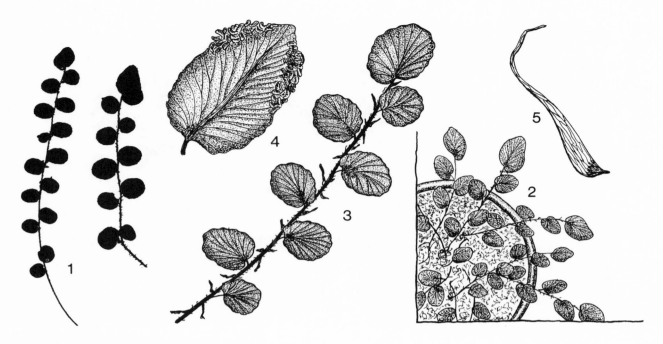

## *Pellaea rotundifolia*—**Button Fern**

Leaf slender, 1-pinnate, 12 to 18 inches long, with 12 to 20 pairs of round or nearly round, alternately spaced, waxy, dark green pinnae. Petiole and rachis densely covered with short and occasional long, brown scales. Apical pinna is often oblong-orbicular.

The leaves of this plant, with their button-like pinnae, bear little resemblance to many ferns. The leaves are not erect as in many of the *Pellaea* but low and spreading, growing over the sides of the container or hanging basket.

When first noticeable, the crosiers are small and heavily scale-clad. Their partially concealed, button-shaped pinnae of new leaves are red-green when young, but quickly change to waxy, dark green before they are fully grown. Leaves grow rapidly from a spreading rhizome; succeeding leaves become longer and sturdier.

Pinnae are nearly round to oblong-orbicular in shape. The apical pinnae are inclined to depart more from the normal shape than the other pinnae; some of these appear almost as though two odd-shaped pinnae had fused together. Venation is dichotomous; because of the leathery nature of the pinnae, the veins are difficult to see.

SORI: Marginal, located on the underside of pinna. Extend varying distances along the pinna edge but never quite close around the apex. Indusium long and narrow, affording little or no protection for the sporangia. Without a magnifier, the sori appear exindusiate.

CULTURE: Loose, humus soil with ample crocks. Use large-sized pot to accommodate fast growth of rhizome. Keep moist but avoid overwatering. Plant growth may be accelerated with mild winter sunlight. Keep in open shade during summer. Inspect weekly for plant scale on both sides of foliage. Crushing the parasite is the best treatment.

RANGE: New Zealand.

---

1, Leaf silhouettes showing variations of apical pinnae. 2, Potted plant with intertwining leaves. 3, Leaf with alternately spaced, button-shaped pinnae, and scattered scales. 4, Underside of fertile pinna showing venation and marginal sori. 5, Enlarged sketch of long scale.

146

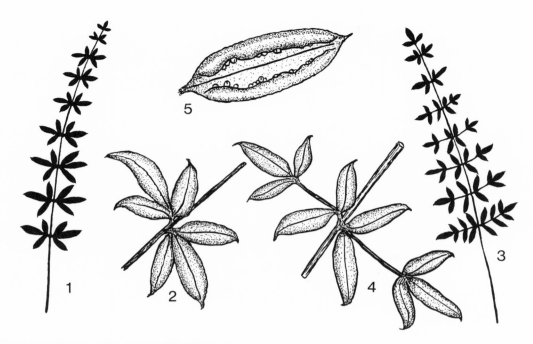

## Pellaea ternifolia—Ternate Cliff-brake
## Pellaea wrightiana—Wright's Cliff-brake

These two Cliff-brakes are somewhat similar in general appearance and habitat. *P. ternifolia* differs in having a leaf 18 inches long with blade narrowly oblong, 2-pinnate at base, pinnate above. Stipe wiry, brown to black, with top surface round to flat. Pinnae opposite, each having very short rachis. *P. wrightiana* has leaves up to 15 inches long, blades narrowly triangular, 2-pinnate, with pinnae divided into two to four opposite pairs of pinnules on elongate rachises. Stipe wiry, chestnut-brown, grooved.

Cliff-brakes comprise a large group of small to medium-sized ferns growing in the dry regions of the temperate and subtropical zones, seeking calcareous to non-calcareous rock for their habitat. In general, they have wiry stipes with colors of yellow, purple, brown or black.

SORI: Sporangia continuous, covered beneath reflexed margin of pinnule. Drying, fertile pinnules develop a pod-like appearance.

CULTURE: Provide elevated rock setting with plants placed in crevices. Water only when soil becomes nearly dry.

RANGE: *P. ternifolia:* Southwestern United States, tropical America. *P. wrightiana:* Southwestern United States and North Carolina, Northern Mexico.

---

1, Leaf silhouette of *P. ternifolia.* 2, Pinnae of same. 3, Leaf silhouette of *P. wrightiana.* 4, Pinnae of same. 5, Typical fertile pinnule.

## Pellaea viridis

Leaf lanceolate, 1-pinnate above, 2-pinnate below, 8 to 30 inches long, 4 to 8 inches wide. Pinnule brilliant, glossy green. Petiole and rachis glossy chestnut-brown to black.

The genus *Pellaea* comprise a large group of ferns having members spread throughout the world in both warm and cold regions. Many of them have dark, wiry petioles, either hairy or smooth, and all have marginal-borne sori.

Growth habits of the species differ greatly. The leaves of some are flat and spreading, particularly *P. rotundifolia*, the Button Fern; others form bushy stands, while there are those, long and slender, that resemble climbing ferns. *P. viridis* var. *viridis* is an excellent houseplant and is especially adaptable to fluorescent light. Leaves of this fern grow rapidly to 30 inches.

Two variants of *Pellaea viridis* are shown here—var. *viridis* and var. *macrophylla*. Both are native to Africa and are more colorful than some of the other *Pellaea*. Their pinnules are brilliant, shiny green with the edges of the sterile pinnules either serrate or crenate. Petioles and rachises, green when young, change to smooth, glossy black by maturity.

Both of these variants grow readily from spores. The first sign of the sporophyte growing from the prothallium is a pair of small, kidney-shaped leaves attached to a black, wiry petiole. These double, juvenile leaves continue for about three or four pairs, when a gradual change to the mature pattern occurs.

---

*Pellaea viridis* var. *viridis:* 1, Leaf silhouette. 2, Apical pinnule showing forked veins leading to crenate margin. 3, Young, sterile basal pinna. 4, Young sporophyte. 5, Underside of fertile pinna showing reflexed margin and maturing sporangia.

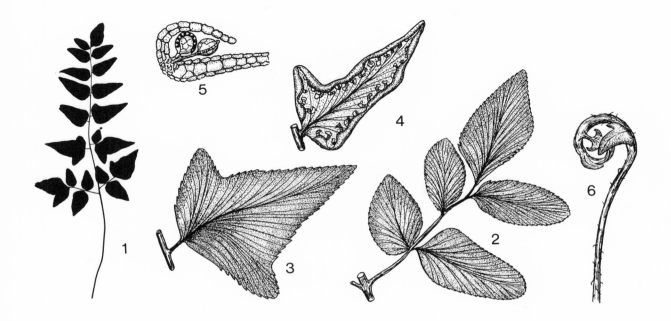

Comparison of the silhouettes of the two variants shows that var. *macrophylla* is composed of fewer but larger and bolder pinnules. As the leaves become larger, the pinnules have well-defined single or double auricles, giving the pinnule a *halberd* or battle-axe appearance. Var. *viridis* has a more delicate pattern.

As small plants, still in 2-inch pots, they are attractive with miniature flowering plants in a window garden. Medium-sized plants, 6 to 8 inches tall, are pretty in combination with the bushier *Pteris cretica* variants when grouped in a brass table planter. Larger plants may be individually displayed on a wrought iron stand. The petioles and rachises of larger plants are exceptionally brittle and may need to be supported.

SORI: In common with *Pteris cretica, Cheilanthes,* and others, all of the *Pellaea* bear their sporangia under the reflexed margin of the pinnule. This membranous edge is a continuation of the pinnule, and is composed of virtually transparent tissue only one or two cells thick.

CULTURE: Loose humus soil to which broken limestone rocks have been added. Good drainage is essential and the soil must be moist at all times. Open shade or filtered sunlight during winter months.

RANGE: Africa.

---

*Pellaea viridis* var. *macrophylla:* 1, Leaf silhouette. 2, Basal pinna showing forked veins leading to serrate edge. 3, Halberd form of sterile pinnule. 4, Underside of fertile pinna showing reflexed margin and maturing sporangia. 5, Enlarged cross-section of the margin showing indusim and sporangia. 6, Unfolding crosier.

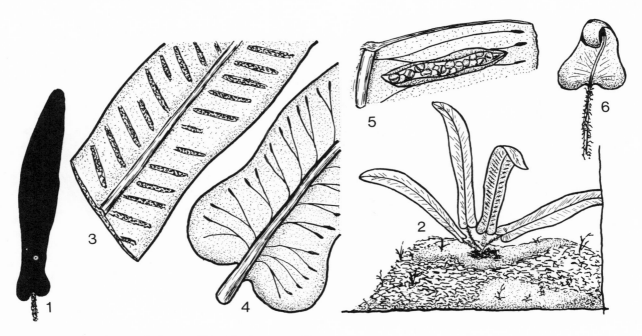

## *Phyllitis scolopendrium*—Hart's-tongue Fern

Leaf strap-like, 6 to 18 inches long, 1 to 2 inches wide, glossy, bright green, somewhat leathery. Tip may be pointed or blunt. Base cordate and often auricled. Veins forking. Evergreen.

*Phyllitis scolopendrium,* because of destruction by collectors, has been recognized as far back as the late nineteenth century as one of America's rarest ferns. While many states have laws protecting all forms of wildlife, such enforcement can only be maintained by education and appreciation of our natural heritage. Some of the early known stations are now depleted or nearly so.

Hart's-tongue Fern is critical as to its habitat, preferring damp limestone rocks and ravines in the proximity of streams or waterfalls. The European varieties are fairly common in England and are often seen on the limestone walls of old churches, in gardens, and in calcareous ravines, as well as in selected areas on the Continent.

SORI: Linear, in close pairs, with elongate indusia face to face growing from contiguous veins.

CULTURE: This fern and the European varieties can be grown in horticulture with proper care. All make interesting focal points, especially when displayed in limestone rock gardens. Natural conditions must be simulated. Slug, snail, and rodent protection must be maintained at all times.

RANGE: New Brunswick, Ontario, New York, Tennessee, Michigan.

---

1, Leaf silhouette. 2, Habitat. 3, Fertile area. 4, Sterile leaf showing vein pattern and hydathode endings. 5, Sori at maturity. 6, Crosier.

150

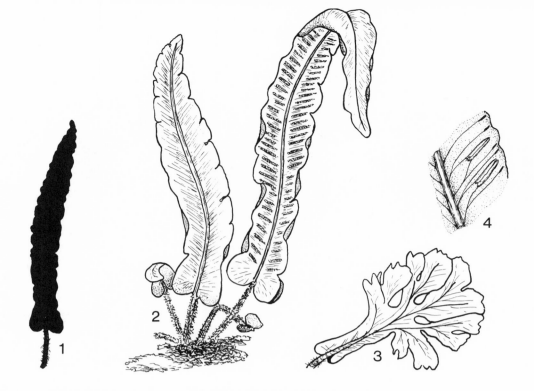

## *Phyllitis scolopendrium* variants—English Hart's-tongue Ferns

Leaf basically strap-like, of widely varying lengths, leathery, glossy, bright green, many with unusual shapes.

Some ferns are prone to mutate, such as our Boston Fern with its many variants. It is possible that the English Hart's-tongue Fern variants could equal or exceed those of the Boston Fern in numbers.

Lowe in his book *Our Native Ferns,* Vol. II, 1869, illustrates 183 variations in the leaf structure of English Hart's-tongue Ferns and further lists an additional 44 varieties, giving botanical names to all. At that time the generic name he used was *Scolopendrium,* although *Phyllitis scolopendrium* had already been introduced. Lowe's colorful illustrations start with the basic English Hart's-tongue Fern, *Scolopendrium vulgare,* a fern with entire but crispy, undulated blades, having petioles heavily clad with golden-brown scales.

One especially interesting variety is var. *Reniforme.* As the name implies, the blade is in the form of a kidney, somewhat vertically elongated. Another very rare variety, and a most magnificent fern, is the var. *Stansfieldii.* Lowe's description states it was raised from spores in 1859 and that "It is quite constant, and when the fronds are in perfection it is the most beautiful of all the varieties of this protean species."

Fortunately, many English Hart's-tongue variants are commercially available in America, all make excellent houseplants and are sufficiently hardy to withstand milder winter climates.

SORI: Linear, in close parallel pairs, with elongate indusia face to face, growing from contiguous veins.

CULTURE: Require moist but well-drained soil to which ground oyster shells have been added.

RANGE: British Isles, Europe.

---

1, Leaf silhouette. 2, Plant with fertile and sterile leaves, and crosiers. 3, Variant with short, crested blade. 4, Fertile area.

## *Pityrogramma triangularis*—Goldback Fern

Leaves 6 to 15 inches long, growing in clusters from tufted rootstock. Blades 2 to 5 inches long, more pentagonal than triangular, 1-pinnate-pinnatifid. Basal pinnae largest and strongly asymmetrical, with longest pinnules or segments being on lower side. Other pinnae either pinnate or pinnatifid. Stipe, rachis and larger midribs smooth, wiry, dark brown to nearly black. Underside of leaf covered with golden or white waxy powder. Free veins carrying sporangia are hidden by heavy powder-covering during early growth.

Goldback Fern is common in our Pacific states, especially in California. It grows at low altitudes along the coast to the damp and higher areas surrounding Yosemite Falls. It may grow as an occasional plant in crevices and humus-filled pockets of great monoliths or in large patches. In prolonged dry seasons the leaves curl, exposing their yellow or silvery-white undersides.

SORI: Naked sporangia grow along simple and forking veins. Small and obscure at first, they break through the waxy undercoating by maturity, becoming more or less confluent.

CULTURE: May be used in a rock garden of temperate areas where natural growing conditions can be simulated.

RANGE: Western North America, Mexico.

---

1, Leaf silhouette.  2, Enlarged view of underside of fertile leaf.  3, Small plants growing in rock crevices.

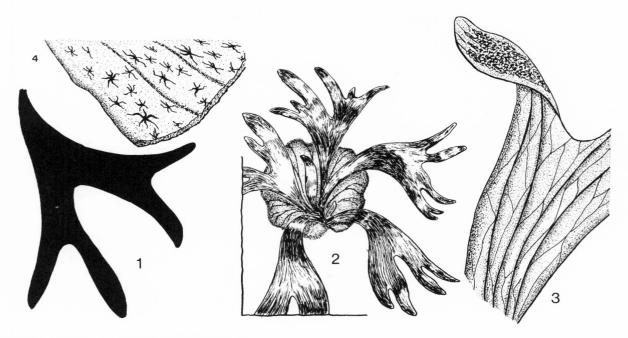

## *Platycerium vassei*—**Staghorn Fern**

Strongly dimorphic. Fertile leaf antler-like, double-forked, deep green, thick, leathery, 12 inches long. Sterile leaf round or shield-shaped.

The genus *Platycerium* comprises a large group commonly known as the Staghorn Ferns. In silhouette, the fertile leaves of many of these plants resemble the branching of an antler rather than the usual fern leaf. These ferns are epiphytic and make their homes in tropical trees in different parts of the world. They find sufficient nutrients in the humus they collect to live independently, and in no way are they parasitic. Sizes and shapes vary tremendously, ranging from little thumb-like antlers to the giant *P. angolense* seen in botanical gardens.

Staghorn Ferns are the curios among the fern family and never fail to draw attention. They grow slowly, and make excellent houseplants. Even if one of the larger species is obtained, its ultimate size should cause no concern.

Strongly dimorphic, the "antlers" are fertile and radiate from the center of several layers of round or kidney-shaped shields that are the sterile leaves. In nature, the shields assume nearly vertical positions either on tree trunks or in crotches of limbs. The outermost shields are green and sometimes inner ones persist two or three deep. Older ones eventually become brown and finally rot. Shields have a definite purpose—they catch and store moisture and any organic material washed into them.

SPORANGIA: Appear on the underside of the "antlers", closely spaced all over the apical lobes. At maturity they become confluent, giving the leaf a brown, velvety surface.

CULTURE: Use a mixture of fibrous material with humus and sand for potting. Place this fern on cork bark and hang vertically to give a natural setting, but careful, periodic watering is essential. Best results require a humid atmosphere. Leaves are capable of absorbing considerable moisture from mist-spraying. Filtered winter sunlight and open shade in summer are recommended.

RANGE: Mozambique.

---

1, Leaf silhouette—fertile leaf.  2, Plant with fertile leaves radiating from shield-like sterile leaves.  3, Portion of fertile leaf showing venation on upper surface and fertile area on upturned underside.  4, Stellate hairs.

153

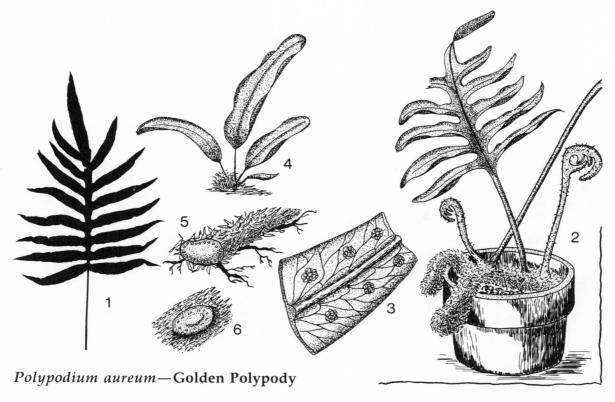

*Polypodium aureum*—**Golden Polypody**

Leaf ovate-lanceolate, growing to 36 inches long, 10 inches wide. Blade coarse, deeply pinnatifid, soft blue-green. Long brown petioles rise at intervals from heavily scale-covered, surface-creeping rhizome. Epiphytic.

Commonly called Rabbit's-foot Fern. Actually, the "rabbit's foot" is the colorful orange-brown or white, scaly rhizome, gnarly and irregular, sometimes 1 inch in diameter. When the sporophyte is barely thumb high, a little scaly tuft covers the apex of the rhizome, the first indication of this distinctive feature. The apical end of the rhizome becomes densely covered with white or lightly colored scales. As the plant grows, the rhizome climbs over and around any obstacles encountered.

Crosiers appear at intervals along the rhizome and unfold their segmented blades and long petioles of light green. Gradually the color changes, and the blade turns to powdery blue-green and the petiole darkens to powdery brown. Leaves are coarse and long-lasting, but eventually become yellow and wither. Petioles are articulate; old leaves need not be cut from the plant as the base of the petiole cleaves from a knob or prominence on the rhizome. When the petiole is removed, a "footprint" or elliptical scar is exposed. Within the scar the ends of the vascular system are always visible.

SORI: Large, golden, exindusiate mounds, uniform in size and spacing.

CULTURE: One of the easiest tropical ferns to grow. Plant in shallow tub or hanging basket and use mixture of sphagnum, humus, and sand. Keep moist. Filtered winter sunlight, open shade in summer. Propagation by spores or rhizome sectioning.

RANGE: Peninsular and tropical Florida; West Indies, Mexico to Argentina.

---

1, Leaf silhouette. 2, Plant with creeping rhizomes and unfolding crosiers. 3, Underside of segment showing naked sori and venation. 4, Young sporophyte; simple, wavy leaves rising from scaly tuft. 5, Portion of rhizome showing scales and roots. Vascular bundles visible on cut end. 6, Petiole scar on rhizome showing vascular ends.

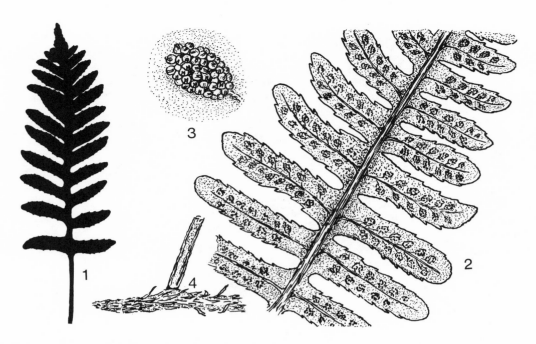

## *Polypodium californicum*—**California Polypody**

Leaves ovate to ovate-oblong, a few inches to over 1 foot long, growing at intervals from a creeping, scale-covered rhizome. Stipe one-third to one-half the length of leaf. Segments few to numerous, papery, oblong-linear, somewhat close, separated by rounded sinuses, ending in blunt to slightly pointed terminals. Margins obscurely to plainly serrate. Evergreen.

Some members of the *Polypodium* genus growing near the west coast are closely related to *P. vulgare*. These are rock-loving plants and have been split into several distinct species. In some cases, overlapping characteristics make identification difficult.

SORI: Slightly oval, exindusiate, nearer to midrib than margin.

CULTURE: Simulate natural growing conditions by growing in rock crevices packed with humus. Water in prolonged dry spells.

RANGE: California, Baja California.

1, Leaf silhouette.  2, Upper portion of blade.  3, Enlarged view of exindusiate sorus. 4, Scale-covered rhizome.

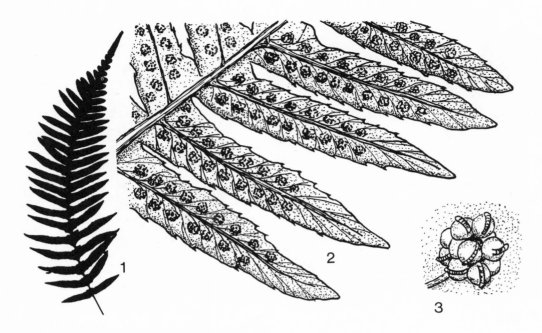

## *Polypodium glycyrrhiza*—Licorice Fern

Leaf broadly lanceolate, 10 to 20 inches long or more, 2 to 4 inches wide, with 12 to 25 pinnatifid segments. Segments long tapering, membranous, much thinner than common polypody. Veins free, forking one or more times, terminating in sharp spines in toothed margins. Stipe slender, straw color when dry.

During the mid-nineteenth century this fern had the common name of Kellogg's Polypody, a name honoring a physician. At that time it was stated that "the root is used as an emolient and expectorant; the taste resembles liquorice." Licorice Fern is common throughout the western and northwestern mountain areas where it grows on shaded damp rocks and bases of trees.

SORI: Round, medium size, nearer midrib than margin. Distribution on segment very uniform. Exindusiate.

CULTURE: Simulate natural habitat by using soil rich in humus, and providing good drainage.

RANGE: Western and northwestern United States.

1, leaf silhouette. 2, Section of leaf showing distribution of sori and spiny, toothed margins of segments. 3, Enlarged view of sorus.

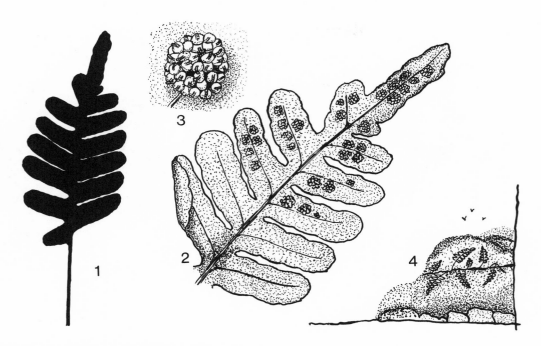

## *Polypodium hesperium*—Western Polypody

Leaves 4 to 15 inches long, growing at intervals from creeping rhizome, with blades ovate-oblong, dark green. Stipe about one-third the length of leaf. Blades deeply pinnatifid, with 4 to 14 pairs of round-tipped, oblong-elliptical segments with margins obscurely to deeply crenate.

This fern is believed to be one of the many variants of *P. vulgare*, and may be quite variable in size and leaf characteristics in different localities. Grows on rocks in crevices filled with humus.

SORI: Round, mostly large and crowded against the midrib, exindusiate.

CULTURE: Simulate natural environment by building elevated rock ledges. Will do best in partial sunlight to open light. Avoid deep shade.

RANGE: Mountainous areas of western North America.

---

1, Leaf silhouette. 2, Upper portion of fertile leaf, showing round-tipped segments and distribution of various-sized sori. 3, Enlarged view of exindusiate sorus. 4, Leaves growing at intervals from creeping rhizome between crevices of large boulders.

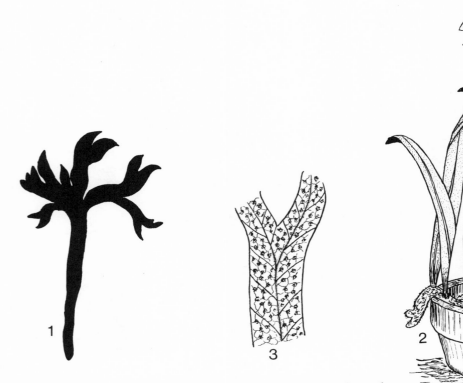

*Polypodium polycarpon* cv. 'Grandiceps'—Crested Polypody

Strap-like leaves, brilliant green, 18 to 24 inches long, 1 to 2 inches wide. Leaves, closely spaced on creeping rhizome, terminate in spreading tassels 6 or more inches wide. Rhizome green, covered with dark brown scales eventually shed, exposing nude surface and leaf scars.

Crested Polypody is a cultivar and, as in many cases, is more beautiful than the species. Its tall stately structure and waxy green-colored leaves resemble the Bird's-nest Fern, while its antler-like terminals resemble the Staghorn Fern, although there is no generic relation to either.

Leaves are strong and erect, growing from rhizomes that continue to cross each other until a solid mass of leaves is formed. Among these leaves there will be long, simple ones resembling the true species, those with once-bifurcated terminals, and others that terminate in wide-spreading tassels.

SORI: Small, scattered, exindusiate.

CULTURE: Excellent houseplant. An 8-inch shallow pot is suggested as best for growing this fern. Start the plant by pinning one or more pieces of active rhizome to the growing medium. Leaf growth is rapid and massive rhizomes are eventually formed. Use a growing medium of peat moss, humus, perlite, and sand. Feed occasionally with emulsified fish oil.

RANGE: Old World tropics; cultivar obtainable from commercial growers.

1, Leaf silhouette.  2, Potted plant.  3, Section of leaf showing fertile area.

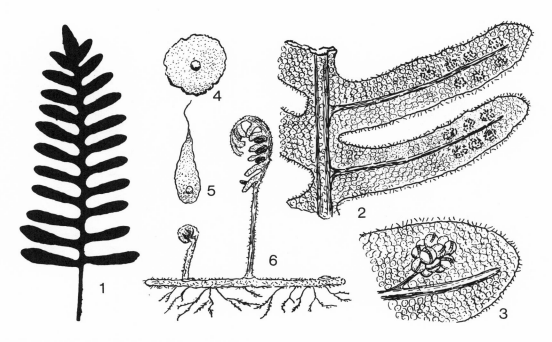

*Polypodium polypodioides*—**Resurrection Fern**

Leaf 4 to 8 inches long, 1 to 2 inches wide, with stipe nearly one-half the length of the blade, growing at intervals from a scaly, creeping rhizome. Blade deeply pinnatifid, having 6 to 20 alternately spaced, oblong to oblong-obtuse segments joined by rounded sinuses. Top surface of segments either naked or with occasional scales. Underside of segment covered with long ovate or roundish, dark center, peltate scales. Essentially epiphytic but does grow on rocks and fallen trees. Leathery. Evergreen.

A true native of the tropics, this fern has migrated through Florida northward to the Carolinas where it grows on live oaks. It also grows in Virginia, withstanding long periods of weather below freezing. In sustained dry periods it appears to die, the leaves curling and changing to light brown. With the return of rain, the leaves regain their normal vigor, giving the species its common name of Resurrection Fern.

SORI: Naked, uniformly spaced in single rows each side of midrib.

CULTURE: Difficult to get established. Requires acid to circumneutral, well-drained soil. Does well in open terrarium when grown on heavy bark slab. Maintain good ventilation in enclosure.

RANGE: Tropical America, common in our southern states, occasionally reaching northward to Virginia.

---

1, Leaf silhouette. 2, Portion of fertile leaf showing distribution of sori. 3, Enlarged view of naked sorus. 4, Enlarged view of round scale. 5, Enlarged view of elongate, peltate scale. 6, Young leaves arising from scale-covered rhizome.

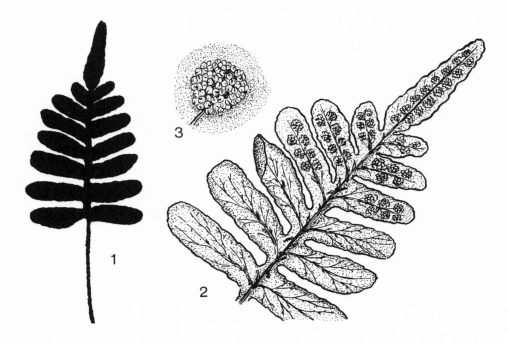

### *Polypodium scouleri*—Leathery Fern

Leaf 2 to 12 inches or more long, with blade and stipe about equal. Blade thick and leathery, deltoid-ovate to broadly ovate, pinnatifid. Segments, 2 to 10 pairs, linear-oblong, extremely blunt, with rounded tip. Margin obscurely serrulate and hard. Apical segment bold and longer than upper segments.

This is one of the small to medium-sized evergreen ferns of the western coast, and is frequently seen along highway embankments, growing either on boulders or at the base of large trees. This species does not usually appear very far inland and can be readily identified by its harsh, leathery texture, and broad, blunt segments.

SORI: Few, very large, round, borne close to midrib on outer end of upper and apical segments.

CULTURE: Can be grown in simulated natural conditions, but other species of *Polypodium* make a better horticultural selection.

RANGE: Far western North America, often in proximity of coast.

1, Leaf silhouette. 2, Upper portion of blade showing soral distribution. 3, Enlarged view of exindusiate sorus.

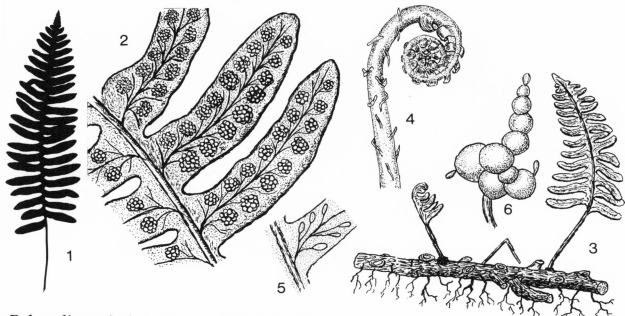

## *Polypodium virginianum*—Common Polypody

Leaf oblong-lanceolate, deeply pinnatifid, 10 inches long, 2 inches wide with alternate, blunt segments. Yellow-green to medium green, leathery. Evergreen.

Literally the word "polypodium" means "many feet" and alludes to the "footprint" scars remaining on the rhizome where the dead leaves have fallen off. Rhizomes grow in a partially exposed manner and in older plants form a dense mat. Where conditions are favorable, this fern covers large boulders, giving it the common name of Rock-cap Fern or Rock Polypody.

It is definitely an evergreen fern, even in severe climates. As the winter becomes colder, the segments curl tighter, exposing the back of the leaf and showing the mature sori. This causes the leaf to appear greenish-brown. The segments become flat again when warm weather returns but the original green color has darkened with age. These old leaves persist long after the new leaves appear.

SORI: Large, round clusters of sporangia lacking indusium, uniformly spaced between the midrib and edge of all but a few of the lower segments. These sori are green-white when young, becoming confluent golden or red-brown circular mounds at maturity.

CULTURE: Grows on both basic and acidic rocks and cliffs. Plant in loose woodland soil in crevices between rocks or at the base of a large rock. Although tolerant of dry spells, an occasional watering will keep it in good condition. Grows best in open shade or alternate sunlight.

RANGE: Newfoundland to eastern Alberta, south to northern Georgia and Arkansas.

---

1, Leaf silhouette. 2, Portion of deeply pinnatifid blade with naked sori and free veining. 3, Rhizome showing leaf, crosier, "footprint" scars, and roots. 4, Tightly coiled crosier and scales on petiole. 5, Hydathodes terminating veins on upper surface of leaf. 6, Paraphysis growing among sporangia.

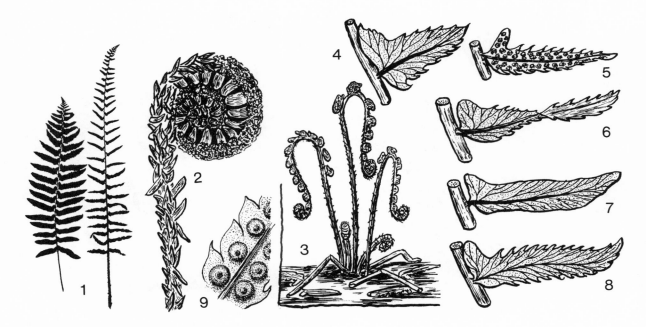

## *Polystichum acrostichoides*—**Christmas Fern**

Dimorphic, leaves lanceolate, 1-pinnate, up to 36 inches long and 5 inches wide, leathery. Various shades of green, ultimately becoming very dark. Evergreen.

Among the first crosiers to be seen in the spring are those of the Christmas Fern. They are tightly coiled and partially concealed beneath long, silvery-white scales. The crosiers droop backward before they are strong and fully grown.

On mature plants, the first leaves rising from the crown are generally fertile, with fertile pinnae numbering as many as twenty-six pairs from the apex. The sterile leaves soon follow. While most leaves are released in the early spring, occasional sterile ones continue to appear during the summer.

The Christmas Fern has many variations and some have been named as forms. Plants have a wide range of color density. Further variations are in the pinnae, particularly in the type of edge, degree of tapering and twisting, and presence of bristle tips. One dominant feature common to all plants is the auricle on the upper side of the pinna.

SORI: Circular, on underside of pinnae, covered with round, centrally attached indusia, arranged in rows on both sides of the midrib. First observed, they are green, sufficiently separated to appear as individual dots. At maturity the sori become confluent, making a velvety, golden-brown covering. The indusia disappear or shrivel so much that the sori might erroneously be considered exindusiate.

CULTURE: Easily grown in a deep woodland, stony mulch. A large, pumpkin-sized stone beside the plant makes an attractive setting. Although a native of shaded areas, the Christmas Fern can tolerate considerable sunlight if the soil is kept reasonably moist.

RANGE: Nova Scotia to southeastern Wisconsin, south to central Florida and eastern Texas.

---

1, Silhouette of broad sterile leaf and narrow fertile leaf. 2, Silvery-scaled, tightly coiled crosier. 3, Early developing crosiers showing drooping position. 4-8, Pinna variants. 9, Early sori.

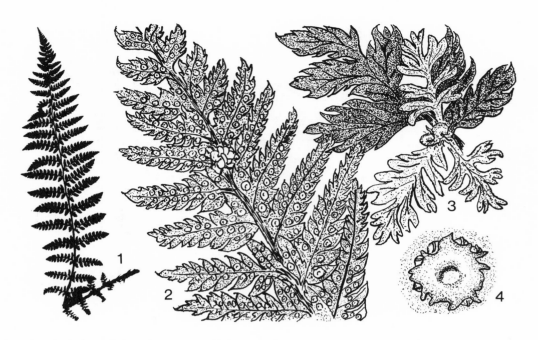

## *Polystichum andersonii*—Anderson's Holly-fern

Leaf 12 to 36 inches long, narrowly elliptic-lanceolate, somewhat reduced at base, pinnate-pinnatifid to 2-pinnate, dark green. Stipe stout, densely covered with medium brown, large scales. Rachis brown, grooved above, with occasional scales. Pinnae alternate, narrowly triangular, having pinnules with veins terminating in long, upturned spines. Proliferating scale-covered buds on rachis near the apical end of leaf are a distinguishing feature in identification of this species. A further diagnostic feature is in the pinnae, in which the basal pinnule on the upper side is longer than the adjoining pinnule.

SORI: Large, nearly midway between midrib and margin, covered with centrally attached, dentate indusium.

CULTURE: This species is a native of cool, moist, rocky slopes. Use humus soil and ample broken stones for a growing medium. This is a beautiful fern, but a poor selection for a garden in a warm, dry area.

RANGE: Northwestern North America

---

1, Silhouette of leaf. 2, Apical section of leaf showing proliferating bud and details of pinnae. 3, Primordial leaves and crosiers of young plant. 4, Sorus with centrally attached dentate indusium.

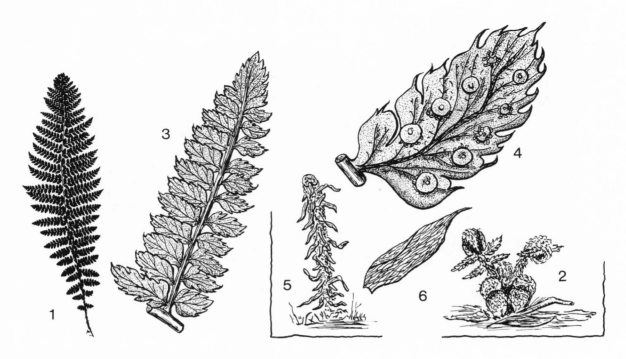

## *Polystichum braunii*—Braun's Holly-fern

Leaf elliptic-lanceolate, 2-pinnate, up to 36 inches long and 8 inches wide. Deep lustrous green, somewhat leathery. Petiole and rachis brown, covered with long, light-brown scales.

Braun's Holly-fern is one of the most handsome northeastern ferns. It grows on the cool, wooded mountain slopes of New England. Unfortunately, with all of its sturdiness, it is not evergreen and the leaves turn brown in late fall.

Crosiers for the following year are formed in a crown by late summer, and their coverings of silvery-white scales are easily seen. During the first few warm days of spring these crosiers grow rapidly. The young leaves droop backwards until they gain sufficient strength, giving the plant a wilted appearance for a short period.

When the leaf is mature, the blade is 2-pinnate nearly the entire length. Spiny bristles tip the little incurved edge-cuts of the pinnules. Long, brown scales densely covering the petiole become more sparse along the rachis. Similar scales appear along the midribs of the pinnae and pinnules. Because of the bristly margin, some of the nineteenth century botanists called this plant the Prickly Shield-fern.

SORI: Round dots uniformly spaced on both sides of pinnule midrib. Indusium round with central attachment. Swelling, darkened sporangia force their way from under the indusium early in summer, gradually obscuring the presence of the indusium.

CULTURE: Plant in cool location. Keep deeply mulched woodland soil moist at all times. Provide occasional mist-spray during hot weather.

RANGE: Newfoundland to northern Wisconsin, southward into the uplands of New England and New York, northeastern Pennsylvania.

---

1, Leaf silhouette. 2, Early crosier showing lower pinnae developing. 3, Upper side of pinna. 4, Arrangement of sori on underside of pinnule. 5, Densely-scaled petiole. 6, Long, brown scale of petiole, enlarged.

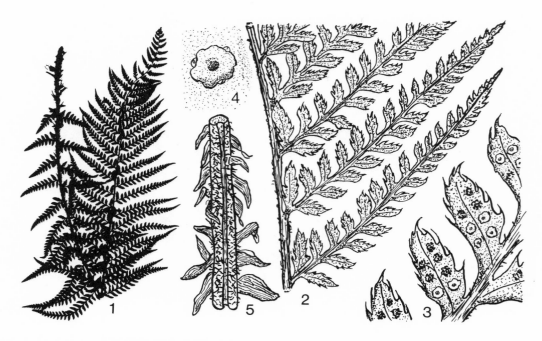

## *Polystichum dudleyi*—Dudley's Holly-fern

Leaves lanceolate, 12 to 44 inches long, 1- to 2-pinnate. Heavy, deeply grooved brown stipes have large chestnut-brown scales at base. Scales decrease in size in upper area of stipe, becoming less frequent, narrowing and becoming more hair-like on rachis. Blade narrows slightly toward base. Veins in pinnules terminate in exceptionally long spines.

This is another fern of the large group of *Polystichum aculeatum* variations. There is little doubt in the minds of fern lovers that the American Holly-ferns are among the most handsome of all species. This species, formerly recognized as one of the variants of *P. aculeatum,* now has species status and accordingly is designated *P. dudleyi.*

SORI: Round, covered with centrally attached thin indusium, having irregular edge and darkened center.

CULTURE: Because of its height and brittle nature, this fern should be grown in a protected area free from high winds. Planted individually, especially at the base of a large rock, it will be a showpiece of the garden. Select a cool, moist growing area where good drainage is assured. For a planting-medium, use a mixture of soil rich in organic material and stones.

RANGE: Shaded, rocky canyons and slopes below 1000 feet in California coastal area.

---

1, Leaf silhouette. 2, Mid-section of leaf. 3, Enlarged section of fertile pinna showing distribution of sori and terminal spines. 4, Enlarged sorus showing dark center. 5, Lower portion of stipe showing deep groove and covering of large and small scales.

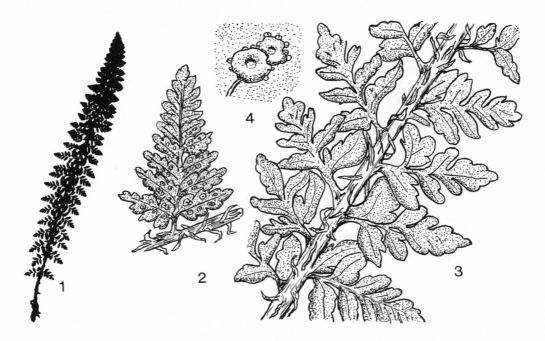

## *Polystichum lemmonii*—Shasta Holly-fern

Leaf 4 to 12 inches long, oblong-lanceolate, 2-pinnate to 2-pinnate-pinnatifid, narrowing slightly from middle to base. Stipe heavily covered with large chestnut-brown scales intermixed with smaller scales and hairs; occasional small scales along rachis. Pinnae deltoid to deltoid-lanceolate, crowded or imbricate; pinnules obtuse, having lobed segments and crenate teeth, without spines.

The genus *Polystichum* comprises a large, worldwide group of ferns often referred to as Holly ferns. Shasta Fern is one of the smaller species but in every way retains the beauty of the genus. D. C. Eaton, in his book "Ferns of the United States and British North American Possesions," Vol. II, 1880, mentions this fern under the common name of Falkland Islands Shield-fern with the botanical names of *Aspidium mohriodes* and *Polystichum mohriodes*. It is interesting to note that, while the Shasta Holly-fern is a native of our western states, it is also established in the distant, cool subantarctic islands found near the tip of South America.

SORI: Large, round, with orbicular indusium attached in center, often imbricate, at times partially covering neighboring sori.

CULTURE: This species is a native of granitic areas, growing in soil among loose rocks. Horticulturally critical, requiring simulated natural growing conditions.

RANGE: Western United States, Falkland Islands.

---

1, Leaf silhouette. 2, Fertile pinna with large sori. 3, Lower portion of rachis, showing pinna distribution and scales on rachis. 4, Enlarged view of sori.

166

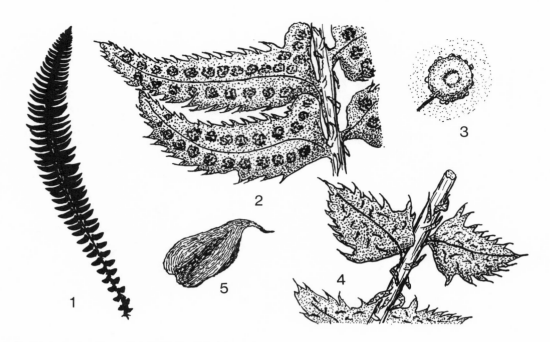

## *Polystichum lonchitis*—**Northern Holly-fern**

Leaf linear-lanceolate, 1-pinnate, 6 to 24 inches long, 1 to 2½ inches wide, narrowing toward the base. Leaves grow from crown formed at the end of short, stout rhizome. Alternately spaced pinnae very numerous and crowded. Basal pinnae markedly triangular, with upper pinnae becoming lanceolate-falcate, the ends turning upward. Prominent auricles on pinnae throughout, except basal area. Free veins terminate in sharp spines. Evergreen.

There are several native holly-ferns of the genus *Polystichum*. With their brilliant, dark green pinnae and contrasting brown-scaled rachis, they comprise the most beautiful of all American ferns. Leaves remain erect until overtaken by heavy frost. The prostrate leaves of *P. lonchitus* continue brilliantly green under snow, and remain so until arrival of new leaves.

SORI: Round, numerous, covered with orbicular, peltate indusium, evenly spaced in rows on pinnae and auricles. As maturity approaches, the indusium becomes funnel-shaped and drops off.

CULTURE: Difficult to grow, not possible in warmer areas. Requires cool, constantly damp soil and air for best growth.

RANGE: Northern areas of United States, northward to Alaska.

---

1, Leaf silhouette.  2, Enlarged view of fertile pinnae.  3, Sorus with orbicular, peltate indusium.  4, Enlarged view of sterile basal pinnae.  5, Chaffy, chestnut-brown scale.

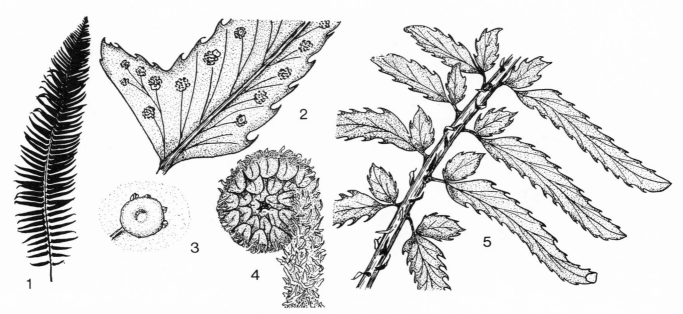

*Polystichum munitum*—**Western Sword-fern**

Leaf 1-pinnate, stiffly erect, harsh feeling, dark green, lanceolate, slightly tapering toward the base, 12 to 50 or more inches long, 2 to 10 inches wide, growing from dense crown. Pinnae alternate, auricled and slightly falcate, with lower pinnae having pinnate auricles. Pinna incised, ending in sharp, incurved prickles. Veins free, forking once or twice. Chaffy petiole covered with ovate-accuminate scales, bright glossy brown, some scales having dark centers. Scales continue on rachis and to lesser degree on underside of pinna. Evergreen.

Western Sword-fern strongly resembles the eastern Christmas Fern, although generally much larger. It is commonly found growing in damp, rich woods and shaded talus slopes of the western coastal mountains. Like the Christmas Fern, it is quite variable in size and pattern of leaves due to differences in ecological conditions.

SORI: Uniformly spaced in a single row on each side of the midrib, the row continuing around the edges of large auricles. Indusium circular, peltate, the margin being either entire or incised.

CULTURE: An unusually beautiful and stately plant rarely appearing in eastern horticulture. It is particularly attractive when displayed as a focal-point plant. Best grown in cool, moist soil, rich in humus and small stones.

RANGE: Alaska to western Montana and California.

1, Leaf silhouette. 2, Fertile pinna after dehiscence. 3, Sorus. 4, Tightly wound crosier. 5, Basal pinnae.

## *Polystichum tsus-simense*—Tsus-sima Holly-fern

Leaf lanceolate, 2-pinnate, 12 inches long, 5 inches wide. Pinnae long tapering. Pinnules sharply cut, terminating in bristles.

Although a native of the Far East, many characteristics of this fern resemble those of the ferns of northeastern America, particularly *P. acrostichoides,* the Christmas Fern, and *P. braunii,* Braun's Holly-fern.

Leaves grow from a partially underground, tufted, dark scale-covered crown. Like those of the Christmas Fern, the crosiers are tightly coiled and densely covered with elongate scales of silvery-white. The gently tapering motif of the leaf also appears in the shape of the individual pinna. The basal pinnule on the upper side of each pinna forms a conspicuous auricle. Pinnule serrations terminate in needle-point bristles or holly-like tips, following the pattern of many of this genus.

The petiole is heavily clad with persistent, long, darkened scales which continue into the rachis, giving the little leaves a shaggy appearance. The scales are composed of many thin, elongate cells, the edge cells terminating as sharp tips.

SORI: Evenly spaced, located about halfway between midrib and edge, covered with round, centrally depressed and attached indusia. Indusia shrivel at maturity exposing dark-colored sporangia.

CULTURE: Rich, loose, humus soil, constantly moist, neutral to slightly acid. Requires cool, shaded location. This fern makes an excellent houseplant; it may be used in combination with flowers or other ferns in window gardens or terrariums. Use smaller plants in dish-gardens.

RANGE: Native of Japan and China, readily available from growers.

---

1, Leaf silhouette. 2, Tightly wound crosier. 3, Upper side of sterile pinna showing large basal auricle. 4, Underside of fertile pinnule showing sori, dichotomous venation and bristle-terminated segments. 5, Scale-covered petiole. 6, Magnified sketch of scale showing sharp ends of cells.

169

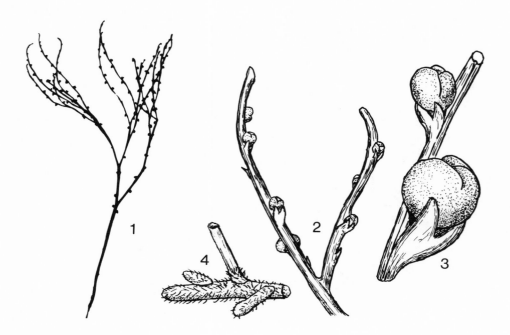

## *Psilotum nudum*—**Whisk Fern**

Stems long and pendulous when growing as an epiphyte, shorter and erect when growing terrestrially or as a potted plant. Length varies, with those upright being 6 to 16 inches, to pendant specimens 30 inches or more. Stems markedly dichotomous, with extremely small appressed leaves alternately spaced throughout stem. Stems grow from a coralloid rhizome devoid of roots, covered with many white hairs.

Coming from a family without fossil record, the Whisk Fern was long thought to be among the most primitive of living vascular plants. More recent study, however, has shown that no relation exists between *P. nudum* and the earliest plant life.

While very unfernlike in appearance, the evolution of the leaf, the subterranean cylindrical gametophyte, multiflagellate sperm and other characteristics make the genus unique and closely associated with the fern family.

SORI: Single globular synangia grow in axils of bifurcate bracts. Synangium formed of three relatively heavy-walled, fused sections.

CULTURE: Easily grown as a greenhouse curiosity, but plant has little horticultural value.

RANGE: Southeastern and southwestern United States, Asia, Africa. Pacific Islands.

1, Leaf silhouette. 2, Terminal end of dichotomous fertile stem. 3, Synangium nested in axil of bifurcate bract. 4, Stem joining coralloid rhizome.

170

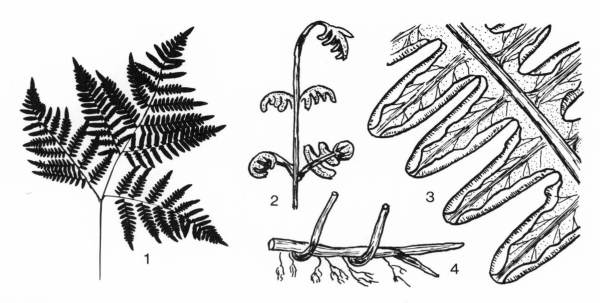

## *Pteridium aquilinum* var. *latiusculum*—Bracken

Leaf coarse, leathery, deep green, 36 to 60 inches long, growing at widely-spaced intervals. Blade ovate-triangular, 3-pinnate or 3-pinnate-pinnatifid. Prominent forked veins readily seen on underside of pinnules. Deciduous.

Bracken, and its many varieties, has a worldwide distribution and where it gains a foothold is likely to take over. Where forest fires occur it quickly recovers due to its deep root system, providing protection for small fauna and other plant life. Grows in open woods and thickets, damp or dry humus, or sandy soil.

SORI: Marginal, continuous with reflexed edge of segment covering sporangia. True indusium from beneath sorus.

CULTURE: Strongly invasive under ordinary growing conditions. Not recommended for small gardens.

RANGE: Newfoundland to Colorado, south to Mississippi, and Mexico.

---

1, Leaf silhouette.  2, Crosier.  3, Fertile pinnule showing marginal sorus and forked venation.  4, Rhizome-root system.

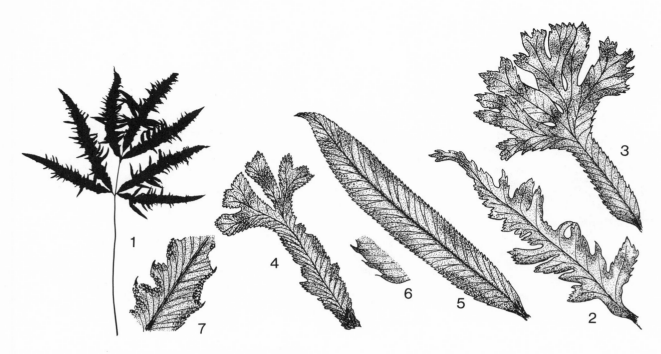

## *Pteris cretica* cultivars—Stove Ferns

*Pteris* is a large genus growing in the tropics and subtropics. Leaves of many species have a fern-like appearance, but others depart from the conventional pattern. All carry dominant generic traits; the strongest is the uninterrupted reflexed margin of the pinna. Some have basal pinnae which are pinnately lobed. Rhizomes are short and scaly, tending to form clumps. Some of the cultivars are bicolored, combining green with silvery- or creamy-white. *Pteris apericaulis* cv. 'Tricolor' is exceptionally colorful and, as the name implies, has three colors—green, white, and red.

Current greenhouse catalogs list many of these ferns as species, varieties, and cultivars of *Pteris*. Former fern literature called them Brakes, Warm Ferns, Stove Ferns, and Old World Ferns. One of these, *Pteris cretica*, is a native of the Mediterranean area, the name of the species having been derived from the Isle of Crete.

*Pteris cretica* has many cultivars, the more recent work of the horticulturist. Some have no common names and their botanical names are not always definitive. This is especially true when a latinized name honoring some person is used, such as cv. 'Wilsonii', cv. 'Wimsettii', and cv. 'Rivertoniana'.

*Pteris cretica*, cv. 'Rivertoniana' and cv. 'Wilsonii'.

Leaves leathery, medium green, 6 to 20 inches long, with two to four opposite pairs of pinnae, and an apical pinna either simple or crested. Cresting and irregularity of edges of pinnae vary with the cultivar.

While considerable similarity exists among these cultivars, the distinguishing features of cv. 'Rivertoniana' are its long, tapering pinnae with their extremely sharply-lobed edges. Some pinnae on the same plant may be less irregular, while others may revert to the wild ancestral form, making identification of young plants difficult. Pinnae of cv. 'Wilsonii' appear to follow the simple shape of the species *cretica* but terminate in widely spread crests.

SORI; CULTURE: Same as Ribbon Brake

SOURCE: Readily available at nurseries.

---

1, Silhouette of leaf, cv. 'Rivertoniana.' 2, Pinna variant. 3, 4, Crested pinnae of cv. 'Wilsonii'. 5, Pinna reversion found on different cultivars. 6, Bristle ending of serrations. 7, Typical marginal sori.

172

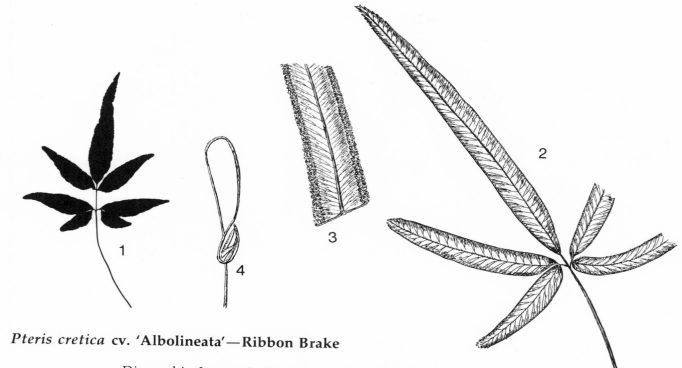

## Pteris cretica cv. 'Albolineata'—Ribbon Brake

Dimorphic. Leaves 1-pinnate, growing to 20 inches in long. Medium green with central, uniform, creamy-white band.

The Cretan brake has several variants, one being the Ribbon Brake, *Pteris cretica* cv. 'Albolineata'. Literally translated this botanical name means "Cretan white-line fern", a name derived from the creamy-white band paralleling the midrib of both its sterile and fertile pinnae.

This fern has many of the *Pteris cretica* features, and it is strongly dimorphic. Sterile leaves have broad lanceolate pinnae with serrate edges. Pinnae of the fertile leaves are slender and tapering and are serrate between the end of the reflexed margins and the apex. Basal pinnae of both fertile and sterile leaves are pinnately lobed on the lower side; the lobes are often as prominent as the supporting pinnae.

SORI: Reflexed margin continuing nearly the entire length of pinna. Confluent sporangia make a deep brown border at maturity.

CULTURE: Good, loose garden soil. Restricted winter sunlight and open shade during summer. Simulate native humidity by occasional mist-spraying. With favorable conditions, these plants grow rapidly and easily reach heights of 12 to 18 inches. Rhizome clumps may be divided and repotted. Remove older leaves by clipping. When small, this is a good plant for a glass window-shelf. Later, transfer to a brass planter with other brakes.

RANGE: The species is native of the Tropics. Cv. 'Albolineata' is obtainable at nurseries.

1, Silhouette of sterile leaf.  2, Long, slender fertile leaf.  3, Underside of pinna showing reflexed fertile margins at maturity.  4, Graceful, double-folded crosier.

173

*Pteris ensiformis* **cv. 'Victoriae'—Victorian Brake**

Strongly dimorphic. Leaves lanceolate, 1-pinnate above, 2-pinnate below. Rich green, variegated, centrally and irregularly banded with silvery-white. Length 8 to 20 inches.

This beautiful little brake has an ancestry traceable to tropical eastern Asia. Its sterile leaves are relatively short and bushy, with pinnae well-proportioned. The fertile leaves are tall and slender, and in healthy plants quite abundant. Like the dimorphic leaves of many ferns, the fertile leaf is interesting and important but the real beauty of the plant is in the sterile leaf. The pinnae of sterile leaves have sharply serrate edges and are well marked with silvery-white bands and wavy margins of deep green. Pinnae of the fertile leaves are exceptionally slender, with serrate edges only near the apical ends where the reflexed margins are no longer present.

SORI: Sporangia located beneath reflexed margin. At maturity they become confluent and appear as dark brown borders on the underside of pinna.

CULTURE: Good, loose garden soil with small stones, kept moist at all times. Diffused winter sunlight, open shade in summer. Grows best in cool room where humidity is high. Remove old leaves. Leaves of plants under fluorescent lights may grow from 6 to 18 inches during the winter months. Propagation is by splitting of rhizome or from spores. By having a variety of sizes available, many delightful decorative applications will be found. Do not nurse shabby plants; start with fresh stock.

RANGE: Cultivar obtainable from most nurseries.

---

1, Leaf silhouettes, (left) fertile, (right) sterile.  2, Upper side of fertile pinna.  3, Enlarged section of underside of fertile pinnule showing reflexed margin. 4, Sterile pinna.

174

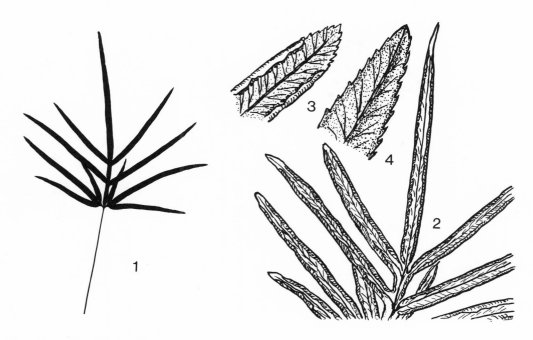

## *Pteris multifida*—**Spider Brake**

Leaf 10 to 20 inches long, blade ovate to deltoid, 6 to 12 inches long, pinnate. Upper pinnae linear, pinnatifid, from winged rachis. Basal pinnae pinnate, with 1 or 2 linear pinnules.

The Spider Brake, like many species in the *Pteris* genus, is a native of Asia that has escaped into our southern area and over the years has become naturalized. Its horticultural interest is in the simplicity of its spider-like blades. These ferns are easy to grow under almost any home condition and, when grouped with seasonal flowering plants, provide an excellent background.

SORI: Continuous along margin, starting from base and terminating just short of serrate tip.

CULTURE: Prefers loose, humus-rich soil to which pieces of old mortar or cement have been added. When grown in a greenhouse or Wardian case, this plant will volunteer on just about any damp surface. Pick the volunteers and plant in individual 3-inch pots for home use or "give-aways."

RANGE: North Carolina to Texas; Asia.

---

1, Leaf silhouette.  2, Apical end of fertile leaf.  3, Enlarged view of pinna showing fertile edge and serrate tip.  4, Terminal of sterile pinna.

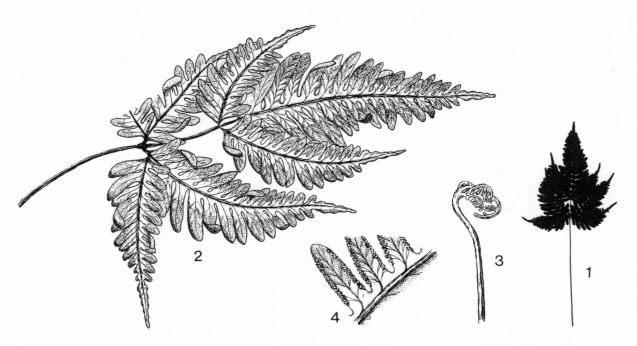

## *Pteris quadriaurita* cv. 'Argyraea'—Silver Brake

Leaf 18 inches long, blade nearly deltoid, 1-pinnate-pinnatifid. Variegated, light green to blue-green, with central band of silvery-white.

Although the species is reported to have leaves growing 5 feet high and 30 inches wide in its native land, this cultivar seldom exceeds one-third of this size when grown as a houseplant. The moderate height and bicolored foliage of the Silver Brake make it a desirable plant for use alone or as a background for flowering plants. Even when small, this fern has sufficient contrast in its colors to make it an attractive miniature on a glass window shelf.

The leaf of the Silver Brake with its modified basal pinna is a departure from the conventional. Replacing the innermost lower segment on each basal pinna is a large, deeply pinnatifid pinnule. This unusual pinnule tends to spread downward and outward. All of the pinnae, and also these unusual pinnules, are long and gracefully tapering.

SORI: Young sporangia are fully hidden beneath reflexed margins of segments. They form a colorful reddish-brown border at maturity when fully exposed.

CULTURE: Potting soil composed of sand, peat moss, garden soil and small amount of bone meal. Keep moist. Partial winter sunlight and open shade in summer. Growth can be accelerated by growing under fluorescent lights 14 hours daily.

Like so many of the genus *Pteris,* this fern propagates readily from spores. Where the plant is in close association with others, little sporophytes from air-borne spores often grow on the surface of the soil and the sides of nearby clay pots. When the little ferns become about 1-inch high, transplant them into small pots.

RANGE: Species—Tropics. Cultivar—obtainable from nurseries.

---

1, Leaf silhouette. 2, Sketch of leaf indicating light, silvery central band and edge of blue-green. 3, Opening crosier. 4, Underside of pinna showing maturing sori and venation.

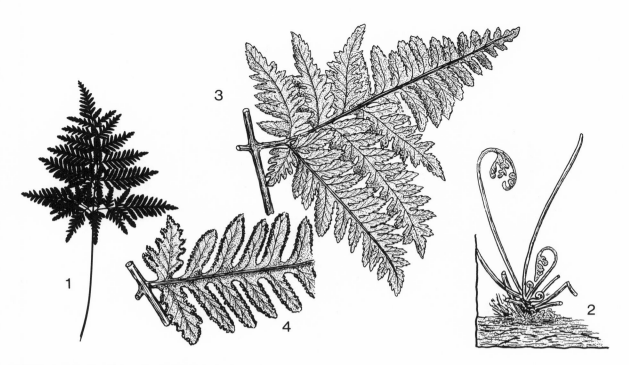

## *Pteris tremula*—**Trembling Brake**

Leaf coarse, blade deltoid or nearly so, 1-pinnate above, 2-, 3-pinnate below, yellow-green to medium green. Plants range from small table specimens to large, spreading decorator sizes.

Also known as the Australian Brake or Bracken, it is one of the largest brakes. Although of much softer texture than *Pteridium aquilinum* var. *latiusculum,* the Northeastern Bracken, it has leaves that grow to 6 feet. Larger plants of this fern are used by floral decorators for weddings, receptions, banquets, and on speakers' platforms. In the home, plants of medium size are best on pedestals in light corners or near windows. Young plants 6 or 8 inches tall have yellow-green leaves and blend nicely with other taller and darker Pteris species when put in a table planter.

The Trembling Brake grows fast and always has many crosiers ready to unfold. Accelerate growth and improve the appearance of the plant by removing old, shabby leaves. Since the leaves are quickly replaced, occasional ones may be picked for winter floral arrangements.

SORI: Sporangia grow beneath reflexed margin of pinnae, forming dark outline at maturity.

CULTURE: Loose, rich, moist garden soil. Winter sunlight to alternate sun and shade in summer. Mist-spraying twice daily will help growth where humidity is low. As crowns increase in size, new ones will appear nearby. Separate these by cutting with a sharp knife and start new plants. Young sporophytes growing from self-sown spores are often seen at the base of plants or in neighboring pots. Put these in 2-inch pots; before long they will look attractive in the pebble tray.

RANGE: Australia, New Zealand, Tasmania.

---

1, Leaf silhouette. 2, Rhizome crown, crosiers, and stubble. 3, Detail of basal pinna showing serrate margins and venation of pinnules. 4, Maturing sori on underside of pinna.

## *Pteris vittata*—**Ladder Brake**

Leaf 8 to 30 inches long, dark green, with lanceolate blade. Pinnae opposite, linear, abruptly ending somewhat pointed. Solitary terminal pinna pointing upward. Pinnae horizontal to strongly ascending, with long upper pinnae. Length of lower pinnae gradually decreasing until short basal pinnae are reached. Rachis and stipe densely covered with white, hair-like scales. Free veins, forking once to margin.

This fern is an Asiatic escapee and has become so strongly established in our southern-southwestern states as to appear as a native species. It has preference for lime and can be found commonly in the mortar of brick walls, foundations, cemetery mausoleums, outcroppings of limestone, and the edge of sinkholes, as well as in open pine forests.

SORI: Marginal, continuous from base of pinna, terminating within short distance of apical tip. Indusium formed by reflexed margin is thin and more or less disappears as sporangia increase in size.

CULTURE: Readily grows as potted plant for the greenhouse or light room of moderate temperature. Use growing medium of equal parts of loam, limestone chips, peat moss and sand.

RANGE: South Carolina to Louisiana, southern California; Asia.

---

1, Leaf silhouette. 2, Apical section of fertile leaf, upper side. 3, Apical end of sterile pinna showing sharp, serrate margin. 4, Apical end of fertile pinna showing reflexed marginal covering of sporangia and serrate tip. 5, Basal sterile pinnae. 6, Base of plant showing heavy white-hair covering of stipe.

## *Rumohra adiantiformis*—**Leather Fern**

Leaf elongate-triangular, 3-pinnate, dark green, having harsh, leathery texture. Grows to 12 inches when potted, 36 inches under native conditions.

The Leather Fern is a member of the lesser known genus, *Rumohra*. It has tightly wound crosiers, all heavily covered with long, silvery-white scales; these grow from a creeping and ascending rhizome. Many of the scales darken with age but remain on the petiole and rachis after the leaf is fully expanded. Leaves are long-lasting, and as they become older have a harsh feeling unlike many of the ferns.

Broad, heavy-set leaves are closely spaced, which gives the plant a sturdy, bushy appearance. Larger leaves do not readily wilt when picked; annually thousands of these are sold commercially for floral arrangements and table decorations. A few leaves removed from a large plant will not be missed; use them with cut flowers or winter-grown bulbs for attractive table pieces.

SORI: Inconspicuous, small, round, greenish mounds when young. With further growth, centrally depressed and attached white indusia become prominent. At maturity, the indusia shrivel and expose the fully developed, brown sporangia.

CULTURE: Moist soil composed of leaf mold, topsoil, and coarse building sand to which small stones and a little bone meal have been added. As the fern increases in size, transfer to a larger pot or divide to start new plants.

RANGE: Subtropical Southern Hemisphere.

---

1, Leaf silhouette.  2, Unfolding scale-covered crosier.  3, Sterile pinna showing incised edges and venation of pinnules.  4, Underside of fertile pinna showing sori. 5, Enlarged immature sorus with centrally attached indusium.

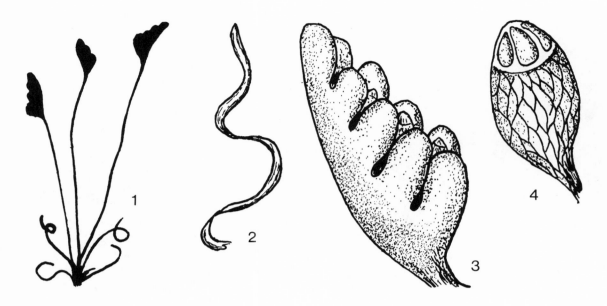

### *Schizaea pusilla*—Curly-grass Fern

Strongly dimorphic. Sterile leaf evergreen, 2 inches long, slender, curly, grasslike, with flattened section. Fertile leaf deciduous, 3 to 4 inches long, erect, uncurled, with 3 to 8 finger-like, obliquely ascending segments at apex. Segments concave or trough-like, with hair covering partially concealing 8 to 10 large ovate sporangia.

Rare. One of the smallest ferns, strongly unfern-like in appearance. Growth somewhat limited to the edges of sphagnum bogs where soil is sandy and highly acid.

SORI: Free end of sporangium terminated by apical ring-cap.

CULTURE: Growing conditions of this fern are so critical it is almost impossible to grow when removed from habitat.

RANGE: Newfoundland, Nova Scotia, New Jersey, and northeast tip of Long Island, New York.

---

1, Leaf silhouette.  2, Sterile leaf.  3, Blade of fertile leaf.  4, Sporangium.

## *Thelypteris hexagonoptera*—Broad Beech-fern

Leaf 10 to 24 inches long, 2-pinnatifid. Blade triangular, virtually equilateral, yellow-green to medium green, slightly hairy.

Commonly called Southern Beech Fern. The blade consists of large, pinnatifid segments rather than pinnae, oppositely located and wing-connected on each side of the rachis. Base of the blade, as seen in a flattened specimen, is about the same length or slightly longer than the sloping sides. While the upper segments gracefully taper to their tips and are deeply lobed, the basal segments are double-tapering, attaining their maximum width near the center. Characteristic of the Beech Ferns, these basal pinnae stretch obliquely outward and downward in relation to the blade.

The crosiers continue to rise throughout the spring and summer. They have a peculiar vernation—rather than the conventional uncoiling, the segments open diagonally upward while the apical section unfolds vertically. Prior to obtaining full height, the petiole is densely covered with long, dark brown scales. As the petiole lengthens, the scales become smaller and widely separated. Elongate, white or light brown scales are borne on the upper rachis, on the midribs of the segments and the lobes. Leaves appear at ½- to 2-inch intervals on a creeping-branching rhizome. The dense, intertwining growth gives the colony a compact appearance. The veins are simple or forked, many terminating at the sori while others continue to the margins of the lobes.

SORI: Small, round, not uniform in size, generally situated somewhat irregularly between the midrib and the margin of lobe. Indusium lacking. Wide variation in number of sporangia.

CULTURE: Grows best in a partially shaded location in deep, rich, acid humus soil. Keep soil moist to extend the growing season. This species has a shallow rhizome and spreads rapidly.

RANGE: Eastern Texas to northernmost Florida, north to Minnesota and Quebec.

---

1, Leaf silhouette.  2, Deeply pinnatifid basal and second segments, showing wing-connection along rachis.  3, Sori on lobe, indusia lacking.  4, Crosier covered with long brown scales.

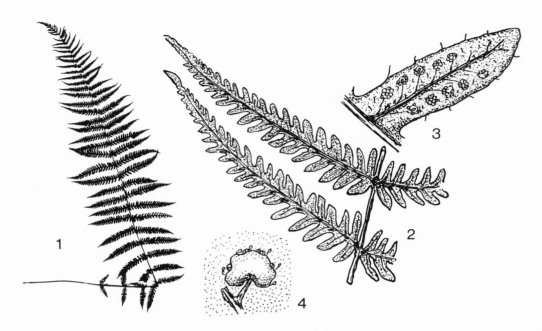

## *Thelypteris nevadensis*—Nevada Wood-fern

Leaves 12 to 30 inches long, arising in small tufted groups from short, creeping rhizome. Blade lanceolate, light green, soft, with sessile pinnae. Pinnae long and tapering, becoming shorter and more distant as base is approached. Veins mostly simple, with underside of segment slightly hairy.

In many ways *T. nevadensis,* the Nevada Wood-fern, is markedly similar to its eastern relative, *T. noveboracensis,* New York Fern. Here are two ferns where careful study will show that many of the features of one have been repeated in the other, the main difference being in the rhizome. Instead of the leaves arising from a tufted base, the leaves of the New York Fern are more widely spaced along a creeping rhizome.

SORI: Small, uniformly spaced in single rows nearer to the margin than the midrib. Indusium irregular in outline, with stalked glands along margin.

CULTURE: Excellent for horticultural applications. Being slow in spreading, little danger exists of crowding other species. Plant in well-drained, rich woodland soil, in areas having alternate shade and sunlight.

RANGE: Northwestern North America, to Nevada and California.

1, Leaf silhouette. 2, Mid-section area showing spacing of pinnae and their connection to rachis. 3, Enlarged view of segment, showing distribution of sori and hair. 4, Enlarged view of sorus with irregularly-shaped indusium and marginal glands.

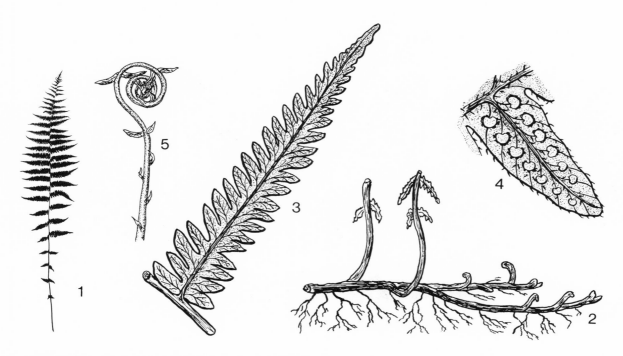

## *Thelypteris noveboracensis*—New York Fern

Leaf elliptic-lanceolate, 1-pinnate-pinnatifid, 12 to 24 inches long, 3 to 6 inches wide, having 20 to 46 pairs of alternately spaced, deeply segmented pinnae. Yellow-green to medium green.

Also known as the Tapering Fern. The alternate common name of this species has been well chosen because of its graceful, double-tapering form. Starting at the tip, the pinnae increase in length until the widest section of the leaf is reached near the middle. Below the middle, the pinnae become shorter and more widely spaced until the tiny, wing-like basal pinnae are reached.

Each long and tapered pinna is deeply pinnatifid, having about 12 to 32 blunt segments. The petiole continues green until nearly reaching the rhizome and is very short in relation to the leaf. The entire leaf is pubescent. Close examination will reveal a light fuzz on the rachis. Bristle-like hairs fringe the edge of the segments and are also scattered on both surfaces. Occasional indusial hairs and tiny glands are present in the early part of the season. Veining is free and both forked and simple veins appear on the same pinna.

This fern is generally found in damp woods, thickets and edges of swamps. It tolerates rare inundations but does not ordinarily stand in water. It appears as isolated leaves rising from a creeping rhizome or in thick patches growing from dense, intertwining rhizomes.

SORI: Distinct, similar to the genus *Dryopteris* except smaller. Early in the season the indusia are kidney-shaped, centrally attached. At maturity they become reduced in size, and if still present are quite inconspicuous. Dehiscence occurs in early summer.

CULTURE: Deep, rich humus soil, slightly acid. Plant where there is no danger of crowding out other species. Withstands considerable sun if kept moist. One of the first ferns to become brown in the early fall.

RANGE: Newfoundland to Minnesota, south to Georgia and Arkansas.

---

1, Leaf silhouette. 2, Rhizome with current petioles and developing crosiers. 3, Upper side of deeply pinnatifid pinna. 4, Enlarged segment, underside, showing sori and hairs. 5, Crosier showing light brown scales and small basal pinnae.

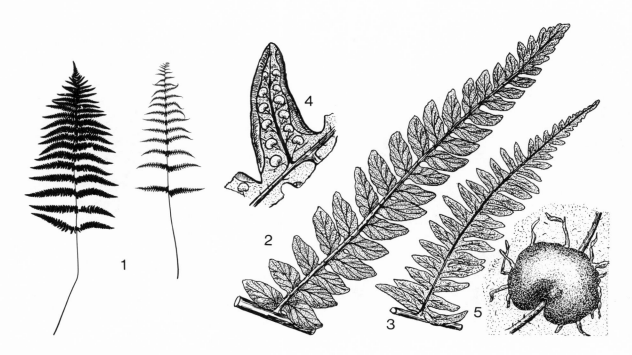

## *Thelypteris palustris*—**Marsh Fern**

Leaf lanceolate, erect, 1-pinnate-pinnatifid, light green to yellow-green, later becoming darker. Length 12 to 40 inches, width 5 inches. Dimorphic.

Also known as Meadow Fern and Snuffbox Fern. This fern grows in marshy meadows and wet thickets. Typical of the species, both fertile and sterile leaves have exceptionally long petioles; in many cases the petioles are much longer than the blades. Plants adjust their height to surrounding vegetation. Those growing in dense hedges force their way to the light and may have leaves 48 inches long with petioles over 30 inches. The basal segments of the pinnae are often longer than the other segments.

The leaves exhibit their dimorphism in an unusual manner. Early each spring a dense stand of light green sterile leaves appears. By late June fertile leaves rise above the sterile ones which have darkened with maturity. Fertile pinnae have the edges of their segments rolled, forming pointed ends, which gives the leaves a wilted look. The segments of the sterile leaves remain flat.

SORI: Uniformly spaced along the midrib of the segments, partially covered by the reflexed margins of the segment. Kidney-shaped indusia have sparsely ciliated edges. Dehiscence occurs in mid-summer.

CULTURE: Excellent fern for swampy area of woodland garden. Spreads rapidly. Soil slightly acid, kept very wet. Not suitable for small garden unless spreading is guarded.

RANGE: Newfoundland to Manitoba, south to Georgia and Oklahoma.

---

1, Leaf silhouettes, (left) sterile, (right) fertile. 2, Sterile pinna. 3, Fertile pinna, upper side. 4, Fertile segment showing sori and forking veins. 5, Indusium with ciliated margin.

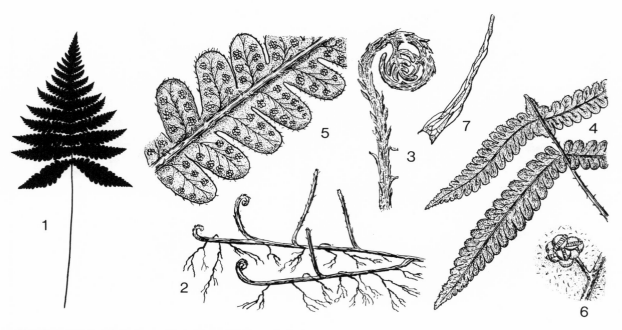

## *Thelypteris phegopteris*—Long Beech-fern

Leaf 12 to 16 inches long and 5 inches wide. Blade narrow, triangular, 2-pinnatifid above, 1-pinnate-pinnatifid below, light green, later changing to yellow-green. Petiole yellow-brown.

Also known as Narrow or Northern Beech-fern. There are two widely known Beech Ferns, the Long or Northern, and the Broad or Southern. Although similar, their well-defined features make positive identification certain.

The blade of the Long Beech-fern is composed of opposite, deeply pinnatifid segments above a single pair of pinnatifid basal pinnae. The upper segments are joined with a narrow wing which extends along both sides of the rachis, terminating above the lowest segment. In relation to the plane of the blade, the basal pinnae of both beech ferns stretch obliquely outward and downward.

The crosiers when first seen have a dense covering of dark brown scales. Similar to the Broad Beech-fern, this fern has the same peculiar diagonal-vertical vernation. As the triangular blade finishes unfolding, the basal pinnae assume their final position.

Young petioles and rachises are densely covered with dark brown scales but, as the petioles grow, the scales become sparse. Later, it is only with a magnifier that the fine pubescence of the entire leaf can be seen.

SORI: Composed of small groups of unprotected sporangia situated along the margins of lobes of the upper segments and the two basal pinnae.

CULTURE: Planted in woodland mulch, it is one of the easiest ferns to grow. Its ever-spreading rhizome should be restrained with a barrier when planted with other ferns. Leaves at close intervals along the rhizome give the planting a dense, matted appearance.

RANGE: Southward only in cool situations, Newfoundland to Alaska, south at low altitudes to southeastern Pennsylvania, and in the mountains to Macon County, North Carolina and Sevier County, Tennessee, west to Washington.

---

1, Leaf silhouette. 2, Advancing rhizome with closely spaced, ascending petioles. 3, Scale-covered crosier. 4, Basal pinnae and lowest lobed segments. 5, Enlarged sketch of fertile segment showing sori, veining, and tiny hairs. 6, Naked sorus at end of simple vein. 7, Enlarged sketch of petiole scale.

185

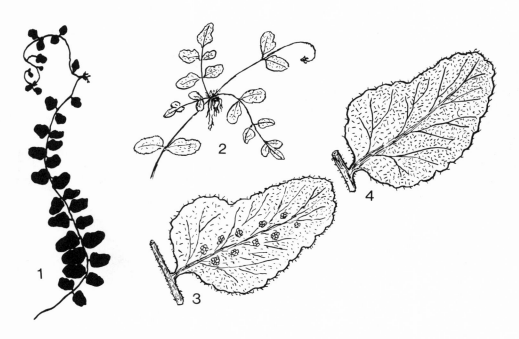

## *Thelypteris reptans*—**Creeping Fern**

Leaves, variable in size and shape, grow as clusters from tufted rootstock. Blades 3 to 12 inches long, ovate-lanceolate to linear-lanceolate, pinnate to pinnate-pinnatifid. Pinnae blunt or with shallowly blunt lobes, slightly to prominently auricled, covered with minute stellate hairs. Vegetative proliferation at apical tip or along vine-like rachis.

Throughout the world there are ferns having names suggesting forms of locomotion, such as "creeping," "walking," and "climbing." In all cases, the ultimate object is to create a new plant during the same season, rather than depending solely on time-consuming sexual reproduction through spore germination and growth. Colony formation of these different ferns may be by elongation of leaf, extension of rachis, continuing growth of rhizome, or spores. This creeping habit marks *T. reptans*.

SORI: Small, round, sparse, exindusiate or nearly so, along the midrib.

CULTURE: Requires growing-medium with ample limestone chips. Keep medium damp at all times, but avoid overwatering.

RANGE: Florida, Caribbean region.

---

1, Leaf silhouette. 2, Apical end of blade, showing juvenile plant growing from junction of pinnae and rachis, and apical budding. 3, Fertile pinna showing small, sparse, exindusiate sori. 4, Sterile pinna showing veining and small white-hair covering on surface and edge.

## *Thelypteris simulata*—**Massachusetts Fern**

Leaf yellow-green, oblong-lanceolate, 8 to 24 inches long, 3 to 6 inches wide, pinnate-pinnatifid, growing from creeping rhizome. Veins simple, non-forking. Deciduous.

*Thelpyteris simulata* is a member of the Marsh Fern group and is much less common than either *T. noveboracensis* or *T. palustris.* It prefers the highly acid soil and sphagnum moss of the near coastal swamps and bogs. It occasionally appears at the edge of hemlock or spruce swamps, but shuns calcareous regions. Its specific name, *simulata,* alludes to the similarity to a small sun form of the Lady Fern.

Among its more obvious features are the oblong-lanceolate blade, more like *T. palustris* than the full tapering blade of *T. noveboracensis,* and the basal pinnae, which are markedly narrower toward their bases. Venation is simple, with nonforking veins all reaching the margins of the segments.

SORI: Round and distinct, large, widely spaced, midway between midrib and margin. Indusium kidney-shaped, minutely glandular-ciliate, sometimes disappearing at maturity.

CULTURE: Not readily grown in horticulture because of high acid and moisture requirements. Where a ground-cover fern is desired, either of the other two ferns is recommended as a favorable substitute.

RANGE: Prince Edward Island to Alabama, to Quebec, New York, and West Virginia; central Wisconsin.

---

1, Leaf silhouette.  2, Basal section of leaf.  3, Fertile segment showing sori and venation.  4, Portion of sterile segment.

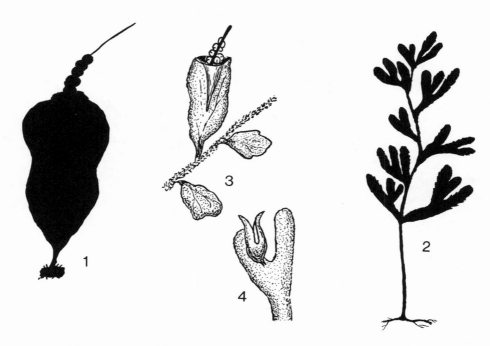

### *Trichomanes petersii*—Peter's Filmy-fern
### *Hymenophyllum tunbridgense*—Tunbridge's Filmy-fern

Filmy ferns comprise a large group of unconventional appearing and seldom seen ferns. In general, these ferns, with their extremely thin blades are classified in a large, worldwide family known as the *Hymenophyllaceae.* This family divides into several genera, the most prominent being *Trichomanes* and *Hymenophyllum.*

These ferns usually have small leaves and grow erect or prostrate from long, creeping rhizomes having either minute roots or hairs. Occasionally growing as terrestrial plants, they are more likely to be found on large damp rocks or the moist bark of trees. Both genera, because of the thinness of their blades, are most sensitive to their natural environment and will quickly die if removed.

SORI: Peter's Filmy Fern: Sporangia with oblique annuli growing around a central receptacle, ultimately extend from a conical indusium.
Tunbridge's Filmy Fern: Sporangia contained in bivalvate indusium having two lips which spread at maturity to allow dehiscence of spores.

CULTURE: Virtually impossible unless critical growing condition of high humidity is maintained at all times.

RANGE: *T. petersii*—Southeastern United States
*H. tunbridgense*—Southeastern United States; tropical America; Eurasia

---

1, Leaf silhouette, Peter's fern. 2, Leaf silhouette, Tunbridge's fern. 3, Fertile leaf of No. 1 showing bristle and sporangia emerging from conical indusium. 4, Fertile leaf of No. 2 showing characteristic bivalvate indusium.

188

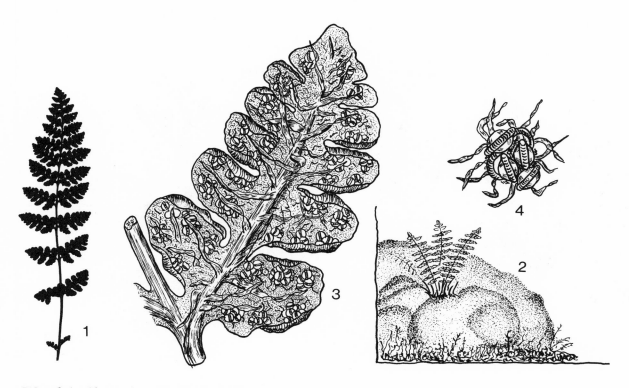

## *Woodsia ilvensis*—**Rusty Woodsia**

Leaf lanceolate, 1-pinnate-pinnatifid, bluntly lobed, 3 to 6 inches long, 1 inch wide. Light gray-green becoming yellow-brown to rusty-brown on underside.

Also known as Rusty Cliff-fern. This is a cliff-growing fern found dwelling at higher altitudes, usually on or at the base of dry, bare rocks where other ferns would be unlikely to survive. Lack of moisture accelerates changing of the color to rust, and prolonged droughts leave nothing but mats of short, brown stubble. With the return of refreshing rains the plant is restored to full vigor.

Although there are some differences between *Woodsia ilvensis* and *W. obtusa,* the most obvious is in their height. More definitive, however, is the character of their petioles. Unlike the blunt-lobed species, Rusty Woodsia has an articulate petiole, the joint being about 1 inch above the ground.

While the upper sides of the deeply lobed pinnae are soft gray-green, the undersides are deep rust. This color change is the result of a dense covering of long, intertwining, dark brown scales borne on the midrib. Maturing sori are almost obscured by the partially reflexed lobes and the matting of the scales.

SORI: Partly covered by long scales and fine hairs from the segment. Sporangia rest on the indusium which has deeply cut, elongate segments. Segments tightly wrap around young sporangia, later disappearing beneath them.

CULTURE: Excellent plant for rock gardens, either between or at base of larger stones. Circumneutral, loose soil. Open shade to alternate sunlight. Do not overwater, but avoid sustained dry periods.

RANGE: Baffin Land and Labrador to Alaska, south to Chester County, Pennsylvania, and at higher altitudes along mountains to northwesternmost North Carolina, Iowa.

---

1, Leaf silhouette. 2, Habitat among large boulders. 3, Underside of pinna showing reflexed margin and long brown scales partially obscuring sori. 4, Long indusial segments coming from beneath sporangia.

189

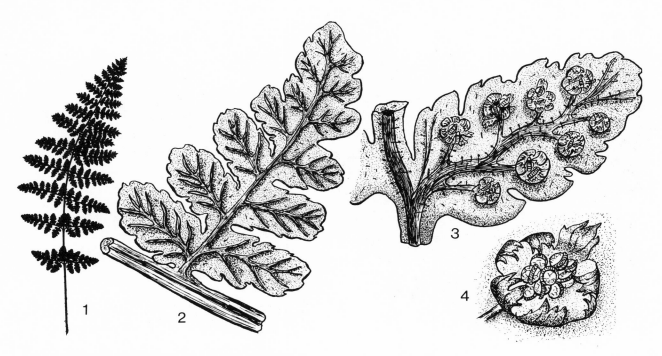

## *Woodsia obtusa*—Blunt-lobed Woodsia

Leaf lanceolate, 2-pinnate, gray-green, 12 to 16 inches long, 3 inches or more wide. Pinnae composed of bluntly lobed pinnules or segments. Lower rachis dark gray-green, changing to dark yellow-green at base of petiole.

Also known as Blunt-lobed Cliff-fern. The upper pinnae are elongate-triangular, while the basal pinnae are shorter and nearly deltoid. Pinnules, instead of having pointed ends like those of many ferns, are *obtuse* or blunt. Both the common and the botanical names are derived from this characteristic.

Tiny white glands and hairs cover both surfaces of the leaf; it is the abundance of these *trichomes* that gives the grayish tint to the pale-green leaf. The lower portion of the petiole has scattered, long brown scales; higher on the petiole and rachis the scales become less frequent and their color changes to silvery-white.

In its habitat this plant grows in circumneutral soil or along limestone ridges where leaf mold has slowly accumulated in pockets and crevices. Each season, new growth rises from the stubble of the previous year's petioles.

SORI: Clusters of sporangia rest upon the indusia, and when young are completely wrapped by long, pointed indusial segments. Toward maturity, the indusium is nearly covered by expanding sporangia and is difficult to see.

CULTURE: Easy to grow and small enough to make a pleasing addition to the rock garden or border. Open shade to moderately shady location. Circumneutral soil.

RANGE: Nova Scotia to eastern Minnesota, south to northern Florida, the elevated parts of the Gulf states, Texas and Arizona.

---

1, Leaf silhouette. 2, Upper side of obtuse, deeply lobed pinnule showing strong venation. 3, Underside of segment showing glands and partly covered sori. 4, Enlarged sorus with indusium.

190

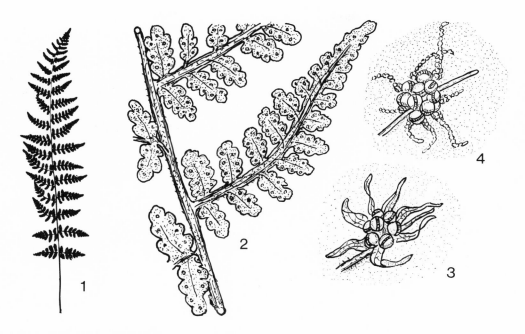

## Woodsia scopulina—Rocky Mountain Woodsia
## Woodsia oregana—Oregon Woodsia

Leaves of the Rocky Mountain Woodsia and Oregon Woodsia are markedly similar, having oblong-linear to oblong-ovate, pinnate-pinnatifid to 2-pinnate-pinnatifid blades. Leaf height ranges between 3 to 4 inches and 10 to 12 inches. Stipes yellow-brown, approximately one-third the length of leaf, and in both species inarticulate. Stipe and blade of *W. scopulina* pubescent, with white hairs and short stalked glands. Underside of blade of *W. oregana* may be sparsely to quite glandular.

SORI: Round, uniformly spaced toward the margin of pinnule. The most positive identifying feature of these ferns is their indusial covering which can only be seen with a magnifying glass. Indusia of *Woodsia* are composed of varying types of segments growing from under the sori. When the sporangia are immature, the white broad to narrow segments more or less cover the sori. At maturity, the indusia are pushed back and disappear, the sporangia becoming confluent, covering the underside of the leaf. The indusia of *W. scopulina* appear to be deeply cleft into a number of flat, lanceolate segments, while those of *W. oregana* are narrow, thread-like chains of cells.

CULTURE: Difficult to maintain in horticulture unless natural growing conditions can be closely simulated.

RANGE: Rocky areas of northern and western United States, southern and northwestern Canada.

---

1, Leaf silhouette of *W. scopulina*. 2, View of typical pinna. 3, Sorus of *W. scopulina*. 4, Sorus of *W. oregana*.

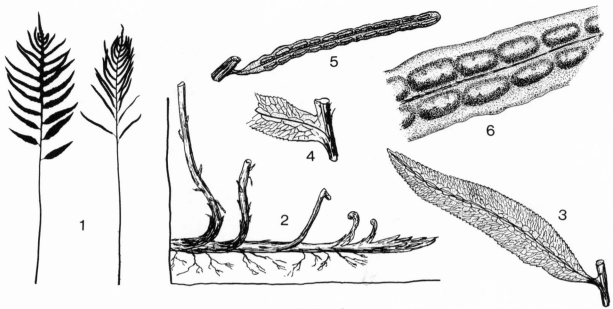

## Woodwardia areolata—Narrow-leaved Chain-fern

Strongly dimorphic. Sterile leaf oblong-lanceolate, pinnatifid above, 1-pinnate below, 24 inches long. Glossy, dark green. Some resemblance of sterile leaf to that of the sensitive fern.

The crosiers of this fern appear late in the spring and are heavily covered with light brown scales. These scales persist on both the petiole and rachis, becoming widely spaced as the leaf attains full height. The upper part of the sterile leaf is pinnately segmented. Near the base, the blade becomes pinnate and one or more pinnae are present. The fertile blade is similar in segment-pinna spacing, although these sori-bearing leaflets are very narrow by comparison. When young, both leaves are reddish-green; later the color changes to deep green.

The beauty of the leaf structure is appreciated by examining the edge and venation with a magnifier, particularly when the leaflet is held before a light. Strong, well-defined, elongate *areoles* are aligned along the midrib, with smaller areoles extending toward the edge. The edge has small, sharply cut serrations pointing toward the apex.

Similar to the Virginia Chain-fern, this species sends up crosiers at intervals along an extending rhizome. The massed appearance of the colony is caused by the leaves growing from a dense, intricate growth of underground rhizomes.

SORI: Inconspicuous when young, lying in a chain-like formation along the midrib, and swelling to form elongate mounds as maturity is approached. Sori are protected by elongate indusia that are free on the midrib side.

CULTURE: Because of its tendency to spread, this fern should be planted in a large area. Provided with an acid, swampy soil, it is easy to grow. Tolerates strong, open sunlight if soil and moisture requirements are met.

RANGE: Chiefly near coast, Florida to Texas, Arkansas, and Nova Scotia; also rare inland to Missouri and Michigan.

---

1, Leaf silhouettes, (left) sterile, (right) fertile. 2, Extending rhizome, with petioles and young crosiers growing at intervals. 3, Sterile pinna, lower, showing net-veining and stalk-connection to rachis. 4, Base of upper sterile segment showing wing-connection. 5, Fertile lower pinna. 6, Enlarged sketch of 5 showing covered, elongate, mound-like sori.

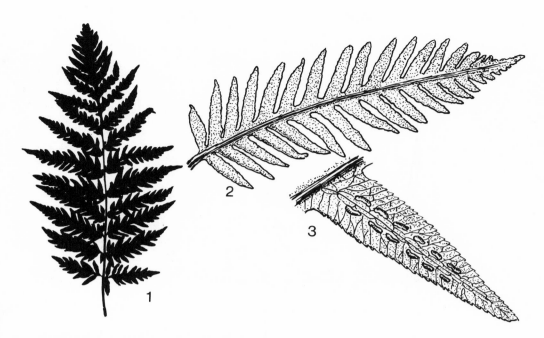

## *Woodwardia fimbriata*—Giant Chain-fern

Leaves lanceolate, light green, becoming much darker at maturity, 3 to 6 feet or more long, pinnate-pinnatifid, slightly narrowing to the base. Pinnae 8 inches or more in length. Segments long and tapering, becoming pointed at the end, with edges sharply saw-toothed. Brown scale-covered rhizomes may be creeping or somewhat erect and crown-forming. Evergreen.

Giant Chain-fern is a large, coarse-leaved fern found growing in the damp areas of western United States. This plant is most attractive when used as a focal point. Generally, cultivated plants do not attain the height of those found growing under natural conditions. As with all large ferns, this species should not be grown in a natural wind passage where breakage of leaves may occur.

SORI: Oblong to linear, forming one or more conspicuous rows parallel to midrib. Indusium tightly covers sorus when young, later becoming free and breaking to allow dehiscence of spores.

CULTURE: Loose, humus-rich soil. This fern should have constantly moist soil; where drainage is good there is little danger of overwatering.

RANGE: Western North America, British Columbia, to California and Arizona.

---

1, Leaf silhouette. 2, Sterile pinna. 3, Fertile segment with chain-like distribution of sori.

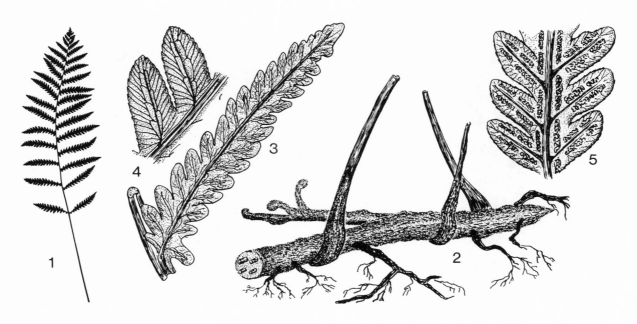

## *Woodwardia virginica*—**Virginia Chain-fern**

Leaf oblong-lanceolate, 1-pinnate-pinnatifid, dark green to yellow-green, leathery. Length 36 to 48 inches or more.

Although different in many ways, this fern may be mistaken for the Cinnamon Fern. Unlike the Cinnamon Fern, which is one of the first signs of spring, the Virginia Chain-fern appears much later amid the stubble of last year's growth. When first seen, the crosiers are naked and reddish-brown; this color persists until the leaf is fairly well developed. The leaf becomes dark green at maturity, with the rachis green-brown. The lower end of the petiole is dark brown, changing to black as it enters the earth.

The leaf is 1-pinnate; the deeply pinnatifid pinnae have blunt, stubby segments. Each leaf has about twenty alternate pairs of pinnae. The venation, which differs from so many ferns, forms a well-defined pattern readily seen. Some veins form areolae nearly parallel to the midrib, and other veins starting here become free, forming forks leading to the margin of the segment.

The rhizome of this chain fern is unusually strong and dense and can only be removed from its native swamp with great effort.

SORI: Elongate mounds parallel to midribs, in chain formation. Long indusia are free on the midrib side. Indusia disappear at maturity. As the sori become confluent the chain-like pattern is less obvious.

CULTURE: Grows well in the swampy woodland garden. It can be a vicious spreader. Planted in a restricted area of a drier garden, it should have acid soil and be kept moist at all times. Where soil and moisture are satisfactory, it can tolerate unlimited sunlight.

RANGE: Coastal Plain from Florida to Texas and to Long Island, and sporadically northward to Nova Scotia, inland to Bruce Peninsula, Ontario, and southern Michigan.

---

1, Leaf silhouette. 2, Underground scaly, branching rhizome. 3, Upper side of pinna. 4, Venation of segment. 5, Enlarged view of segments showing chain formation of sori.

194

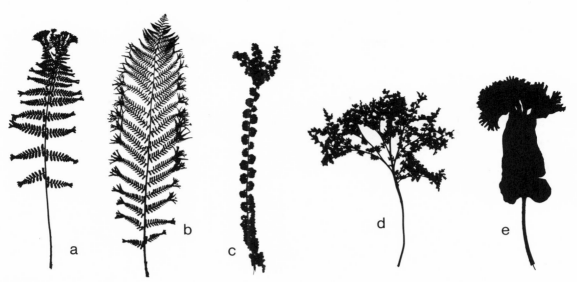

## English Crested Ferns

During the last century, English horticulturists have developed many novel variations of some of their commonly found native hardy ferns. These cultivars are characterized by simple or elaborate apical tassels adorning the leaves, or by crested tips of the pinnae; they are often referred to as "crested ferns."

Crested ferns are about as hardy as their progenitors. A group of crested ferns makes an unusual planting, and when individual plants are mixed with native ferns the difference is readily appreciated. In all cases, the culture is the same as for the parent species.

Genera of some crested ferns are quickly recognized, especially where a simple tassel is the only major change. Others are more complex and can only be identified after careful observation.

The most common crested ferns are from the genera *Athyrium, Dryopteris, Polystichum, Phyllitis,* and *Polypodium.* All of these, with their many variations, can be obtained from growers in this country specializing in fancy ferns. Unfortunately there is no contemporary American literature on the subject, but dealers' catalogs and guide sheets give helpful information regarding the selection and care of these cultivars.

The silhouettes of a few crested ferns are shown here. In the plants a, b, and e, the resemblance to lady, male, and hart's-tongue ferns is easily recognized. Plants c and d, both originating from the lady fern, show little resemblance to the wild species.

a. *Athyrium filix-femina* cv. 'Cristulatum'. Beautiful dwarf form. Leaves 8 inches long, with apex dividing into rounded crest 2½ inches in diameter. Pinnae narrow and minutely finger-crested.

b. *Dryopteris filix-mas* cv. 'Cristata'. The crested variety of the male fern is one of the best to grow and has been previously discussed.

c. *Athyrium filix-femina* cv. 'Frizellae'. Leaves 14 inches long, uniformly narrow. Pinnae small, fan-shaped, having dentate edges, alternately spaced, giving blade a spiral appearance.

d. *Athyrium filix-femina* cv. 'Acrocladon'. This dwarf variation seldom exceeds 1 foot in height. Its rich green leaves form bushy plants desirable for rock gardens or stone borders.

One nineteenth century English botanist called this plant the "Queen of the Lady Ferns" saying, "Indeed its exquisite foliage is unequaled in the whole range of English botany, and at the present time it is at once the rarest and most remarkable of the British filices."

e. *Phyllitis scolopendrium* cv. 'Cristatum'. Leaf grows to about 8 inches. Similar in pattern to our native northeastern Hart's-tongue Fern except beautifully crested at apex. Grows best in cool shaded area, in circumneutral soil over limestone.

195

# 11. Composite Descriptive Summary

| NAME | LEAF | SORUS | SOIL | LIGHT | REMARKS |
|---|---|---|---|---|---|
| *Acrostichum aureum* | Dark green, lanceolate 1-pinnate L: 6'-12' W: 12" | Sporangia cover entire under-surface of pinna | Very wet, acid | Full sun to alternate | Not desirable for garden use |
| *Acrostichum danaeifolium* | | | Very wet, acid | Full sun to alternate | Not desirable for garden use |
| Adder's-tongue, Engelmann's | See *Ophioglossum engelmannii* | | | | |
| Adder's-tongue fern | See *Ophioglossum vulgatum* | | | | |
| *Adiantum capillus-veneris* | Soft, green, fan-like pinnules ovate-lanceolate 1-pinnate above 2-pinnate below L: 3"-12" | Beneath reflexed margin of pinnule | Loose, moist, woodland mulch with added broken limestone | Subdued or filtered sunlight for short periods | Divide and repot occasionally |
| *Adiantum hispidulum* | Fan-like pinnules rose-colored when young, changing to green. 2-pinnate L: 6"-12" | Beneath reflexed margin of pinnule | Loose, moist, woodland mulch with added broken limestone | Subdued or filtered sunlight for short periods | Divide and repot occasionally |
| *Adiantum jordanii* | Ovate, 2-, 3-pinnate L: up to 18" | Beneath reflexed cleft edges | Humus-rich, well-drained | Avoid prolonged sunlight | |
| *Adiantum pedatum* | Soft, light to medium green. Rachis forked and diverging, 5 to 7 pinnate pinnae on each side. L: 12"-26" | Beneath reflexed, deeply cleft margin of pinnule | Rich humus, constantly moist | Medium shade | Spreads slowly. Deciduous |

| NAME | LEAF | SORUS | SOIL | LIGHT | REMARKS |
|---|---|---|---|---|---|
| *Aglaomorpha meyenianum* | Deep green, oblong-lance-olate, pinnatifid. Strongly dimorphic. L: 12"-24" W: 6" | Round, uniformly spaced in stubby lobes of segments. Exindusiate | Moist, rich neutral humus. Use "log-cabin" box for best drainage | Open shade or filtered sunlight during winter | Epiphytic |
| Anderson's holly-fern | See *Polystichum andersonii* | | | | |
| *Anemia adiantifolia* | Medium green, triangular 2 pinnate-pinnatifid or 3-pinnate | Sporangia borne on 2 separate vertical panicles | Loose, humus-rich, circum-neutral | Alternate sunlight | |
| *Arachniodes aristata* | Ovate-deltoid 3-, 4-pinnate L: 12"-20" W: 9"-12" | Round, covered with circular indusium | Damp, rich in humus | Open light. Filtered winter sunlight | Excellent accent plant |
| *Asplenium bradleyi* | Oblong-lanceolate. 1-pinnate. L: 4"-7" | Linear, short. Indusiate | Crevices of acid rock | Medium shade | Rare, hybrid |
| *Asplenium bulbiferum* | Medium soft-green. Petioles black. Oblong-lanceolate, 2-, 3-pinnate Dimorphic L: 24" W: 9" | Linear, with elongate indusium | Moist, rich, loose neutral soil | Open shade | Propagate from young plants growing on leaves |
| *Asplenium × ebenoides* | Lanceolate, long, tapering. L: 4"-9" | Linear. Indusiate | Limestone cliffs and outcroppings | Alternate light and shade | Rare, hybrid. Leaves variable. Evergreen |
| *Asplenium montanum* | Deltoid-ovate to lanceolate. 1-, 2-pinnate. L: 4"-8" | Linear. Indusiate | Crevices of non-calcareous rocks | Sheltered areas | Grows out of mat of dead leaves. Evergreen |
| *Asplenium nidus* | Glossy, brilliant green. Simple, narrowly to broadly elliptical. L: 12" W: 2" | Linear, with elongate indusium, forming herringbone pattern. | Rich, damp humus. Occa-sional mist spray where room humidity is low | Open shade | Excellent house-plant |
| *Asplenium pinnatifidum* | Lanceolate, narrow. L: 6"-9" | Linear. Indusiate | Crevices of non-calcareous rocks | Medium shade | Rare, hybrid. Evergreen |
| *Asplenium platyneuron* | Deep green, slender, double-tapering. 1-pinnate L: 6"-20" W: 1"-2" | Linear, elongate, in herringbone pattern. Indusiate | Loose, circum-neutral wood-land soil. Tolerates limited dry spells | Medium shade to alternate sunlight | Sterile leaves evergreen |
| *Asplenium pumilum* | 3-lobed L: 2½"-5" or more | Elongate, indusium-covered | Prefers limestone setting | Alternate sunlight | |
| *Asplenium ruta-muraria* | Deltoid-ovate. 2-, 3-pinnate. L: 6" | Linear. Indusiate | Moist calcareous cliffs and ledges | Alternate light and shade | Evergreen |

| NAME | LEAF | SORUS | SOIL | LIGHT | REMARKS |
|---|---|---|---|---|---|
| *Asplenium trichomanes* | Deep green, slender, 1-pinnate L: 6″ W: ½″-¾″ | Linear, elongate, in herringbone pattern. Indusiate | Humus with small pieces of limestone. Requires good drainage | Medium shade to alternate sunlight | Grows best when between limestone chunks |
| *Asplenium viride* | Bright green, linear-lanceolate. L: 2″-5″ | Linear, few. Indusiate | Damp cal-careous rocks and talus | Shade | Subevergreen |
| *Athyrium alpestre* | Oblong-lanceolate, 2-pinnate-pinnatifid L: 12″-30″ W: 3″-6″ | Round, very small. Indusium lacking or rare | Humus-rich, cool-moist | Alternate to open sunlight | |
| *Athyrium filix-femina* | Yellow-green to medium green. Broad, lanceolate 2-pinnate L: 36″ W: 15″ | Linear, elongate to horseshoe shape forming herringbone pattern. Indusiate | Neutral to slightly acid. Keep moist | Medium shade to alternate sunlight if soil is kept moist | Deciduous. Spreads slowly |
| *Athyrium niponicum* | Gray-green-wine, lanceolate. 2-pinnate L: 24″ W: 8″ | Linear, elongate to slightly curved, in herringbone pattern. Indusiate | Neutral to slightly acid. Keep moist | Medium shade to alternate sunlight | Spreads slowly. Deciduous |
| *Athyrium pycnocarpon* | Brilliant to deep green, lanceolate 1-pinnate L: 30″-48″ W: 6″ Dimorphic | Linear, elongate, in herringbone pattern. Indusiate | Neutral mulch containing broken pieces of limestone. Keep moist. | Shade | Spreads slowly. Deciduous |
| *Athyrium thelypterioides* | Yellow-green to brilliant green, elliptic-lance-olate. 1-pinnate-pinnatifid L: 36″ W: 7″ | Linear, elongate, in herringbone pattern. Indusiate | Neutral or slightly acid. Keep moist | Tolerates some sun if soil is constantly damp. | Spreads rapidly. Deciduous |
| Bear's-foot fern | See *Humata tyermannii* | | | | |
| Bear's-paw fern | See *Aglaomorpha meyenianum* | | | | |
| Beech-fern, broad | See *Thelypteris hexagonoptera* | | | | |
| Beech-fern, long | See *Thelypteris phegopteris* | | | | |
| Bird's-foot fern | See *Pellaea mucronata* | | | | |
| Bird's-nest fern | See *Asplenium nidus* | | | | |
| Bladder-fern, bulblet | See *Cystopteris bulbifera* | | | | |
| Bladder-fern, crested | See *Cystopteris bulbifera* var. *crispa* | | | | |
| Bladder-fern, fragile | See *Cystopteris fragilis* | | | | |

| NAME | LEAF | SORUS | SOIL | LIGHT | REMARKS |
|------|------|-------|------|-------|---------|
| *Blechnum occidentale* | Reddish-green when young, changing to medium green. Ovate-lanceolate. 1-pinnate L: 12"-24" W: 2"-3" | Linear, continuous band on each side of midrib. Indusium continuous. | Loose, woodland mixture with small limestone chips. Keep moist. Good drainage essential. | Open shade | Small plants good for terrarium |
| *Blechnum spicant* | Linear, tapering each way from middle. 1-pinnatifid L: 30" W: 1"-3" | Continuous, both sides of midrib | Mulch soil with small stones | Alternate sunlight. Avoid deep shade | |
| *Bommeria hispida* | Pentagonal, 1-, 2-pinnatifid L: 4"-6" W: 1"-3" | Exindusiate, along veins | Desert conditions | Sun, with some shade from boulders | Not suggested for garden |
| Boston ferns | See *Nephrolepis exaltata* cultivars | | | | |
| *Botrychium dissectum- f. dissectum* | Blade triangular. L: 4"-12" | Spherical, sessile, borne on panicle | Damp, acid | Open woodlands | Evergreen |
| *Botrychium dissectum- f. obliquum* | Fleshy, ternate. L: 4"-15" | Spherical, sessile, borne on panicle | Damp, acid | Open woodlands and thickets | Appears in early summer. Evergreen |
| *Botrychium lanceolatum* | Blade triangular, sessile. L: 5"-7" | Spherical, sessile, borne on panicle | Cool, damp, rich humus | Open woods and meadows | Deciduous |
| *Botrychium lunaria* | 1-pinnate, variable. L: 2"-6" | Spherical, sessile, borne on panicle | Dry pastures and open wastelands | Alternate light and shade | Rare. Deciduous |
| *Botrychium matricariifolium* | Fleshy. L: 2"-12" | Spherical, sessile, borne on panicle | Dry to moist thickets | Open woods | Appears early in spring. Deciduous |
| *Botrychium multifidum* | Fleshy, ternate. L: 4"-15" | Spherical, sessile, borne on panicle | Slightly acid | Open clearings and thickets | Appears in early summer. Evergreen |
| *Botrychium simplex* | Light green, fleshy. L: 1"-6" | Spherical, sessile, borne on panicle | Moist woodland humus | Open shade | Very small. Deciduous |
| *Botrychium virginianum* | Yellow-green to rich green. Triangular, somewhat horizontal L: 6"-30" | Sporangia spherical, sessile, borne on pannicle | Rich, moist, woodland soil, neutral to slightly acid | Medium to deep shade | Succulent. Protect from slugs and rodents. Deciduous |
| Bracken | See *Pteridium aquilinum* var. *latiusculum* | | | | |
| Brake, ladder | See *Pteris vittata* | | | | |
| Brake, ribbon | See *Pteris cretica* cv. 'Albolineata' | | | | |
| Brake, silver | See *Pteris quadriaurita* cv. 'Argyraea' | | | | |
| Brake, spider | See *Pteris multifida* | | | | |

| NAME | LEAF | SORUS | SOIL | LIGHT | REMARKS |
|------|------|-------|------|-------|---------|
| Brake, trembling | See *Pteris tremula* | | | | |
| Brake, Victorian | See *Pteris ensiformis* cv. 'Victoriae' | | | | |
| Button fern | See *Pellaea rotundifolia* | | | | |
| *Camptosorus rhizophyllus* | Medium green, elongate, tapering, simple. L: 4"-12" | Linear, elongate, arranged in random positions. Indusiate | Circumneutral. Grows best between limestone rocks. Avoid overwatering | Shade to alternate sunlight | Protect from slugs. Evergreen |
| *Ceratopteris pteridoides* | Triangular, L: 5"-10" or more | Sporangia hidden in horn-like segments | Shallow, still water | Full sunlight | For small water garden. Can be aggressive |
| Chain-fern, giant | See *Woodsia fimbriata* | | | | |
| Chain-fern, narrow-leaved | See *Woodwardia areolata* | | | | |
| Chain-fern, Virginia | See *Woodwardia virginica* | | | | |
| *Cheilanthes gracillima* | Linear-lanceolate 2-pinnate L: 3"-10" | Continuous, marginal | Critical soil condition | Alternate sunlight | Underside of leaf has dense hair covering |
| *Cheilanthes lanosa* | Medium yellow-green, lanceolate 2-pinnate L: 6"-8" W: 1"-2" | Located beneath reflexed margin of pinna | Circumneutral. Tolerates short dry periods | Open shade | Leaf covered with segmented hairs. Deciduous |
| *Cheilanthes siloquosa* | Triangular-oblong to pentagonal, 2-, 3-pinnate. L: 3"-10" | Continuous, marginal | Critical soil condition | Alternate sunlight | Good for rock garden |
| Christmas fern | See *Polystichum acrostichoides* | | | | |
| Cinnamon fern | See *Osmunda cinnamomea* | | | | |
| Cliff-brake, purple | See *Pellaea atropurpurea* | | | | |
| Cliff-brake, slender | See *Cryptogramma stelleri* | | | | |
| Cliff-brake, ternate | See *Pellaea ternifolia* | | | | |
| Cliff-brake, Wright's | See *Pellaea wrightiana* | | | | |
| Climbing fern | See *Lygodium palmatum* | | | | |
| Climbing-fern, Japanese | See *Lygodium scandens* | | | | |
| Coffee fern | See *Pellaea andromedifolia* | | | | |
| Copper fern | See *Bommeria hispida* | | | | |
| Creeping fern | See *Thelypteris reptans* | | | | |

| NAME | LEAF | SORUS | SOIL | LIGHT | REMARKS |
|---|---|---|---|---|---|
| *Cryptogramma acrostichoides* | Ovate, strongly dimorphic. 1-, 3-pinnate L: 3"-6" | Continuous, marginal | Loose, humus-rich | Alternate sunlight | Good for rock garden |
| *Cryptogramma stelleri* | Ovate to ovate-deltoid. L: 2"-6" | Beneath reflexed margin of pinnule | Crevices of damp limestone ledges | Open | Soil condition critical |
| Curly-grass fern | See *Schizaea pusilla* | | | | |
| *Cyrtomium falcatum* | Holly-like, deep shiny green, leathery. Oblong-lanceolate. 1-pinnate. L: 12"-24" W: 6"-9" | Round, many, irregularly spaced. Indusium circular | Loose, woodland soil with sand and pebbles to insure good drainage. Water daily | Open shade. Plant outside in summer | One of the finest houseplants |
| *Cystopteris bulbifera* | Yellow-green, long tapering, 2-pinnate L: 24"-36" | Round, numerous. Arched indusium forms little bladder | Cool, damp humus, neutral to slightly alkaline | Open shade | Numerous small bulblets on underside of leaf. Deciduous |
| *Cystopteris bulbifera* var. *crispa* | Yellow-green tapering, L: 12" 2-, 3-pinnate | Numerous. Bladder-like indusium, glandular | Same as *C. bulbifera* | Open shade | Spreads rapidly by bulblets. Deciduous |
| *Cystopteris fragilis* | Medium green, lanceolate 2-pinnate L: 10" W: 3" | Round, few, irregularly spaced on conspicuous veins. Arched indusium forms little bladder | Cool, loose, neutral or slightly acid | Open shade | May discolor in hot weather, becoming green with cool, damp weather. Deciduous |
| *Davallia fejeensis* cv. 'Plumosa' | Deltoid, 2-, 3-pinnate, feathery L: 12"-20" | Sporangia grow out of semi-cylindrical indusium. | Humus-rich with sphagnum | Alternate sunlight | Excellent houseplant |
| *Davallia pentaphylla* | Deep green. 1-pinnate with 5 to 7 pinnae. Dimorphic L: 9"-12" | Semi-cylindrical, opening at margin | Principally neutral humus, constantly damp | Open shade, or filtered sunlight in winter | Excellent for "log-cabin" box or cork bark plaque |
| Deer fern | See *Blechnum spicant* | | | | |
| *Dennstaedtia punctilobula* | Yellow-green, feathery, lanceolate. 2-pinnate L: 20"-32" W: 11" | Open, cup-shaped indusium containing few sporangia | Slightly acid, damp woodland mulch | Open shade. Alternate sunlight where soil is constantly damp | Strong spreading tendencies. Deciduous |
| *Doryopteris pedata* var. *palmata* | Brilliant green with chestnut-brown petiole. Spear-shaped segments. Strongly dimorphic L: 9"-12" W: 4"-6" | Marginal, continuous, making pretty brown border at maturity | Rich, damp humus, well drained | Open shade | Prefers high humidity. Mist-spray essential in drier atmosphere |

| NAME | LEAF | SORUS | SOIL | LIGHT | REMARKS |
|---|---|---|---|---|---|
| *Dryopteris arguta* | Ovate to deltoid-lanceolate, 2-pinnate-pinnatifid L: 24" W: 14" | Large indusium, shield-shaped with narrow sinus | Cool, damp woodland soil | Alternate sunlight | Excellent focal point for garden |
| *Dryopteris* × *bootii* | Oblong-lanceolate. 2-pinnate. L: 36" W: 6" | Round, with kidney-shaped indusium. Glandular | Wet woods, swampy area | Medium shade | Hybrid between *D. cristata* and *D. intermedia* |
| *Dryopteris campyloptera* | Ovate to nearly deltoid. 2-, 3-pinnate. L: 24"-36" W: 12" | Round, with kidney-shaped indusium. Glabrous or few glands | Damp humus-rich soil or swampy woodland | Medium shade | Occasionally found on rocky slopes |
| *Dryopteris clintoniana* | Oblong-lanceolate. 1-pinnate-pinnatifid. L: 24"-36" W: 9" | Round, with kidney-shaped indusium. Glabrous | Wet woods, swamps | Medium shade | Marked resemblance to *D. cristata* but larger |
| *Dryopteris cristata* | Dark green, leathery, erect, linear-lanceolate 1-pinnate- pinnatifid. L: 30" W: 5" Dimorphic | Round, covered with shield-shaped indusium | Slightly acid, constantly damp, loose woodland mulch | Open to deep shade | Native in boggy areas. Somewhat evergreen |
| *Dryopteris erythrosora* | Ovate-lanceolate, 2-pinnate L: 30" W: 15" | Round, with red kidney-shaped indusium | Circumneutral rich humus, constantly moist | Medium shade | One of the most beautiful of all shield ferns |
| *Dryopteris filix-mas* | Oblong-lanceolate. 1-, 2-pinnate. L: 12"-36" W: 8" | Round, indusium smooth or minutely glandular | Rich woods, limestone slopes | Medium shade | Rarity increasing. Sterile leaf evergreen |
| *Dryopteris filix-mas* cv. 'Cristata' | Medium green, ovate-lanceolate 1-pinnate-pinnatifid L: 28" W: 8" | Round, covered with shield-shaped indusium | Neutral, moist woodland soil | Open shade to alternate sunlight | Stands considerable long, cold weather, but not of evergreen status |
| *Dryopteris fragrans* | Lanceolate. 2-pinnate. L: 4"-12" W: 2½" | Round, indusium covered with glands | Cool, north-facing slopes | Exposed areas | Rare. Strongly aromatic |
| *Dryopteris goldiana* | Deep green, leathery, ovate-oblong 1-pinnate-pinnatifid L: 48" W: 14" | Round with shield-shaped indusium along midrib | Circumneutral rich humus, constantly moist | Cool, open to medium shade | May reach 60" under favorable conditions. Deciduous |
| *Dryopteris intermedia* | Deep green, oblong-lanceolate. 2-pinnate above 3-pinnate below L: 30" W: 10" | Round, with shield-shaped indusium | Deep, rocky soil, rich in humus. Neutral or slightly acid | Open to medium shade | Evergreen or nearly so |
| *Dryopteris marginalis* | Dark blue-green, leathery, deep veined. Lanceolate to ovate-oblong. 2-pinnate L: 20" W: 8" | Round, with shield-shaped indusium, at margin of lobe | Deep, stony, well mulched moist compost. Circumneutral | Open shade to alternate sunlight | Evergreen |

| NAME | LEAF | SORUS | SOIL | LIGHT | REMARKS |
|---|---|---|---|---|---|
| *Dryopteris spinulosa* | Deep green, oblong-lanceolate. 2-pinnate above 3-pinnate below L: 30" W: 7" | Round, with shield-shaped indusium near pinnule midrib | Rich, stony humus. Moist, slightly acid | Open shade. Short periods of sunlight if in moist soil | Evergreen or nearly so |
| Filmy-fern, Peter's | See *Trichomanes petersii* | | | | |
| Filmy-fern, Tunbridge's | See *Hymenophyllum tunbridgense* | | | | |
| Glade fern | See *Athyrium pycnocarpon* | | | | |
| Glade-fern, silvery | See *Athyrium thelypterioides* | | | | |
| Goldback fern | See *Pityrogramma triangularis* | | | | |
| Goldie's fern | See *Dryopteris goldiana* | | | | |
| Grape-fern, dissected | See *Botrychium dissectum* f. *dissectum* | | | | |
| Grape-fern, lance-leaved | See *Botrychium lanceolatum* | | | | |
| Grape-fern, matricary | See *Botrychium matricariifolium* | | | | |
| Grape-fern, multifid | See *Botrychium multifidum* | | | | |
| Grape-fern, ternate | See *Botrychium dissectum* f. *obliquum* | | | | |
| Grape-fern, simple | See *Botrychium simplex* | | | | |
| *Gymnocarpium dryopteris* | Deltoid, ternately compound L: 8"-16" | Small, round exindusiate | Damp woodland soil | Alternate light and shade | Rachis and blade without glands. Common |
| *Gymnocarpium robertianum* | Deltoid or nearly so, 2-pinnate-pinnatifid L: 8"-16" | Small, round, exindusiate | Damp woodland soil | Alternate light and shade | Rachis and blade densely glandular. Rare |
| Hammock fern | See *Blechnum occidentale* | | | | |
| Hard fern | See *Blechnum spicant* | | | | |
| Hart's-tongue fern | See *Phyllitis scolopendrium* | | | | |
| Hart's-tongue fern, English | See *Phyllitis scolopendrium* variants | | | | |
| Hay-scented fern | See *Dennstaedtia punctilobula* | | | | |
| *Hemionitis palmata* | Palmate, 2"-5" across, 5 divisions | Net-like pattern following veins | Moist, well-drained, rich in humus | Open light. Filtered winter sunlight | Propagate from vegetative buds |
| Holly-fern Anderson's | See *Polystichum andersonii* | | | | |
| Holly-fern, Braun's | See *Polystichum braunii* | | | | |
| Holly-fern, Dudley's | See *Polystichum dudleyi* | | | | |
| Holly-fern East Indian | See *Arachniodes aristata* | | | | |

| NAME | LEAF | SORUS | SOIL | LIGHT | REMARKS |
|---|---|---|---|---|---|
| Holly-fern, Japanese | See *Cyrtomium falcatum* | | | | |
| Holly-fern, northern | See *Polystichum lonchitis* | | | | |
| Holly-fern, Shasta | See *Polystichum lemmonii* | | | | |
| Holly-fern, Tsus-sima | See *Polystichum tsus-simense* | | | | |
| *Humata tyermannii* | Dark green, elongate-triangular. 3-pinnate. L: 6"-9" W: 4"-5" | Circular, covered with flap-like indusium attached at base. | Neutral, rich humus, preferably in porous clay pot or "log-cabin" box | Open shade. Alternate winter sunlight | Long, white scale-covered rhizomes add beauty to plant |
| *Hymenophyllum tunbridgensis* | Pinnate to 1-pinnate-pinnatifid. Blade tissue-like. L: 1"-2" W: ½" | Sporangia contained in bivalvate indusium | Prefers damp rocks or moist tree base | Shade | Requires constant dampness |
| Indian's dream | See *Cheilanthes siloquosa* | | | | |
| Interrupted fern | See *Osmunda claytoniana* | | | | |
| Ivy-leaved fern | See *Hemionitis palmata* | | | | |
| Lace fern | See *Cheilanthes gracillima* | | | | |
| Lady fern | See *Athyrium filix-femina* | | | | |
| Lady fern, alpine | See *Athyrium alpestre* | | | | |
| Leather fern | See *Acrostichum aureum* | | | | |
| Leather fern | See *Rhumohra adiantiformis* | | | | |
| Leather fern, giant | See *Acrostichum danaeifolium* | | | | |
| Leathery fern | See *Polypodium scouleri* | | | | |
| Licorice fern | See *Polypodium glycyrrhiza* | | | | |
| Lip-fern, hairy | See *Cheilanthes lanosa* | | | | |
| *Lygodium palmatum* | Vinelike. L: 24"-60" | Beneath over-lapping indusia | Swampy, wet, acid | Open | Climbs and twines on other plants |
| *Lygodium scandens* | Yellow-green to medium green. Vinelike with both fertile and sterile pinnae on same rachis. 3-, 4-pinnate. L: indeterminate | Egg-shaped capsule individually hidden beneath imbricated sheath | Loose, well drained, slightly acid | Open shade in summer. Filtered winter sunlight | Good houseplant. Provide trellis near window |

| NAME | LEAF | SORUS | SOIL | LIGHT | REMARKS |
|---|---|---|---|---|---|
| Maidenhair, California | See *Adiantum jordanii* | | | | |
| Maidenhair, common | See *Adiantum pedatum* | | | | |
| Maidenhair, rosy | See *Adiantum hispidulum* | | | | |
| Maidenhair, southern | See *Adiantum capillus-veneris* | | | | |
| Male fern | See *Dryopteris filix-mas* | | | | |
| Marsh fern | See *Thelypteris palustris* | | | | |
| *Marsilea quadrifolia* | 4 equal clover-like segments L: 4"-8" | Clam-shaped sporocarps grow at base | Pond mud or wet marsh | Full sunlight | Interesting plant for water garden. Can be invasive |
| Massachusetts fern | See *Thelypteris simulata* | | | | |
| *Matteuccia struthiopteris* | Deep green, leathery, elliptic-lanceolate 1-pinnate-pinnatifid L: up to 60" Strongly dimorphic | Fully hidden on fertile leaf during growing season | Moist, humus-rich, sandy soil. Circumneutral | Open shade. Alternate sunlight if soil is moist | Spreads rapidly. Native in swamps and alluvial flats along streams. Deciduous |
| Moonwort | See *Botrychium lunaria* | | | | |
| Mother fern | See *Asplenium bulbiferum* | | | | |
| *Nephrolepis exaltata* | Yellow-green to medium green. Exceptionally long and narrow. 1-pinnate L: 24"-72" W: 3" | Round, covered with circular to kidney-shaped indusium attached on midrib side | Loose garden soil with crocks. Keep moist | Wide range between partial sunlight and open shade | Excellent house-plant. Start new plants from stolons |
| *Nephrolepis exaltata*— cultivars | Medium green. Some similar to parent stock, others more bushy and multi-pinnate | Similar to parent if present, with probably sterile spores | Loose garden soil with crocks. Keep moist | Wide range between partial sunlight and open shade | Excellent house plants. Start new plants from stolens |
| New York fern | See *Thelypteris noveboracensis* | | | | |
| Oak fern | See *Gymnocarpium dryopteris* | | | | |
| Oak fern, limestone | See *Gymnocarpium robertiana* | | | | |
| *Onoclea sensibilis* | Yellow-green to green, deltoid-ovate. Pinnatifid L: 12"-30" Strongly dimorphic | Enclosed in bead-like pinnules | Neutral or sub-acid, moist | Open shade. Tolerates full sunlight if in marshy area | Spreads rapidly. Deciduous. Cold evenings turn leaves brown |
| *Ophioglossum engelmannii* | Elliptical L: 2"-8" | Double-rank columnar synangium | Humus-gravel | Open sunlight | Not suitable for horticulture |

206

| NAME | LEAF | SORUS | SOIL | LIGHT | REMARKS |
|---|---|---|---|---|---|
| *Ophioglossum vulgatum* | Ovate or elliptic. L: 3″-12″ | Double-rank columnar synangium | Moist open woods, damp meadows | Open | Spreads from fleshy roots |
| *Osmunda cinnamomea* | Yellow-green to deep waxy green, oblong-lanceolate 1-pinnate-pinnatifid. L: 24″-36″ W: 6″-8″ Strongly dimorphic | Spherical capsules closely spaced on edges of segments | Acid, constantly damp | Open shade | Native in boggy areas and along edges of ponds. Deciduous |
| *Osmunda claytoniana* | Yellow-green to waxy green, oblong-lanceolate. 1-pinnate-pinnatifid. L: 24″-36″ W: 6″-8″ Dimorphic | Spherical capsules closely spaced on edge of pinna segments. | Acid, constantly moist | Open shade to alternate sunlight in damper soil | Native in swampy areas where it grows 60″ tall. Deciduous |
| *Osmunda regalis* var. *spectabilis* | Deep green, ovate-lanceolate. 2-pinnate. Dimorphic L: 36″-48″ W: 12″ | Spherical capsules closely spaced on terminal panicle | Highly acid, constantly moist | Shade to alternate sunlight when growing in bogs | Native in swampy areas and along streams where it grows to 72″. Deciduous |
| Ostrich fern | See *Matteuccia struthiopteris* | | | | |
| Painted-fern, Japanese | See *Athyrium niponicum* | | | | |
| Parsley fern | See *Cryptogramma acrostichoides* | | | | |
| *Pellaea andromedifolia* | Triangular-ovate 2-, 3-pinnate L: 4″-18″ | Continuous, beneath reflexed margin | Prefers calcareous rocks, good drainage | Alternate sunlight | Rock garden applications |
| *Pellaea atropurpurea* | Gray-green, lanceolate 1-pinnate above 2 pinnate below L: 6″-15″ W: 4″ | Marginal. Reflexed edges of pinnule cover sporangia | Circumneutral or slightly alkaline | Open shade to alternate sunlight | Native on limestone. Evergreen |
| *Pellaea mucronata* | Broadly ovate-lanceolate 2-, 3-pinnate L: 6″-20″ | Continuous, beneath reflexed margin | Loose humus-rich with good drainage | Alternate sunlight | Rock garden applications |
| *Pellaea rotundifolia* | Waxy, dark green. 1-pinnate with nearly round pinnae. L: 12″-18″ W: 2″ | Marginal, extending various distances but not closing at apex | Loose, neutral humus soil with ample crocks. Keep moist but avoid excessive watering | Mild winter sunlight. Open shade in summer | Leaves flat, spreading |
| *Pellaea ternifolia* | Narrowly oblong 2-pinnate at base. L: 18″ | Continuous beneath reflexed margin | Elevated rock setting with humus | Alternate sunlight | Rock garden applications |

| NAME | LEAF | SORUS | SOIL | LIGHT | REMARKS |
|---|---|---|---|---|---|
| *Pellaea viridis* var. *viridis* var. *macrophylla* | Bright green, with chestnut-brown petiole. Lanceolate. 1-pinnate above 2-pinnate below L: 10"-30" W: 4"-8" | Marginal, virtually surrounding entire pinnule | Loose humus with broken limestone | Filtered sunlight during winter. Open shade in summer | Beautiful house-plants. Petioles inclined to be brittle |
| *Pellaea wrightiana* | Narrowly triangular 2-pinnate L: 15" | Continuous beneath reflexed margin | Elevated rock setting with humus | Alternate sunlight | Rock garden applications |
| *Phyllitis scolopendrium* | Strap-like. L: 6"-18" W: 1"-2" | In parallel linear lines | Limestone rocks and ravines | Shade | Very rare. Evergreen |
| *Phyllitis scolopendrium* variants | Strap-like, leathery, glossy | Linear, in parallel pairs | Well-drained humus; add limestone chips | Open light. Filtered winter sunlight | Crested variants make unusual houseplants |
| Pine fern | See *Anemia adiantifolia* | | | | |
| *Pityrogramma triangularis* | Pentagonal or triangular 1-pinnate-pinnatifid L: 6"-15" | Exindusiate, along veins. Confluent at maturity | Humus rich | Alternate sunlight | Gold or white waxy powder on underside |
| *Platycerium vassei* | Deep green, simple. L: 12" Strongly dimorphic | Brown patches of confluent sori near terminals of leaf segments | Mixture of fibrous material, humus and sand. Plant in "log-cabin" box or on cork bark plaque | Filtered sunlight during winter. Open shade in summer | An unusual fern, suitable for house-growing |
| Plume davallia | See *Davallia fejeensis* cv. 'Plumosa' | | | | |
| *Polypodium aureum* | Soft, blue-green, deeply pinnatifid. Ovate-lanceolate. L: 20"-36" W: 10" | Golden mounds uniformly spaced on back of segments | Loose garden soil or mixture of sand, humus, and sphagnum. Keep moist but well drained | Filtered sunlight during winter, open shade in summer | Excellent plant for either hanging basket or pedestal |
| *Polypodium californicum* | Ovate to ovate-oblong deeply pinnatifid L: 6"-12" or more | Slightly oval, exindusiate, nearer to midrib than margin | Prefers rock crevices | Alternate sunlight | |
| *Polypodium glycyrrhiza* | Broadly lanceolate. Segments long-tapering. L: 10"-20" or more W: 2"-4" | Round exindusiate, nearer midrib than margin | Prefers rock crevices. Grows on base of trees | Alternate sunlight | Rock Garden applications |
| *Polypodium hesperium* | Ovate-oblong deeply pinna-tifid. Segments oblong-elliptical, round tipped. L: 4"-15" | Round, exindusiate, crowded against midrib | Prefers rock crevices. Grows on base of trees | Alternate sunlight | Rock garden applications |

| NAME | LEAF | SORUS | SOIL | LIGHT | REMARKS |
|---|---|---|---|---|---|
| *Polypodium polycarpon* cv. 'Grandiceps' | Strap-like, leathery, glossy, L: 18"-24" W: 1"-2" | Round, exindusiate, scattered | Moist, well-drained, rich in humus | Open light. Filtered winter sunlight | Unusual leaves make this an attractive species |
| *Polypodium polypodioides* | Oblong-lanceolate, deeply pinnatifid. Oblong-obtuse segments joined by rounded sinuses. L: 4"-8" W: 1"-2" | Round, exindusiate uniformly spaced in single rows along midrib | Essentially epiphytic but does grow on ground | Alternate sunlight | Evergreen. Revives after rainy period |
| *Polypodium scouleri* | Deltoid-ovate to broadly ovate. Segments extremely blunt with rounded tips. L: 2"-12" | Few, very large, exindusiate, close to midrib | Humus-rich | Alternate sunlight | Less attractive for garden use |
| *Polypodium virginianum* | Yellow-green to medium green, oblong-lanceolate. Deeply pinnatifid L: 10" W: 2" | Large, round, uniformly spaced. Exindusiate. | Moist, circumneutral to slightly acid. Tolerates short dry periods | Open shade to alternate sunlight | Evergreen |
| Polypody, california | See *Polypodium californicum* | | | | |
| Polypody, common | See *Polypodium virginianum* | | | | |
| Polypody, crested | See *Polypodium polycarpon* cv. 'Grandiceps' | | | | |
| Polypody, golden | See *Polypodium aureum* | | | | |
| Polypody, western | See *Polypodium hesperium* | | | | |
| *Polystichum acrostichoides* | Various shades of green, darkening with age. Lanceolate. 1-pinnate Dimorphic L: 24"-36" W: 3"-5" | Round, covered with centrally attached indusium. Closely spaced on upper pairs of pinnae | Circumneutral, moist, stony woodland mulch | Open shade. Tolerates some direct sunlight where moisture is sufficient | Evergreen |
| *Polystichum andersonii* | elliptic-lanceolate L: 12"-36" | Round, with centrally attached dentate indusium | Cool, moist humus, stony | Open shade | One of the most beautiful of Northwestern ferns |
| *Polystichum braunii* | Deep, lustrous green, leathery. Elliptic-lanceolate. 2-pinnate L: to 36" W: 8" | Round, covered with centrally attached indusium uniformly spaced along midrib of pinnule | Cool, moist, deep woodland soil | Shade | One of our most beautiful northeastern ferns. Deciduous |
| *Polystichum dudleyi* | Lanceolate 1-, 2-pinnate L: 12"-44" | Round, covered with centrally attached thin indusium | Rich humus, stony mixture, cool, moist | Alternate sunlight | Excellent garden selection |

209

| NAME | LEAF | SORUS | SOIL | LIGHT | REMARKS |
|---|---|---|---|---|---|
| *Polystichum lemmonii* | Oblong-lanceolate 2-pinnate to 2-pinnate-pinnatifid L: 4"-12" | Large, round with centrally attached indusium | Rich humus, stony mixture, cool, moist | Alternate sunlight | Excellent garden selection |
| *Polystichum lonchitis* | Linear-lanceolate 1-pinnate L: 6"-24" W: 1"-2½" | Round, numerous, evenly spaced in rows on pinnae and auricle | Cool, damp, humus-rich soil | Alternate sunlight | Evergreen |
| *Polystichum munitum* | Lanceolate, 1-pinnate. L: 12"-50" W: 2"-10" | Round, covered with centrally attached indusium in single row each side of midvein | Cool, moist, rich in humus | Open shade, best with limited sunlight if kept moist | Stately, use as focal point. Do not crowd. |
| *Polystichum tsus-simense* | Deep green, lanceolate 2-pinnate. L: 12" W: 5" | Round, covered with circular, centrally attached indusium | Loose mulch, neutral to slightly acid | Open shade or filtered winter sunlight | Good plant for terrarium |
| *Psilotum nudum* | Long dichotomous stems, leaves rudimentary L: 6"-30" or more | Globular synangium grows in axil of bract | Humus, well drained | Alternate sunlight | Avoid overwatering |
| *Pteridium aquilinum* var. *latiusculum* | Ovate-triangular, coarse, leathery. L: 36"-60" | Continuous, at margin of segment | Wet or dry, humus or sandy | Open | Can be very weedy. Deciduous |
| *Pteris cretica* cultivars | Medium green, forming bushy, decorative plants. L: 6"-20" | Marginal, along greater part of pinnae | Good, loose garden soil | Open shade or filtered winter sunlight | Use at base of taller, flowering plants |
| *Pteris cretica* cv. 'Albolineata' | Medium green with central creamy-white band. 1-pinnate. Dimorphic. L: 8"-20" | Marginal, along greater part of pinna | Good, loose garden soil | Open shade or filtered winter sunlight | |
| *Pteris ensiformis* cv. 'Victoriae' | Deep green, variegated with irregular areas of silvery-white. Lanceolate. 1-pinnate above 2-pinnate below. Strongly dimorphic L: 8"-20" | Marginal, on slender pinnae | Good, loose garden soil | Open shade or filtered winter sunlight | Use in small planter or dish garden |
| *Pteris multifida* | Ovate to deltoid L: 10"-20" | Continuous along margin | Neutral soil with pieces of cracked cement or limestone | Alternate sunlight | Easy to grow. Makes a good potted houseplant |

| NAME | LEAF | SORUS | SOIL | LIGHT | REMARKS |
| --- | --- | --- | --- | --- | --- |
| *Pteris quadriaurita* cv. 'Argyraea' | Light green to blue-green, variegated with cental band of silvery-white. Triangular, 1-pinnate, with few large pinnae. L: 18″ | Marginal, on under edges of segments. Indusium continuous | Good garden soil with bone meal added | Open shade or filtered winter sunlight | Easy to grow, especially with ample humidity |
| *Pteris tremula* | Yellow-green to medium green, coarse. 1-pinnate above 2-, 3-pinnate below. Small table plant eventually becoming large floor plant | Marginal, on underside of segments. Indusium continuous | Good garden soil with bone meal added | Open shade or filtered winter sunlight | Easy to grow. Large plants excellent for backgrounds |
| *Pteris vittata* | Lanceolate, pinnae opposite, ladder-like L: 8″-30″ | Continuous, beneath reflexed margin | Grows on old masonry and any circum-neutral soil | Open sunlight if kept moist | Common, easy spreading. Grows readily from spore volunteers |
| Rabbit's-foot fern | See *Polypodium aureum* | | | | |
| Rattlesnake fern | See *Botrychium virginianum* | | | | |
| Resurrection fern | See *Polypodium polypodioides* | | | | |
| Royal fern | See *Osmunda regalis* var. *spectabilis* | | | | |
| *Rumohra adiantiformis* | Dark green, elongate-triangular. Leathery. 3-pinnate L: 12″-20″ | Round, uniformly spaced, covered with circular indusium | Moist leaf mold, topsoil and coarse sand | Open shade or filtered winter sunlight | Leaves good for cut-flower arrangements |
| *Schizaea pusilla* | Grass-like. L: 2″-4″ | Few, in fertile hand-like leaf | Very critical as to habitat | Open | Cannot be grown away from habitat |
| Sensitive fern | See *Onoclea sensibilis* | | | | |
| Shield-fern, Boott's | See *Dryopteris* × *boottii* | | | | |
| Shield-fern, Clinton's | See *Dryopteris clintoniana* | | | | |
| Shield-fern, crested | See *Dryopteris cristata* | | | | |
| Shield-fern, English crested | See *Dryopteris filix-mas* cv. 'Cristata' | | | | |
| Shield-fern, fragrant | See *Dryopteris fragrans* | | | | |
| Shield-fern, intermediate | See *Dryopteris intermedia* | | | | |
| Shield-fern, Japanese red | See *Dryopteris erythrosora* | | | | |

| NAME | LEAF | SORUS | SOIL | LIGHT | REMARKS |
|---|---|---|---|---|---|
| Shield-fern, marginal | See *Dryopteris marginalis* | | | | |
| Shield-fern, mountain | See *Dryopteris campyloptera* | | | | |
| Shield-fern, spinulose | See *Dryopteris spinulosa* | | | | |
| Spear-leaved fern | See *Doryopteris pedata* var. *palmata* | | | | |
| Spleenwort, Bradley's | See *Asplenium bradleyi* | | | | |
| Spleenwort, dwarf | See *Asplenium pumilum* | | | | |
| Spleenwort, ebony | See *Asplenium platyneuron* | | | | |
| Spleenwort, green | See *Asplenium viride* | | | | |
| Spleenwort, lobed | See *Asplenium pinnatifidum* | | | | |
| Spleenwort, maidenhair | See *Asplenium trichomanes* | | | | |
| Spleenwort, mountain | See *Asplenium montanum* | | | | |
| Spleenwort, Scott's | See *Asplenium* × *ebenoides* | | | | |
| Spleenwort, wall-rue | See *Asplenium ruta-muraria* | | | | |
| Staghorn fern | See *Platycerium vassei* | | | | |
| Stove ferns | See *Pteris cretica* and cultivars | | | | |
| Sword fern | See *Nephrolepis exaltata* | | | | |
| Sword-fern, Western | See *Polystichum munitum* | | | | |
| *Thelypteris hexagonoptera* | Yellow-green to medium green. Triangular, broad. 2-pinnatifid L: 10"-24" W: 12"-15" | Small, round, irregularly spaced. Exindusiate | Rich woodland acid soil, moist throughout season | Open shade | Spreads rapidly. Deciduous |
| *Thelypteris nevadensis* | Lanceolate 1-pinnate-pinnatifid L: 12"-30" | Small, in single rows. Indusium irregular in shape, with glands | Rich, loose, woodland soil, moist | Alternate sunlight | Spreads very slowly |
| *Thelypteris noveboracensis* | Yellow-green to medium green, elliptic-lanceolate. 1-pinnate-pinnatifid. L: 12"-24" W: 3"-6" | Small, round, covered with kidney-shaped indusium | Deep, rich, moist humus, slightly acid | Open shade to alternate sunlight if moist | Spreads rapidly. Turns brown early. Deciduous |

212

| NAME | LEAF | SORUS | SOIL | LIGHT | REMARKS |
|---|---|---|---|---|---|
| *Thelypteris palustris* | Yellow-green to medium green, lanceolate. 1-pinnate-pinnatifid. L: 12″-40″ W: 5″ Dimorphic | Small, round, covered with kidney-shaped indusium | Deep, rich, moist humus, slightly acid | Open shade to alternate sunlight if moist | Spreads rapidly. Deciduous |
| *Thelypteris phegopteris* | Yellow-green to medium green. Triangular, narrow. 2-pinnatifid above, 1-pinnate-pinnatifid below. L: 12″-16″ W: 5″ | Small, round, irregularly spaced. Exindusiate | Loose mulch, circumneutral, moist through-out season | Open shade | Spreads rapidly. Deciduous |
| *Thelypteris reptans* | Ovate, lanceolate to linear-lanceolate L: 3″-12″ | Round, small, sparse. Exindusiate or nearly so | Humus-rich soil with limestone chips | Alternate sunlight | Spreads readily by budding at apical tip |
| *Thelypteris simulata* | Oblong-lanceolate. L: 8″-24″ W: 3″-6″ | Round, with kidney-shaped indusium | Highly acid bogs and swamps | Open | Height conforms to surrounding growth |
| *Trichomanes petersii* | Fan-like, tissue-thin L: ½″ W: ¼″ | Sporangia grow on bristle out of funnel-like indusium | Prefers damp rocks or moist bark | Shade | Requires constant moisture |
| Walking fern | See *Camptosorus rhizophyllus* | | | | |
| Water fern | See *Ceratopteris pteridoides* | | | | |
| Water fern, European | See *Marsilea quadrifolia* | | | | |
| Whisk fern | See *Psilotum nudum* | | | | |
| Wood fern, coastal | See *Dryopteris arguta* | | | | |
| Wood fern, Nevada | See *Thelypteris nevadensis* | | | | |
| Woodsia, blunt-lobed | See *Woodsia obtusa* | | | | |
| *Woodsia ilvensis* | Light gray-green, rusty-brown on under-side, lanceolate. 1-pinnate-pinnatifid. L: 3″-6″ W: 1″ | Round, partially obscured by long, brown scales. Seg-mented indusium from beneath, wrapping sorus | Circumneutral, well drained, slightly moist. Avoid overwatering | Open shade to alternate sunlight | Tolerates limited dry spells. Deciduous |
| *Woodsia obtusa* | Gray-green, lanceolate. 2-pinnate. L: 12″-16″ W: 3″ | Round. Cleft indusium from below | Moist, circumneutral. | Open shade | Evergreen to some extent |
| *Woodsia oregana* | Oblong-linear to oblong-ovate L: 3″-12″ | Sori round with segmented indusium from beneath | Simulate native conditions | Alternate sunlight | Difficult to maintain in horticulture |

| NAME | LEAF | SORUS | SOIL | LIGHT | REMARKS |
|---|---|---|---|---|---|
| Woodsia, Oregon | See *Woodsia oregana* | | | | |
| Woodsia, Rocky mountain | See *Woodsia scopulina* | | | | |
| Woodsia, rusty | See *Woodsia ilvensis* | | | | |
| *Woodsia scopulina* | Oblong-linear to oblong-ovate L: 3"-12" | Sori round with segmented indusium from beneath | Simulate natural conditions | Alternate sunlight | Difficult to maintain in horticulture |
| *Woodwardia areolata* | Glossy, medium to dark green. Sterile leaf oblong-lanceolate. Pinnatifid above, 1-pinnate below. L: 24" W: 5" Strongly dimorphic | Borne in chain formation on long, narrow pinnae. Covered with continuous indusium | Boggy, acid soil | Open shade. Tolerates considerable sunlight when in boggy soil | Spreads rapidly forming dense, heavy rhizomes. Deciduous |
| *Woodwardia fimbriata* | Lanceolate, 1-pinnate-pinnatifid L: 36"-72" W: 15" | Oblong to linear, chain-like with indusium parallel to midvein | Loose, humus-rich, constant moisture. Little danger of overwatering | Full sunlight | Protect from high wind |
| *Woodwardia virginica* | Deep green to yellow-green depending on light. Oblong-lanceolate. 1-pinnate-pinnatifid. L: 36"-48" W: 5" | Borne in chain formation along midrib of segments. Indusium elongate | Boggy, acid soil | Open shade. Tolerates considerable sunlight when in boggy soil | Spreads rapidly forming dense, heavy rhizomes. Deciduous |

# Glossary

*acuminate:* gradually tapering to a point

*alternate:* in reference to pinnae that are borne at regular intervals at different levels on the rachis

*anastomosing:* connected by cross-veins, and forming a network

*antheridium* (pl. *antheridia*): the male organ of the fern, located on the underside of the prothallium, producing the motile sperm or spermatozoid

*annulus:* an elastic cellular ring partially or completely surrounding the sporangium of some ferns

*apex:* the tip, point or summit of a leaf, pinna, or pinnule

*apical:* relating to the apex or tip

*apogamous:* developed without fertilization

*aquatic:* growing in water, totally or partially submerged

*arboreal:* living or situated among trees

*archegonium* (pl. *archegonia*): the female organ of the fern, located on the underside of the prothallium, producing the egg cell

*areole:* the space marked out between anastomosing veins

*articulate:* jointed, having a node or joint

*auricle:* an ear-shaped appendage or lobe

*axil:* the angle formed between any two parts

*basal:* pertaining to the base, the lowermost or bottom

*bipinnate:* doubly or twice-pinnate; sometimes indicated as 2-pinnate

*bipinnatifid:* doubly or twice-pinnatifid; sometimes indicated as 2-pinnatifid

*blade:* the expanded portion of a leaf or frond

*bulbil—bulblet:* a small bulb; a bulb-like body, especially one borne on the rachis or pinna midrib

*ciliate:* marginally fringed with hairs

*circinate:* coiled from the apex downward, as the leaf of a young fern

*circumneutral:* about neutral, said of a soil with chemical reaction of pH7

*cleft:* deeply cut

*compound:* in reference to a leaf—the blade composed of separate leaflets

*confluent:* blending together so as to appear as one

*cordate:* heart-shaped, especially referring to the base

*costa:* the midrib of a blade, pinna, or pinnule that is not compound

*crenate:* having a toothed margin with rounded teeth

*cristate:* in reference to fern leaves—the apex of the blade or pinna repeatedly forked

*crocks:* small pieces of broken clay pots added to potting soil to aid drainage and ventilation

*crown:* a circular arrangement of closely spaced leaves

*crosier:* the young coiled leaf of some ferns

*cultivar:* a named horticultural variety as distinguished from a natural variety of a species. As an example, *Athyrium filix-femina* var. *rubellum* represents a natural variety while *Nephrolepis exaltata* cv. 'Bostoniensis' is a horticultural variety.

*cuneate:* wedge-shaped, narrowly triangular with the acute angle downward

*deciduous:* falling off or withering at the end of the growing season

*dehiscence:* method of opening of sporangium to discharge spores at maturity

*deltoid:* broadly triangular, like the Greek letter delta

*dentate:* toothed, usually with the teeth directed outward

*dichotomous:* forking regularly into two nearly equal parts

*dimorphic:* occurring in two different forms, as the fertile and sterile leaves of some ferns

*entire:* in reference to the edge or margin of a leaf having no teeth, lobes, or divisions

*evanescent:* gradually disappearing

*epiphyte:* a plant growing on or attached to another plant, but not parasitic

*evergreen:* remaining verdant throughout the year

*exindusiate:* a sorus without an indusium, the sporangia naked

*falcate:* sickle or scythe-shaped, flat and curved, gradually tapering toward end

*fern:* a flowerless, vascular plant reproducing itself by means of spores borne on its leaves, and differing from flowering plants in that it is a one-celled organism twice in its life cycle

*fertile:* bearing spores

*fiddlehead:* name commonly applied to the crosier because of its resemblance to a violin scroll

*flabellate* or *flabelliform:* fan-shaped or broadly wedge-shaped

*flexuous:* curved alternatively in opposite directions

*form:* A minor variant of a species (Latin: *forma*)

*free:* referring to veins that do not unite

*frond:* a fern leaf, including the petiole and blade

*gametophyte:* the stage in the life cycle of the fern that develops the organs that bear the sex cells (sperms and eggs)

*genus* (pl. *genera*): a group of species having close resemblance in one or more characteristics

*glabrous:* smooth, especially without hairs

*gland:* a small appendage or protuberance containing or secreting special substances

*glaucous:* covered with a whitish or bluish bloom

*habitat:* the place in which a plant grows naturally

*hastate:* shaped like an arrowhead, with the basal lobes pointed outward at wide angles. Halberd-shaped

*herbaceous:* Leaf-like in color and texture

*hispid:* provided with rigid or bristly hairs or with bristles

*hydathode:* an opening on the epidermal surface of a leaf to allow exudation of water

*imbricate:* overlapping vertically or spirally, as shingles on a roof

*incised:* sharply and more or less deeply cut

*indusiate:* covered by an indusium

*indusium:* the membranous covering of a sorus

*inferior:* lower or below

*lanceolate:* shaped like a lance-head, several times longer than wide, broadest toward the base and narrowed to the apex

*leaf:* the leaf of a fern (often designated as a frond) usually consists of an expanded blade, which may be simple or compound, and a stalk called a petiole or stipe

*leaflet:* a primary division of a compound leaf

*life cycle:* the orderly sequence of growth stages of a fern from spore to prothallium, to sporophyte, to spore

*linear:* long and narrow, with parallel margins

*lobe:* more or less rounded division of a leaf, pinna, or pinnule

*margin:* the border or edge of a leaf, pinna, or pinnule

*midrib:* the main axis in a leaf or part of a leaf

*morphology:* the form and structure of an organism or any of its parts

*naked:* without covering; a sorus that is not covered by an indusium

*node:* the point on a rhizome at which a leaf is produced

*oblique:* unequal-sided or slanting

*opposite:* situated in pairs along the rachis or midrib

*obtuse:* blunt or rounded at the end

*orbicular:* circular in outline

*ovate:* shaped like the outline of an egg, having the broader end at the base

*palmate:* radiately lobed or divided like the fingers on a hand

*panicle:* a branched portion of a fertile leaf that bears sporangia on stalks

*paraphysis* (pl. *paraphyses*): a slender sterile filament borne among sporangia

*parasitic:* growing on and deriving nourishment from another plant

*pedate:* palmate, with additional lateral portions

*pendent* or *pendulous:* more or less hanging downward

*peltate:* shield-shaped, attached to the stalk at or near the center of the lower surface

*petiole:* the supporting stalk of a fern, the stipe

*pH soil test:* a chemical indication of soil acidity. Soil having a pH value of 7 is neutral. A decrease in pH denotes acidity, while an increased pH indicates alkalinity.

*pilose:* bearing long, soft hairs

*pinna* (pl. *pinnae*): the primary division of a compound leaf

*pinnate:* in reference to a blade that is compound, with the pinnae arranged regularly on each side of the rachis

*pinnatifid:* cut almost to the rachis or midrib

*pinnule:* a secondary pinna; one of the pinnately arranged divisions of the pinna

*prothallium* (pl. *prothallia*): the outgrowth of a spore, usually a somewhat flat, heart-shaped, multicelled organism, containing both male (antheridial) and female (archegonial) cells and, when fertilized, capable of giving rise to a new sporophyte

*pteridophyte:* a member of the pteridophyta or group containing the ferns, clubmosses, and their allies

*pubescent:* covered with short soft hairs; downy

*rachis* (pl. *rachises*): the axis of a compound blade

*reflexed:* in reference to the margin of a segment, turned downward and under

*reniform:* kidney-shaped

*rhizome:* a horizontal or underground stem

*rootstock:* an underground stem, a rhizome

*rupestral:* growing on rock

*scale:* a small, thin, dry, and membranous epidermal outgrowth

*segment:* one of the divisions or lobes of a leaf

*serrate:* having sharp teeth pointing forward

*sessile:* without a stalk

*simple:* of one piece; undivided; not compound

*sinus:* the cleft or recess between two lobes

*sorus* (pl. *sori*): a group or cluster of sporangia; a fruit-dot

*sperm, spermatozoid:* the flagellated, male germ cell found in the antheridium

*spinulose:* bearing small, spine-like processes

*sporangium* (pl. *sporangia*): the organ in which spores are borne

*spore:* an asexual reproductive cell. In contrast to a seed, it bears no embryo or undeveloped young plant

*spore-mother-cell:* the cell which gives rise to the tetrad of four spores
*sporophyte:* the spore-bearing plant in the life cycle of the fern
*sport:* a vegetative variation from the normal
*station:* a particular location for a specific plant
*sterile:* without sori
*stipe:* the petiole, or stalk, of the fern leaf, bearing the blade
*stolon: a runner that is inclined to root and produce buds*
*succulent:* fleshy, juicy
*superior:* above or higher
*synagium:* a specialized spore container of some primitive ferns in which 2 or more thick-walled sporangia have become fused to form a single body
*terminal:* borne at the end or apex
*ternate:* in three sections or parts
*terrestrial:* growing on the ground
*tetrad:* a group of four spores developed from one spore-mother-cell
*tomentose:* with dense, woolly, matted hairs
*trichome:* a hair-like outgrowth of the epidermis
*vascular:* having vessels or ducts, i.e. xylem and phloem
*veins:* thread-like vascular elements in the leaf-tissue
*vernation:* the arrangement of the leaf while in the crosier
*viable:* capable of maintaining life

# Fern Selector

*Fern Selector No. 1—Choosing Ferns for Your Home*

## FERNS AS FOCAL POINTS

| | |
|---|---|
| *Asplenium nidus*<br>Bird's-nest Fern | Simple, glossy, brilliant green leaves with contrasting dark costas. |
| *Cyrtomium falcatum*<br>Japanese Holly-fern | Glossy green leaves, strongly resembling sprigs of hybrid holly. |
| *Davallia fejeensis*<br>cv.'Plumosa'<br>Plume Davallia | Feathery leaves grow at intervals from creeping, scale-covered rhizome. Articulate leaves eventually drop off and are replaced by young leaves growing from extending rhizome. |
| *Nephrolepis exaltata*<br>cultivars<br>Boston ferns | Most popular of all house ferns. Articulate pinnae fall from older leaves. Wire-like runners may be clipped to improve appearance. |
| *Humata tyermannii*<br>Bear's-paw Fern | Similar to plume fern. Articulate leaves vary in color from green to bronze-green and grow from exposed scale-covered rhizome. |
| *Platycerium* species<br>Staghorn ferns | Thick leaves of odd shapes make these ferns the curios of ferndom. Wall mounting on cork-bark plaques gives these ferns a natural appearance. Some species readily adapt to home conditions if given proper care. |
| *Polypodium aureum*<br>Rabbit's-foot Fern | A large, coarse-leaved species best displayed as a pedestal plant. |
| *Polypodium polycarpon* cv.<br>'Grandiceps'<br>Crested Polypody | Simple, dark green, leathery strap-like leaves with prominent crested terminals. |

## FERNS FOR HANGING BASKETS

| | |
|---|---|
| *Adiantum capillus-veneris*<br>Southern Maidenhair<br>Fern | One of the prettiest of all house ferns. Somewhat critical of the dry atmosphere of average home. |

219

*Asplenium bulbiferum*
New Zealand
Mother-fern

Beautiful soft green, feathery leaves Central leaves upright. As "baby" ferns appear, the added weight causes outer leaves to become pendant.

*Davallia fejeensis* cv.
'Plumosa'
Plume Davallia
*Humata tyermannii*
Bear's-paw Fern

These two old world favorites are excellent for hanging baskets.
Eventually the basket will disappear beneath the colorful, scale-covered rhizomes.

*Nephrolepis exaltata*
cultivars
Boston ferns

Excellent specimens for hanging baskets. Best grown from window bracket where light level is higher. Some sunlight during winter months is beneficial.

*Pellaea rotundifolia*
New Zealand
Button-fern

Dark green with button-like pinnae. Center leaves upright; older leaves flowing and pendulous.

## FERNS FOR THE AQUARIUM

*Ceratopteris pteridoides*
Water Fern

Rapid grower; excellent oxygenating plant for the fish tank.

*Marsilea quadrifolia*
European Water-fern

Clover-like leaves, some floating, others emerging from water. Very attractive.

Both of these species are aquatic ferns and normally grow in full sunlight. A 14-hour cycle of fluorescent light at about 18 inches will be sufficient for indoor growing.

## FERNS FOR PLANTERS

*Blecknum occidentale*
Hammock Fern

Crosiers and young leaves are pinkish green, turning to medium green at maturity.

*Pellaea rotundifolia*
New Zealand
Button-fern

Combine smaller plants of this species with other ferns or winter flowering plants.

*Phyllitis scolopendrium*
Hart's-tongue Fern

Smooth, medium green, tongue-like leaves. There are many different English cultivars that make attractive arrangements in planters.

*Polystichum tsus-simense*
Tsus-sima Holly-fern

Like many species of the *Polystichum* genus, this fern is a member of the holly-fern group. It has dark green leaves with segments ending in spiny tips; it readily adapts itself to average home conditions.

*Pteris cretica* cultivars
Stove ferns

These cultivars vary greatly in leaf architecture and color. Try a combination of the Victorian brake, silver brake and ribbon brake.

Note: By filling the planter with damp peat moss and submerging the clay pot containers, the roots will be constantly damp and the foliage will have increased humidity.

## FERNS FOR THE TERRARIUM

*Adiantum* species
Maidenhair ferns

Small assorted specimens removed from spore-growing table make delightful terrarium plants. They will last about two years before outgrowing the container.

| | |
|---|---|
| *Polystichum tsus-simense*<br>Tsus-sima Holly-fern | Grown as a terrarium plant, and not overwatered or overfed, this species can remain in the enclosure for about two years. |
| *Pteris cretica* cultivars<br>Stove ferns | Since these species are rapid growers, an open-dish garden is recommended. |
| *Thelypteris reptans*<br>Creeping Fern | This fern is best grown as a single plant, as it quickly spreads by young ferns proliferating at the leaf terminals of the parent. Add small chunks of weathered limestone to provide a natural appearance. |

## *Fern Selector No. 2*

### INDOOR FERNS ARRANGED IN ORDER OF EASE OF GROWING

| | |
|---|---|
| *Asplenium nidus* | Bird's-nest Fern |
| *Cyrtomium falcatum* | Japanese Holly-fern |
| *Polypodium aureum* | Rabbit's-foot Fern |
| *Nephrolepis exaltata* cultivars | Boston ferns |
| *Davallia fejeensis* cv. 'Plumosa' | Plume Fern |
| *Polypodium polycarpon* cv. 'Grandiceps' | Crested Polypody |
| *Pellaea rotundifolia* | New Zealand Button-fern |
| *Platycerium species* | Staghorn ferns |
| *Polystichum tsus-simense* | Tsus-sima Holly-fern |
| *Pteris cretica* species | Stove ferns |
| *Asplenium bulbiferum* | New Zealand Mother-fern |
| *Pellaea viridis* | False Holly-fern |
| *Adiantum hispidulum* | Rosy Maidenhair Fern |
| *Adiantum capillus-veneris* | Southern Maidenhair Fern |

Note: This list can be considered as only a general guide, as atmospheric conditions of the average home vary greatly. As an example, if any of the maidenhair ferns shown at the end of the list are kept in a cool room where the atmospheric moisture content is higher, the plants will make a luxuriant showing with ordinary care.

## *Fern Selector No. 3*

### OUTDOOR FERN CLASSIFICATION

**Ground Covers**

| | |
|---|---|
| *Dennstaedtia punctilobula*<br>Hay-scented Fern | One of the best ground-cover ferns. Up early in the spring, first appearing with fuzzy, white, hair-covered crosiers, it spreads rapidly. Grows well in rocky soil; leaves turn beautiful golden brown in autumn. |
| *Thelypteris hexagonoptera*<br>Broad Beech-fern<br>*Thelypteris phegopteris*<br>Narrow Beech-fern | Beech ferns do best when grown in well-mulched soil and partial shade. Once started, they will form a dense cover. |
| *Thelypteris noveboracensis*<br>New York Fern | This fern is similar to the beech ferns in growing habit. Leaves, yellow-green in color, are long tapering and will continue to grow until frost. |

| | |
|---|---|
| *Thelypteris palustris*<br>Marsh Fern | Somewhat similar in growth habit to the New York Fern, but prefers a marshy soil. |

## Erosion Protection

| | |
|---|---|
| *Blecknum spicant*<br>Deer Fern or Hard Fern | A dimorphic species with leaves growing from heavy rhizome. |
| *Matteuccia struthiopteris*<br>Ostrich Fern | Large fern with plume-like leaves growing from a crown. Forms vigorous, deep root system by extending network of stolons. Tolerates full sunlight when grown in swampy areas. |
| *Onoclea sensibilis*<br>Sensitive Fern | This fern is sensitive to cold nights of late spring and early fall. Best when used as erosion protection along banks of streams. |
| *Polystichum acrostichoides*<br>Christmas Fern | Slow in spreading, but green prostrate leaves remain all winter to protect sloping area. |
| *Woodwardia areolata*<br>Narrow-leaved<br>Chain-fern | This fern has dimorphic leaves, sterile leaves appearing somewhat similar to *Onoclea sensibilis.* |
| *Woodwardia fimbriata*<br>Giant Chain-fern | Large, strong-leaved specimen. Especially good where water erosion is a problem. |
| *Woodwardia virginica*<br>Virginia Chain-fern | A good species for use in wet areas. Vigorous root system can tolerate long periods of inundation. |

## Rock Garden Suggestions

A rock garden can be one of the most interesting parts of the garden. This is a place where small species can be displayed to advantage that might otherwise be lost in a larger garden.

Use local native species to get the garden started, gradually learning the preference for each fern. There are enough species of both the eastern and western areas of our country to satisfy the beginner. As knowledge is gained, ferns from different areas may be added. In my garden in the northwest hill area of New Jersey, I have been successful with most native plants. Some plants of the western states will take hold while others phase out. Study carefully and, if possible, duplicate the rock habitat of each species before planting. Some ferns are indifferent to soil conditions; others are most critical.

Rock-loving species of both the eastern and western parts of our country are not common and could soon be depleted if extreme caution is not used in their removal. It is good to purchase plants from a reputable grower; better still to grow your own from spores, sharing and exchanging your young sporophytes with your friends. Among the rock-loving species try some of the following:

Eastern Area:

| | |
|---|---|
| *Camptosorus rhizophyllus* | Walking Fern |
| *Cheilanthes lanosa* | Hairy Lip-fern |
| *Cystopteris bulbifera* | Bulblet Bladder-fern |
| *Cystopteris bulbifera*<br> var. *Crispa* | Crested Bladder-fern |
| *Cystopteris fragilis* | Fragile Bladder-fern |
| *Pellea atropurpurea* | Purple Cliff-brake |
| *Pellaea glabella* | Smooth-stemmed Cliff-brake |

Western Area:

| | |
|---|---|
| *Cheilanthes gracillima* | Lace Fern |
| *Cheilanthes siloquosa* | Indian's Dream |
| *Cryptogramma acrostichoides* | Parsley Fern |
| *Cystopteris fragilis* | Fragile Bladder-fern |
| *Pellaea andromedifolia* | Coffee Fern |
| *Pellaea mucronata* | Bird's-foot Fern |
| *Polystichum lonchitis* | Northern Holly-fern |
| *Polystichum tsus-simense* | Tsus-sima Holly-fern |
| *Woodsia ilvensis* | Rusty Woodsia |
| *Woodsia oregana* | Oregon Woodsia |
| *Woodsia scopulina* | Rocky Mountain Woodsia |

## Ferns as Focal Points

Many of the larger ferns make excellent focal points for the garden. In general, they will do well where there are two or three hours of direct sunlight each day, supplemented with partial shade during the remainder of the day. If possible, avoid natural wind passages as some ferns are easily broken. A large stone beside each plant not only enhances the individual beauty of the fern but also provides some protection from animals and wind. Adding protective stakes or wire enclosures destroys the natural appearance of ferns and should be avoided. Below is a list of ferns that do not spread or spread very slowly:

| | |
|---|---|
| *Athyrium niponicum* | Japanese Painted-fern |
| *Dryopteris arguta* | Coastal Wood-fern |
| *Dryopteris clintoniana* | Clinton's Shield-fern |
| *Dryopteris erythrosora* | Japanese Red Shield-fern |
| *Dryopteris filix-mas* | Male Fern |
| *Dryopteris filix-mas cultivars* | Male Fern cultivars |
| *Dryopteris goldiana* | Goldie's Fern |
| *Dryopteris marginalis* | Marginal Shield-fern |
| *Dryopteris spinulosa* | Spinulose Shield-fern |
| *Polystichum acrostichoides* | Christmas Fern |
| *Polystichum andersonii* | Anderson's Holly-fern |
| *Polystichum braunii* | Braun's Holly-fern |
| *Polystichum lemmonii* | Shasta Holly-fern |
| *Polystichum munitum* | Western Sword-fern |

## Ferns as aids to Architecture

Below is a list of ferns which, when used with careful planning, will add to the beauty of the house and its horticultural arrangement. All of the species mentioned are of the larger and bolder type. They are up early in the spring and, if kept moist during prolonged dry periods, will last until late autumn. As a suggestion, try some in front of an old-fashioned high porch; the ferns will appear to lower the architectural lines. Where older broad-leaved evergreens have become leggy, the ferns will fill in the barren area. Don't overlook the smaller ferns for house and driveway borders.

| | |
|---|---|
| *Athyrium niponicum* | Japanese Painted-fern. Border planting |
| *Dryopteris goldiana* | Goldie's Fern. Damp, rocky soil |
| *Matteuccia struthiopteris* | Ostrich Fern. Damp acid soil |
| *Osmunda cinnamomea* | Cinnamon Fern. Damp acid soil |
| *Osmunda claytoniana* | Interrupted Fern. Damp acid soil |
| *Woodwardia fimbriata* | Giant Chain-fern. Damp acid soil |

# Index